TPO写作全解

WRITING

孟炎　赵波　编著

中国人民大学出版社
· 北京 ·

PREFACE
前言

    TPO（TOEFL Practice Online: 托福在线练习）是托福出题机构——ETS 官方唯一认可的、可以让考生体验真实考试的练习材料，题目基本都是之前考过的真题，比如 TPO 24 为 2017年 11 月 12 日大陆考题，TPO 32 为 2011 年 2 月 26 日大陆考题，TPO 33 为 2016 年 10 月 16日大陆考题，TPO 41 为 2017 年 12 月 10 日大陆考题，TPO 42 为 2013 年 4 月 12 日北美考题，TPO 46 为 2014 年 4 月 12 日大陆考题，TPO 49 为 2014 年 8 月 30 日大陆考题。其难度、出题思路和逻辑跟目前真题相差不多，因此是广大托福考生备考的必备材料。

    TPO 1~34 和 TPO 40~50 为官方推出的之前考过的真题，参考价值很大，本书做了详细解析，但是 TPO 35~39 中的题目出处不明，据坊间传闻为之前 TPO 跟少数流出真题拼凑而成，参考价值不大，因此本书没有做解析。

    针对综合写作题目，笔者对阅读和听力要点的笔记进行了梳理，以便考生在使用时，对照自己的笔记进行校对和反思，为了便于记笔记，笔记中有些单词使用了不完全拼写，比如 "consistent" 记为 "consistnt"，"value" 记为 "valu" 等。另外，还提供了优质范文，考生可以摘取其中的地道表达来丰富自己的答题模板。

    针对独立写作题目，笔者做了观点和理由的罗列，撰写了用词地道可模仿性强的参考范文，并绘制了范文每个段落的思维导图，以便考生能够更好地把握全文的逻辑，从而学以致用。每篇范文后，精选了地道表达，供考生学习。

    本书使用方法如下：

    综合写作部分，考生可以随机挑选一篇进行模考练习，然后参考书中提供的阅读和听力要点，对照是否有要点信息遗漏，若有遗漏，反思原因。最后对照范文，校对自己所写的作文是否出现句义不清的情况，学习范文中给出的模板性语言，最终形成个性化的模板，在后续练习中不断强化，直至提笔而出。

    独立写作部分，考生可以先审题，列出自己的提纲，再参考书中所提供的观点和思路，汲取自己未想到的思路。然后，通读范文，根据思维导图分析清楚范文中每句话的功能，不断内化每段段内的写作套路和方法。最后，背诵范文后面摘抄的地道表达，并在自己的写作中进行应用，逐步提升写作的语言质量。

编者

目录

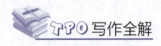

独立写作

托福写作简介

托福写作包含两个任务，综合写作和独立写作，具体如下图所示：

任务类型	任务介绍		
Task 1 综合写作 （基于阅读和听力）	阅读： 3 分钟内读完一篇 230~300 词的学术文章	听力： 听一篇时长 2 分钟左右 230~300 词的学术讲座	写作： 20 分钟内对所读所听内容做一个 150~225 词的总结
Task 2 独立写作 （基于知识和经验）	×	×	写作： 30 分钟内写出一篇 300 词以上的议论文

综合写作

综合写作技巧讲解

综合写作简介

	主题	出题形式	阅读时间	听力时间	写作时间
任务一	学术讲座	阅读＋听力＋写作	3 mins	2 mins	20 mins

答题具体步骤

写作任务类型	任务步骤描述
任务一 综合写作 读 → 听 → 写	● 阅读：3 分钟内阅读一篇 230 到 300 单词的学术文章，并记笔记 ● 听力：听一篇时长 2 分钟左右的讲座，讲座与阅读文章主题相同，角度不同，并记笔记 ● 写作：20 分钟内总结听力重要信息，解释其与阅读信息的关系，篇幅建议 150 到 225 单词，超出上限也不扣分

　　注意：目前所有 TPO 中的综合写作阅读和听力文章都是反驳关系，所以考生在备考时，仅需要熟悉反驳的套路即可。

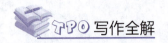

综合写作例题演示（OG 第三套样题）

◆ 1. 阅读

（1）界面/阅读文本

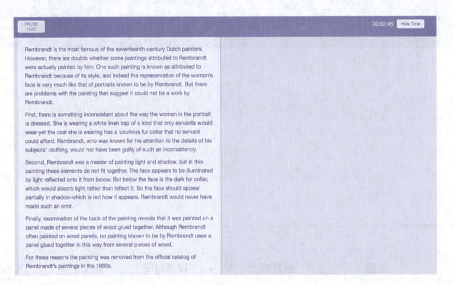

（2）阅读技巧

综合写作阅读的核心原则：在 3 分钟内，阅读信息读得越详细越好，目的是更好地预判听力信息。

阅读文章结构 99% 都是总—分结构，极少出现总—分—总结构。无论哪种结构，阅读时重点关注的都是前四个段，因为首段包含阅读主观点，第二、三、四段包含支持主观点的分论点和细节。

阅读文章的信息分布如下图所示：

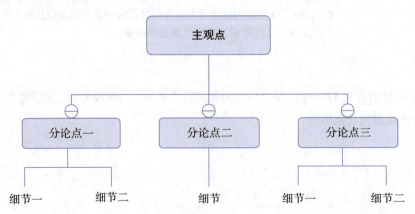

下面为考生讲述一些快速定位以上三层信息的技巧。

主观点：

a）位于首段偏后部分

b）呈现形式有三种：现象解释型（如 TPO 23 黄松减少的原因）；问题解决型（如 TPO 15 控制蔗蟾蔓延的方法）；事件态度型（如 TPO 1 四天工作制的好处）

分论点：

a）位于第二、三、四段，具体位置不定，所以不能仅按照位置来断定

b）呈现形式一般为：原因理由 & 解决方案

细节：

a）位于第二、三、四段

b）切记每一个分论点下面的细节数量是≥1 个

（3）阅读笔记

Reading

MP	Painting not by Rmbrndt
1	分论点一：detail inconsistent 细节：fur collar not match clothing of servants
2	分论点二：light and shadow not fit 细节：dark fur collar below face not fit face illuminated by light
3	分论点三：wood panels 细节：painting use several wood panels glued together but Rmbrndt never use

注解：

Rmbrndt= Rembrandt

◆ 2. 听力

（1）界面

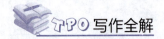

（2）听力文本

Narrator

Now listen to part of a lecture on the topic you just read about.

Professor

Everything you just read about *Portrait of an Elderly Woman in a White Bonnet* is true, and yet, after a thorough reexamination of the painting, a panel of experts has recently concluded that it's indeed a work by Rembrandt. And here's why.

First, the fur collar. X-rays and analysis of the pigments in the paint have shown that the fur collar wasn't part of the original painting. The fur collar was painted over the top of the original painting about a hundred years after the painting was made. Why? Someone probably wanted to increase the value of the painting by making it look like a formal portrait of an aristocratic lady.

Second, the supposed error with light and shadow. Once the paint of the added fur collar was removed, the original painting could be seen. In the original painting the woman is wearing a simple collar of light-colored cloth. The light-colored cloth of this collar reflects light that illuminates part of the woman's face. That's why the face is not in partial shadow. So in the original painting, light and shadow are very realistic and just what we would expect from Rembrandt.

Finally, the wood panel. It turns out that when the fur collar was added, the wood panel was also enlarged with extra wood pieces glued to the sides and the top to make the painting more grand—and more valuable. So the original painting is actually painted on a single piece of wood—as would be expected from a Rembrandt painting. And in fact, researchers have found that the piece of wood in the original form of *Portrait of an Elderly Woman in a White Bonnet* is from the very same tree as the wood panel used for another painting by Rembrandt, his *Self-Portrait with a Hat*.

（3）听力要点

听力与阅读是相反的关系，所以听力的主观点和分论点，基本可以通过阅读反推，所以并不重要，<u>最重要的部分是：听力每个分论点下面的细节。</u>

（4）听力笔记

	Reading	Listening
MP	Painting not by Rmbrndt	×
1	分论点一：detail inconsistent 细节：fur collar not match clothing of servants	pigments analysis show fur collar added 100 years later→ display noble lady → increase value
2	分论点二：light and shadow not fit 细节：dark fur collar below face not fit face illuminated by light	original painting wear light color cloth to illuminate face→ light and shadow fit
3	分论点三：wood panels 细节：painting use several wood panels glued together but Rmbrndt never use	1) add fur collar → enlarge wood panel → painting value ↑ 2) this painting panel & panel of R's another painting from the same tree

◆ **3. 写作**

（1）界面

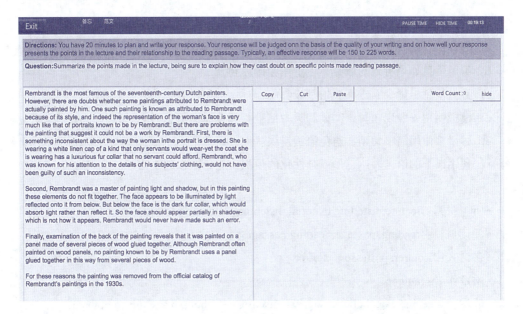

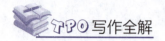

（2）问题

Summarize the points made in the lecture and be sure to explain how they cast doubt on specific points made by the reading passage.

（3）模板

Para 1:

The reading material believes that ___（阅读主观点）___. Nevertheless/ However, the lecture states that ＋听力主观点 .

Para 2:

Firstly, the reading material holds that ___阅读分论点 1 ＋解释___. However, the speaker contradicts the idea of the reading. He/She thinks that ___听力分论点 1___ because ___听力细节 1___.

Para 3:

Secondly, the reading material points that ___阅读分论点 2 ＋解释___. However, according to the speaker, the reading material's idea does not hold water. He/ She believes that ___听力分论点 2___ for ___听力细节 2___.

Para 4:

Thirdly, the reading material argues that ___阅读分论点 3 ＋解释___. However, the speaker holds the opposite opinion by saying that ___听力分论点 3___. This is because ___听力细节 3___.

（4）写作注意事项

a) 阅读信息要同义改写，且不要过多。

b) 听力信息如果听到的原文，尽量用原词原句。

c) 听力信息尽量全面，不要怕啰唆。

d) 模板使用一般现在时，阅读和听力信息与阅读原文信息时态一致。

e) 尽量多使用简单句型，避免语法错误。

f) 利用以下的语言表达，形成个性化的模板，避免模板过于雷同。

• 听力材料：lecture, listening material, listening, listening passage

• 阅读材料：reading, passage, reading passage

• 讲话人：lecturer, professor, speaker

• 文章作者：author

• 陈述：state, indicate, believe, suggest, discuss, talk about, make the point that, say…

• 驳斥：refute, disagree with, cast doubt on, challenge, oppose, conflict with, deny the statement of, contradict…

• 支持：support, enhance, uphold, justify…

• 转折：in contrast, however, on the other hand, but, in opposition…

• 列举：first, second, third, first of all, secondly, also, finally…

（5）参考答案

The reading passage believes that <u>the painting was not created by Rembrandt</u>. However, the lecturer argues that <u>it is Rembrandt who did the painting.</u>

Firstly, the reading material holds that <u>the woman in the portrait could not afford such luxurious fur collar and Rembrandt was very cautious about the details of his subjects' clothing. As a result, he would not have made such an obvious mistake.</u> However, the speaker contradicts the idea of the reading. She thinks that <u>based on the X-ray of the painting, the fur was not on the original painting. Actually, it was added on top of the original painting about 100 years ago so that the painting could represent the aristocrat lady and be more valuable.</u>

Secondly, the reading material points out that <u>the light and the shadow do not fit together, and Rembrandt as a great artist would not have made such an error.</u> However, according to the speaker, the reading material's idea does not hold water. She believes that <u>the woman in the original painting wears simple light clothes, which can perfectly illuminate the face of the character. That is, the face in the original painting was obviously not in shadow. The light and shadow are very realistic in the original painting.</u>

Thirdly, the reading material argues that <u>the painting was done on several pieces of wood glued together. Rembrandt had not used woods that were glued together in his previous works.</u> However, the speaker holds the opposite opinion by saying that <u>the pieces of wood were added so that the painting would look more grand and valuable. The original painting was done on a single piece of wood. Moreover, actually the wood of the original painting was found to be from the same tree that provided another piece of wood for the self portrait of Rembrandt with a hat.</u>

综合写作笔记要点 & 参考范文

TPO 1 综合写作

◆ 笔记要点

	Reading	Listening
MP	4 day workweek good	×
1	4 day worker better rest → errors ↓→ company profits ↑	companies spend ↑ e.g. training and medical benefits & more office space and computers
2	same work need more 人 → jobs ↑→ unemployment rate ↓	their employees need overtime e.g. 5 days work finished in 4 day → no additional jobs
3	worker have more free time → life quality ↑	job unstable & promotion chance ↓→ life quality ↓

◆ 参考范文

The reading material and the lecturer in the listening material provide two competing statements on whether it benefits the individual, the company and the economy as a whole if the company is made to allow its employees to work 4 days instead of 5 days a week.

To begin with, the reading material states that shortened workweek brings more profits to the company and hiring more people will not add any payroll cost. However, the lecturer disputes this by arguing that hiring more employees actually does incur huge cost to the company due to the fact

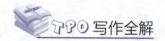

that it has to pay extra money to provide training, medical and health insurance. Plus, more office space and computers are needed to accommodate the increasing number of employees. All the above-mentioned items will add cost to the company and reduce profit.

Furthermore, the reading material states that shortened workweek helps to lower the unemployment rate and a new employee could be hire at the 80 percent rate. Nonetheless, the lecturer posits that hiring can be very costly to the company and there are other cost-effective approaches the company can use. For example, they can ask the workers to work overtime and raise their expectations by forcing the workers to finish the 5 days' workload in 4 days. Thus, shortened workweek will not create new jobs.

Lastly, the reading material states that shortened workweek enables the workers to have some free time and enjoy a quality life. In sharp contrast, the lecturer thinks otherwise. Actually, it will reduce their quality of life. Shorter workweek leads to the instability of the employees and they will lose their chance to advance their careers. They will be the first to lose their jobs in an economic depression. Additionally, they are less likely to be promoted as managers since being a manager means that they have to supervise and cover 5 days' work.

TPO 2 综合写作

◆ 笔记要点

	Reading	Listening
MP	team √	×
1	Group 有 more knowledge & resources → more quick and creative solution	long time to reach agreement→ × quick
2	spread responsbility → risky decisions → more creative	influencers: 1) say no to an idea → quickly drop it 2) convince others & ignore other members → if fail blame the team
3	good for members: 1) feel better when have a voice 2) team results > alone results→ better to shine	Recogn to group include free riders → real contributor × like

◆ 参考范文

The reading material states that working in a group has a lot of benefits. However, the lecturer provides relevant evidence to refute these advantages by citing a real story that happened in a company.

Firstly, the reading material states that working in a team can come up with creative solutions since a group of people have a wider range of knowledge. On the contrary, the lecturer states that this is not the case since there is free rider problem and some of the individuals are not willing to contribute, but they still enjoy the benefit of the whole team's achievement. The feeling of real contributors about the group work is the opposite of what the reading material predicts.

Additionally, in the reading material, it is suggested that people tend to make risky decisions when working in groups since the whole group is held accountable for the result. The lecturer, however, thinks working in groups slows down the decision-making process and it takes the group endless time to reach consensus.

Lastly, the reading material believes that team members have a voice in the decision-making process and they are likely to shine. The lecturer, in sharp contrast, argues that one or two influential people in the group dominate the decision-making process, ruling out other creative ideas. These few influencers tend to promote their so-called creative ideas and other group members' opinion might be totally ignored. Ironically, if the project fails, all members will take the blame.

TPO 3 综合写作

◆ 笔记要点

	Reading	Listening
MP	painting not by Rembrandt	×
1	cap & fur collar not consistnt	pigments analys show fur collar add 100 years later→ display noble lady→ increase valu
2	light and shadow × fit: dark fur collar below face not fit face illuminat by light	原 painting wear light color cloth to illuminat face→ light and shadow fit
3	this painting panel use several wood glued but Rmbrnt never use	1) add fur collar → enlarge wood panel → painting valu ↑ 2) this painting panel & R's another painting from same tree

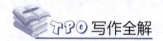
◆ 参考范文

The lecturer and the reading passage hold two competing opinions with regard to whether a portrait was painted by Rembrandt. The reading passage believes that the painting was not created by Rembrandt; however, the lecturer argues against such a claim by citing evidence provided by a panel of experts who have examined the painting thoroughly.

To begin with, in the reading material, it is suggested that the woman in the portrait could not afford such luxurious fur collar and Rembrandt was very cautious about the details of his subject's clothing, and thus he would not have made such an obvious mistake. On the contrary, the lecturer argues that based on the X-ray of the painting, the fur was not on the original painting. Actually, it was added on top of the original painting about 100 years later so that the painting could represent the aristocrat lady and be more valuable.

Additionally, the reading passage claims that the light and the shadow do not fit together and the face of the character appears to be partially in shadow, and Rembrandt as a great artist would not have made such an error. The lecturer, on the other hand, refutes it by affirming that the woman wears simple light clothes, which can perfectly illuminate the face of the character, and the face is obviously not in shadow. The light and shadow are very realistic in the original painting.

Lastly, in the reading passage, it is believed that the painting was done on several pieces of wood glued together. Rembrandt had not used wood that were glued together in his previous works. In opposition, the lecturer claims that the pieces of wood were added so that the painting would look more grand and valuable. The original painting was done on a single piece of wood. Actually, the wood of the original painting was found to be from the same tree that provided another piece of wood for the self portrait of Rembrandt with a hat.

TPO 4 综合写作

◆ 笔记要点

	Reading	Listening
MP	dinosar was endothm	×
1	discovr dinosar fossl in polar regions & only endothm can surviv in cold climates	1) polar when dinosar lived was warm 2) when cold → dinosar migrat to warmer area or hibernat

2	dinosar legs under bodies ≈ leg position of modern endothm	leg position support more weight → dinosars grow to 大 size→ advantg for dinosars
3	dinosar bone have Haversian canal → grow rapid →endothm	growth ring in bones shows periodical growth: rapid grow then no &slow grow ≈ non-endotherm

◆ 参考范文

The lecturer and the reading passage hold two competing opinions with regard to whether dinosaurs were endotherms. The reading passage believes that dinosaurs were endotherms, however, the lecturer argues against such a claim by citing three pieces of contradictory evidence against the reading material.

To begin with, in the reading material, it is suggested that dinosaurs were endotherms since their fossils have been discovered in the Polar Region. On the contrary, the lecturer argues that when the polar dinosaurs existed, the temperature was significantly higher than the current temperature, meaning it was suitable for non-endotherms like dinosaurs to live. Moreover, dinosaurs might have migrated to warmer areas and been able to hibernate like modern-day reptiles.

Additionally, the reading passage claims that the legs of dinosaurs were positioned under its body, not at the body's sides, which was very suitable for running, thus dinosaurs were endotherms. The lecturer, on the other hand, refutes this idea by claiming that the specific position of dinosaur's legs served to support the enormously heavy body, and not for the purpose of running like endotherms.

Lastly, in the reading passage, it is believed that dinosaurs were endotherms given the fact that dinosaurs had Haversian canals, a characteristic of endothermy. In opposition, the lecturer claims that the fact that many dinosaurs had Haversian canals doesn't mean that dinosaurs were endotherms. Actually, the evidence of the growth rings of dinosaurs suggested that during cooler periods they stopped growing or grew much more slowly. However, endotherms grow rapidly even in cool times, suggesting that dinosaurs were not endotherms.

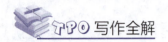

TPO 5 综合写作

◆ **笔记要点**

	Reading	Listening
MP	3 use of stone house	×
1	for living ← 大 house ≈ apartment in Taos	few fire place for cooking for 10 families but rooms for 100 famils
2	store food e.g. maize ← long lasting & size of house suitable	× find maize & container
3	ceremony ← Pueblo Alto heaps of pots ←人 gather to eat and discard the pot	mounds of PA 有 other material × from ceremony e.g. sand & stone → trash heap

◆ **参考范文**

The reading passage proposes three purposes of the "great houses" on the settlements of Chaco Canyon in New Mexico; however, the lecturer in the listening material refutes these three suggested purposes of the "great houses" by providing three contradictory pieces of evidence.

First of all, the reading passage believes that the "great houses" on the settlement of Chaco Canyon were purely residential as the earlier versions of the building seen in more recent Southwest societies. However, the lecturer argues against such a claim. He states that even though the outside of these "great house" does look like residential houses, nonetheless, the number of fireplaces for cooking in these "great houses" could support only 10 families and there were as many as 100 families living in these "great houses" back then. Thus, these "great houses" were not for residential purposes.

Additionally, the reading passage suggests another theory that the Chaco structures were used to store food supplies like grain maize. The lecturer, on the other hand, refutes that by affirming when the Chaco structures were excavated there were no trace of maize or containers. Of course, if the building was used for storage purposes, there would have been maize or maize containers.

Lastly, in the reading passage, it is proposed that the Chaco structure was used for ceremonial purposes since the excavation of the mound revealed deposits of a surprising huge number of broken pots and they might have been discarded after eating festive meals. In opposition, the lecturer claims that this theory is not supported by evidence since there were plenty of construction materials like sand, stone, and construction tools excavated in the mound. Actually, the mound was a trash heap, piled up by things that were not used or garbage that was thrown away. In fact, the pot was also a piece of trash. Thus, the claim that the Chaco structure was used for ceremonial purposes cannot hold water.

TPO 6 综合写作

◆ 笔记要点

	Reading	Listening
MP	online encyclpdia not good	×
1	not accurate ← contributors lack academic background	Errors online easy corrected but error printed remain a long time.
2	information online 改 by users	有 strategy: read-only format & editor monitor changes
3	online encycpd emphasis 小 popular topics → not 分 imprt & unimprt	online has more space → covers various topics & diverse users' interests

◆ 参考范文

The lecturer and the reading passage hold two competing opinions with regard to the advantage of communal online encyclopedias. The reading passage claims that it is less valuable than traditional encyclopedias while the lecturer in the listening material believes that communal online encyclopedias are obviously more effective than traditional ones.

To begin with, in the reading material, it is suggested that communal online encyclopedias lack academic credentials whereas the traditional encyclopedias are generally written by well-trained experts. On the contrary, the lecturer argues that such a claim is not fair since traditional encyclopedias are never perfect and accurate. It is not possible to find documents absent from mistakes. Actually, it is far easier to correct mistakes online while the mistakes on traditional encyclopedias will remain forever.

Additionally, the reading passage claims that online encyclopedias give hackers a chance to fabricate and delete information while traditional encyclopedias are not tampered with. The lecturer, on the other hand, refutes that by affirming that there is a myriad of ways to protect content from

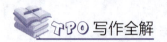

hackers. For instance, crucial facts can be presented in read-only format, which is impossible for hackers to change. Also, special editors are hired to delete malicious changes to the content. Such measures can be very helpful to maintain the authenticity of the contents online.

Lastly, in the reading passage, it is believed that communal encyclopedias focus on topics that are both important and unimportant, which can be misleading while traditional encyclopedias have priorities in terms of what topics to include. In sharp contrast, the lecturer claims that the reason to explain it is that traditional encyclopedias don't have enough space and they just include important topics and exclude unimportant ones. However, in practice, the decisions are made by the so-called scholars and experts, not the majority of the people. Obviously, the online encyclopedias don't have space problem and the topics represent the interest of the common people and the diversity of the topics is its biggest advantage.

TPO 7 综合写作

◆ 笔记要点

	Reading	Listening
MP	US wood companies × ecocertified	×
1	too much ads → American not trust the ecocertification	US 人 trust the products certified by independent organization with reputat
2	eco wood pay certifi agency → more expens than uncertif 木 → US 人 not buy	1) price difference < 5% → US 人 buy 2) envirn protection awarenss ↑
3	Americ 木 sell in US→unnecessy to get ecocert	US 人 interest in eco wood →foreign companies occupy Amric market

◆ 参考范文

The reading passage and the lecturer provide two competing opinions about the likelihood for American wood companies to certify their products issued by international organizations. Though the reading material believes that American companies should not certify their products; however, the lecturer argues that there are obvious reasons for them to do so.

First of all, the reading material states that American consumers don't place so much trust in advertising and it makes no sense for the company to promote their products by stating that their products are certified. However, the lecturer states that consumers don't consider the advertisement as the same one. Instead, they can distinguish the advertisements, in which the claim is made by the company and the ones stated by independent agencies. The American consumers are ecological-minded and they will certainly recognize products that are certified by a reputable international agency. Consequently, consumers will be responsive to the certified products advertised in the commercial.

Secondly, in the reading material, it is believed consumers will choose the uncertified wood since certified products are much more expensive. The lecturer, on the contrary, argues that studies have shown that consumers are sensitive to price when the price discrepancy is high. However, the certified wood will only be 5% more expensive than the uncertified one. Thus, consumers will consider other important factors in this case like whether the product can protect the environment. Thus, consumers might choose certified products.

Lastly, the reading passage holds the opinion that pursuing certification only makes sense if they sell most of their products abroad. However, the lecturer argues this statement doesn't hold water since international consumers are not the major factor here. What is more important is international competition and if American companies are not aware of the international trend of pursuing certification, they will be elbowed out by international competitors and lose their domestic consumers.

TPO 8 综合写作

◆ 笔记要点

	Reading	Listening
MP	Chevalier's memoir not accurate	×
1	C borrow money →he was not rich	C need 几天 convert assets into money
2	memoir written 几 years after the conversation →can't exact	Each night after talking Voltir, C wrote everything & when writing he referred to notes.
3	C's friend bribe to free him →not escape prison	1) C's prisoner have more powerful friends not freed by bribing. 2) ceiling of the prison repaired

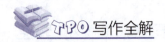

◆参考范文

The reading passage casts doubts about the validity of Chevalier de Seingalt's memoir in three aspects. The lecturer, however, holds three opposing opinions with regard to the argument presented in the reading material and believes that his memoir is actually valid and trustworthy. She also argues that it is impossible for any memoir to be correct in every detail. However, by and large, Chevalier's memoir is reliable.

To begin with, in the reading material, it is suggested that the fact that Chevalier borrowed money from a Swiss merchant contradicts the claim in the memoir that Chevalier was rich and wealthy. On the contrary, the lecturer suggests that the fact that Chevalier got a loan doesn't mean that he was poor since he had enough money to squander on gambling and parties. It took time when he had to sell his property and he had to wait to get the money. During the waiting time, it was normal for him to borrow money.

Additionally, the reading passage casts doubt on the conversation between Chevalier and Voltaire in the memoir since it is impossible for him to remember all the details so clearly after so many years. The lecturer, on the other hand, refutes that by affirming that each night when he had conversation with Voltaire he wrote down their talk and kept notes for years. Witnesses claimed that when he wrote the memoir he referred to his notes and journals. Thus, it is completely possible for him to remember exact phrases from the extended conversation later.

Lastly, in the reading passage, it is suggested that he didn't escape from the prison and it is more likely that the Chevaliers bribed the jailers to free him. In sharp contrast, the lecturer claims that given that there were many others in the prison who were far more powerful than him didn't bribe the jailers to get freedom. Thus, it is unlikely for Chevalier to do so himself. Actually, evidence in certain documents suggests that after he escaped from the prison, some repair work was done about the roof, which affirmed the fact that Chevalier did escape from the prison.

TPO 9 综合写作

◆笔记要点

	Reading	Listening
MP	fuel-cell engines > combstion engin	×
1	fuel-cell use hydrogen from various sourc e.g. 水 & gas	Prodc & store pure liquid hydrogen techn diffic e.g. kept cold −253℃

2	fuel engn only produc 水 →solv pollution	produc pure H_2 burn oil & coal for energ →cause pollution
3	F engin twice efficient than C engines → 人 spend 少 money	F engin need expens platinum →make chemical reaction undergo

◆ 参考范文

The lecturer and the reading passage hold two competing opinions with regard to the fuel-cell engine. The reading passage believes that the fuel-cell engine has several obvious advantages and will soon replace the internal-combustion engine. However, the lecturer argues against such a claim by citing three pieces of evidence accordingly.

To begin with, in the reading material, it is suggested that the main problem of the internal-combustion engine is that petroleum that the engine relies on will soon run out while hydrogen needed for the fuel-cell engine cannot easily be depleted. On the contrary, the lecturer argues that hydrogen is not so readily available even though there is plenty of hydrogen in water; however, it cannot be used directly. Hydrogen has to be in a pure liquid state and it is difficult to produce and store. To be specific, it has to be stored under -253 degrees Celsius, which requires very complicated cooling technology. Thus, it is neither practical nor readily available.

Additionally, the reading passage claims that the fuel-cell engine is environmentally friendly while the internal combustion engine produces carbon dioxide, which causes seriously environmental problems. The lecturer, on the other hand, refutes that by affirming that even though cars with the fuel-cell engine doesn't cause pollution, hydrogen production causes lots of pollution since a significant amount of energy is needed and lots of coal and fuel need to be burnt in order to purify hydrogen.

Lastly, in the reading passage, it is believed that the fuel-cell engine is twice as economical as the internal combustion engine. In sharp contrast, the lecturer claims that the fuel-cell engine is not cost-saving since it requires platinum to facilitate chemical reaction that produces electricity. However, platinum is very expensive. To make matters worse, ways to replace platinum with other materials have been so far unsuccessful.

TPO 10 综合写作

◆ 笔记要点

	Reading	Listening
MP	√ pollution × predation→sea otter ↓	predation
1	source of pollution along Alaskan coast: pollution→水 chemical ↑→otter resistance ↓	predator eat quick → no dead sea otters →
2	1. other species ↓ ← 全 ecostm ← pollution 2. × predator e.g. orca ← eat larger prey e.g. whale	无 whales ← 人 hunt ∴ orca change diet → small sea animals e.g. otters
3	uneven otter decline ← uneven pollutants ← ocean current	otters ↓ or ↑ depends on location accessible to orca: 1) easy access → otter ↓ 2) orca 大 → × access 浅 / rocky area → otter × decline

◆ 参考范文

    The reading passage states that the pollution hypothesis is more likely to explain the decline of the sea otter population in waters along the western coast of North America. However, the professor in the lecture refutes this hypothesis and provides some evidence to justify the predation hypothesis.

    To begin with, in the passage, it is suggested that oil rigs and other sources of industrial chemical are accountable for the decline of sea otter population. However, the professor in the lecture disputes this statement by arguing that since there is no dead bodies of sea otters found along the seashore, predation is more like to explain this. If the decline of otter population is caused by pollution, the dead bodies of sea otters will be washed up to the seashore.

    Secondly, the reading passage holds the opinion that the decline of other mammals like seals and sea lions can be also attributed to environmental pollution like other kinds of whales. In sharp contrast, the professor in the lecture is not in favor of this argument. He states that whales moved to other part of the ocean due to excessive human activities in the area, and it could be that the orca changed their diet and started to prey on small mammals like sea lions, seals and sea otters. So, environmental pollution can't explain the decline of marine animals' population.

    Lastly, in the reading passage, it is believed that based on the pollution hypothesis, ocean currents caused the uneven distribution of pollutants and eventually led to the decline of otter population in some areas while it remained the same in other areas. Nonetheless, the professor in the lecture posits that the fact can be better explained by the limited accessibility of orcas which cannot have access to rocky and shallow waters, where there is no decline in otter population. However, in the places that are accessible to orcas, there is an obvious decline of otter pollution.

TPO 11 综合写作

◆ 笔记要点

		Reading	Listening
MP		literature reading ↓ not good	×
1		reading literature ↓ → the public miss intellectual stimulation	science books & history of high quality and creativity → stimlt intellect
2		reading literature ↓ → lowered the level of culture	1) culture change → 有 other express forms e.g. music and movies 2) speak more directly to 人 concerns
3		reading literature ↓ → good writers and literature works ↓	modern literature difficult to understand → blame authors

◆ 参考范文

　　The lecturer and the reading passage hold two competing opinions with regard to literature reading. The reading passage believes that there are lots of disadvantages of the decline in novel reading. However, the lecturer argues against such a claim by citing three pieces of evidence accordingly.

　　To begin with, in the reading material, it is suggested that less reading time on literature has unfortunate effects on the reading public and the future of literature. On the contrary, the lecturer argues that there are other types of reading that can cause intellectual stimulation besides literature like science, history, and political analysis books. Such books can also stimulate imagination and creativity. So, it is not fair to claim that literature is the only type of good material worth reading.

　　Additionally, the reading passage claims that reading poorly written self-help books brings no benefits and spending more time watching TV, music videos and reading web pages have lowered the level of culture. The lecturer, on the other hand, refutes that by affirming that less novel reading time doesn't mean the lower standard of culture since music and movies are good ways of

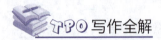

expression. Nonliterary activities don't lower the standard of culture. Currently there are more ways of expression. Moreover, different forms of expression can better address contemporary concerns than literature.

Lastly, in the reading passage, literature is about to decline because of lower standards of readers. In sharp contrast, the lecturer claims that readers should not be blamed for less support for literature. Instead, the authors are largely responsible for this since their works are difficult to understand. It is safe to say that even the earlier generations would have read less of today' novels.

TPO 12 综合写作

◆ 笔记要点

	Reading	Listening
MP	subject of painting = Jane Austen	×
1	1882 JA family permit to use & recog.	1882 JA dead for 70 years → family members × seen JA
2	Face ≈ one of C's sketch of JA ← similar features: e.g. nose mouth	大 family have 多 cousins of JA or children of cousins & resemble JA → paint relative of JA
3	painted in JA teenage = OH active time	portrait canvas sold by a man & sell canvas in London till JA age 27 → painted later

◆ 参考范文

The lecturer and the reading passage hold two competing opinions with regard to whether or not the subject in the painting owned by one of Jane Austen's family members is Jane Austen. The reading passage believes that there are reasons to believe that Jane Austen is the subject. However, the lecturer argues against such a claim by citing three pieces of evidence accordingly.

To begin with, in the reading material, it is suggested that in 1882, Austen's family gave permission to use the portrait as an illustration in an edition of her letters, and her family claimed that the girl in the portrait was Jane Austen. On the contrary, the lecturer argues that the letters were published in 1882, when it was 70 years after Jane died. The family members of Jane Austen would have not seen her themselves. Thus, they could not surely claim that Jane Austen is the subject in the portrait.

Additionally, the reading passage claims that the teenage painting is similar to the one in

Cassandra's sketch, which suggests that Jane Austen is the subject in the painting. The lecturer, on the other hand, refutes that by affirming that it could be some relatives of Jane Austen or their children, who resembled Jane Austen. Actually, some experts do believe that the subject was a distant niece of Jane Austen.

Lastly, in the reading passage, it is believed that the style of painting links to Ozias Humphrey, who was active during the 1780s and early 1790s, when Jane Austen was a girl in the painting. In sharp contrast, the lecturer claims that the similar style cannot explain that the girl is Jane Austen. Other evidence suggests that the stamp on the cloth suggested that it was sold by William Leg. However, records showed that he didn't sell canvases in London when Jane Austen was a teenager. Actually, when he sold canvases in London Jane Austen was already 27 years. Consequently, the claim that the girl in the painting is Jane Austen doesn't hold water.

TPO 13 综合写作

◆ 笔记要点

	Reading	Listening
MP	fossil commerc × good	×
1	privat 人 × allow the public to view fossil → harder to see → interest in fossils ↓	fossils trade → schools & library can buy fossils for the public → can see more fossils
2	buyers richer than scientst → buyer get → scientist × access fossils	scientists identify the value of fossils → pass through scientific experts → nothing missed
3	collectrs untrained → the fossil damaged	fossil collecting by university 少 → without collectors many F × discovered

◆ 参考范文

The reading passage argues that commercialization of fossils, particularly of dinosaurs and other big invertebrates, is detrimental to the general public and the scientists, and three specific reasons are provided to support that. Unfortunately, all of the three reasons are disputed by the professor in the lecture.

To begin with, the reading passage states that since private collectors don't allow the general public to observe fossils, there will be steady decline of interest in fossils and that is a shame. However, the professor refutes that by saying the general public will have greater exposure to

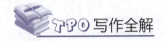

fossils since schools and museums can purchase any kind of fossil they like to collect. They are made accessible to the public. So, what the reading passage argues is totally exaggerated and unconvincing.

Secondly, the reading passage holds that scientists will be deprived of the chance to make new discoveries since they cannot compete with private collectors financially. On the contrary, the professor thinks that doesn't hold water given the fact that it is scientists who identify the value of fossils through examinations and tests. Fossils have to be passed through the hands of the scientists and be evaluated by them before going out on the market. Thus, scientists will not miss out any important discoveries.

Lastly, the reading passage admits that due to the lack of certain knowledge, collectors often destroy valuable evidence with regard to the fossils they unearth. In sharp contrast, the professor disputes that by arguing if private collectors don't even unearth fossils, nobody will because schools and other institutions don't have the means to unearth them. Even though there are some inconsequential damages and sometimes the data collected is not as desirable, it is not a big deal since it is far better to explore fossils than having them undiscovered.

TPO 14 综合写作

◆ 笔记要点

	Reading	Listening
MP	salvage logging good	× good
1	remove dead 木 →make room for fresh → help forest recover	wood decomposition enrich the soil remove → × nutrients
2	remove dead 木 → insect 害 e.g. beetle ↓→ help health	1) beetle lived for 100 years → × major damage. 2) dead 木 provide habitats for 益 birds and insects
3	economy good ← 1) wood for industries 2) more jobs for local 人	1) 小 : ←use expensive helicopters. 2) jobs × long ← outsiders with experience get the job.

◆ 参考范文

The reading passage and the listening material hold competing opinions with regard to the effectiveness of salvage logging. The reading material provides three benefits of salvage logging while listening material argues against these benefits by citing three contradictory pieces of evidence.

Firstly, in the reading material, it is suggested that salvage logging helps forest areas recover from disasters. On the contrary, the lecturer argues that cleaning up the forest after a fire will not be conducive to tree growth. In fact, the decomposition of trees helps to provide nutrients to trees and removing these burnt trees will reduce the nutrients, thus retarding tree growth.

Additionally, the reading passage claims that salvage logging can minimize the danger of insect infestation. The lecturer, on the other hand, refutes that by affirming that rotten wood might not be bad for forest. For instance, beetles living in Alaskan forests don't cause any harm to these forests. Not only do the dead trees provide habitats for insects but also for birds and other insects that are helpful for the forests.

Lastly, in the reading passage, it is believed that salvage logging brings economic benefits and helps to create more jobs. In sharp contrast, the lecturer claims that salvage logging has only short-term economic benefits. Helicopters and other vehicles are expensive to maintain. Also, the jobs created by salvage logging will be more likely to be filled by outsiders than local people.

TPO 15 综合写作

◆ 笔记要点

	Reading	Listening
MP	stop cane toad Central and South Amrica→ Austrlia	×
1	national fence stop CT to other places e.g. rabbit √	小 CT & eggs live stream and rivers → get through fence
2	volunter: 1) CT easier to trap 2) 小 & eggs easy find ← in 水	untrained volunteer → damage other native frogs (endangered) ← not easy tell, esp young
3	virus stop CT matur/ reprodu → Only harm toad	1) virus transpt by resch & pet colectr from Austri to C & S Americ 2) virus → toad ↓ in C & S Americ & vital part of ecosystem

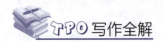

◆ 参考范文

The reading passage proposes three approaches to stop the spread of cane toads in Australia. However, the lecturer argues against such strategies.

To begin with, in the reading material, it is suggested that a national fence can block the advance of the toads. On the contrary, the lecturer argues that a national fence cannot stop the spread of cane toads since their young and eggs can live in streams and rivers, meaning toads can carry their young and eggs from one side to the other side. What's more, only a few young and eggs are needed to get through the fence to establish a population on the other side. Thus, a national fence is not effective.

Additionally, the reading passage claims that volunteers could be successful in trapping and destroying toads. The lecturer, on the other hand, refutes that by affirming that volunteers might catch and destroy the toads. Worse still they might also destroy the native Australian frogs since it is very difficult to distinguish between cane toads and native frogs.

Lastly, in the reading passage, it is believed that a virus can be employed to control the population of cane toads without doing any harm to other infected species. In sharp contrast, the lecturer claims that such a strategy will lead to terrible consequences to original Central and South American cane toads since Australian reptiles and amphibians might be transported to other parts of the world. If pet collectors transport Australian cane toads to Central and South America, it will be a huge ecological disaster and the whole eco-system will be jeopardized.

TPO 16 综合写作

◆ 笔记要点

	Reading	Listening
MP	archaeology 有 problm	new guidelines improved
1	construction projects damage artifacts	before construction archeologists first examine → 有 interest → builders, arch. officials meet to build around them & excavate & document properly
2	insufficient funding problems	companies pay for initial examn & perseveration afterwards → more fund → more research

3	the jobs in archeology hard to find	paid work for archgist ↑ e.g. examin site & draw plan & do research process data

◆ 参考范文

The reading passage believes that the science of archaeology of Great Britain was faced with serious problems and limitations for most of the twentieth century. However, the lecturer argues against such a claim because the new guidelines and rules changed archaeology for the better.

To begin with, in the reading material, it is suggested that many valuable artifacts were lost to construction projects. On the contrary, the lecturer argues that such a claim is not correct since before the start of their construction, archaeological examination would be carried out to check whether there were interesting or valuable relics or not. Then, if there were cultural relics on the construction site, builders and the government would work together to preserve the artifacts. The projects would be built around the artifacts or the relics which were about to be excavated before the construction.

Additionally, the reading passage claims that financial support for archaeological research was inadequate and changes in government priorities brought about periodic reductions in funding. The lecturer, on the other hand, refutes that by affirming that archaeological work was paid by construction companies not the government. Their payment covered the initial examination and the work under the preservation plan. Such funding actually helped researchers to explore a greater range of topics.

Lastly, in the reading passage, it is believed that choosing archaeology was very difficult since there were not enough positions available and lots of archaeological workers were unpaid amateurs. In sharp contrast, the lecturer claims that the new guideline required that archaeological workers be paid. They were paid during every and each process of the archaeological work including preservation, processing of data, and publishing research papers. In fact, the number of archaeologists is now the largest of all times.

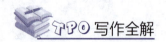

TPO 17 综合写作

◆ **笔记要点**

	Reading	Listening
MP	why bird in US ↓	×
1	人 & settlement ↑→ birds' habitats ↓	other birds ↑ ← 大 & better habitat for seagulls and pigeons & their predators e.g. hawks
2	农 ↑→ birds' habitats ↓	land for agriculture ↓ ← intrduc more productive crops
3	the pesticides pollute birds' food & 水 → kill birds	1) less toxic pesticides 2) geneticly pest-resistant crops

◆ **参考范文**

The reading passage believes that the decline of bird population is attributed to the growth of human population and the use of pesticides. However, the lecturer argues against such a claim by citing three pieces of evidence accordingly.

To begin with, in the reading material, it is suggested that birds' natural habitats will continue to disappear as human population and settlements continue to expand. On the contrary, the lecturer argues that this is not the case since urban expansion does harm to some of the birds, but not to all of them. Actually, urban expansion provides better and larger habitats for other birds like seagulls, and pigeons. It is not unusual to see hawks and falcons preying on pigeons in urban areas. Thus, it is one-sided to claim that urban expansion has uniformly affected all the birds.

Additionally, the reading passage claims that increasing agricultural activities will further the destruction of bird habitats and wilderness areas. The lecturer, on the other hand, refutes that by affirming that there is less land devoted to agriculture. More productive crops have been created and more crops are produced per unit of land, meaning it is not necessary to destroy wild land. Thus, birds' habitats will be preserved instead of being harmed.

Lastly, in the reading passage, it is believed that the increasing use of chemical pesticides will pollute the water and food chain for birds, leading to further decline in birds' population. In sharp contrast, the lecturer claims that the scenario described in the reading will not appear in the future since people are getting more aware of the negative impact of pesticides. Therefore, less toxic pesticides will be used and there is an increasing trend to grow pest-resistant crops. Consequently, pesticides will no longer be needed, which will definitely cause no harm to birds.

TPO 18 综合写作

◆ 笔记要点

	Reading	Listening
MP	how to preserve Torreya	predation
1	reestablish T in 原 habitat North Florda	小 climt 变： global warm → temp ↑ & wetlands 干 → clmt dry
2	move T to 更 north areas	bad outcomes ← e.g. 人 移 black locust → 灭 plants new envrmnt
3	research centr	× resst diseas ← tree popula × 大 & diverse ← centr 无 enough room

◆ 参考范文

The reading passage lists three possible ways to address the decline of Torreya. However, the lecturer believes that all of the three preserving strategies are not satisfactory.

To begin with, in the reading material, it is suggested that the reestablishment of Torreya trees in north part of Florida will be favorable to Torreya's growth because of the specific microclimate. On the contrary, the lecturer argues that climate in the proposed region will be affected by the climate in the larger region because global warming helps to increase temperature in these regions. Also, many parts of Florida is drained and it is getting drier and drier. Thus, it is not possible to have climate similar to the original climate, where it is suitable for Torreya to grow.

Additionally, the reading passage claims that assisted migration can be adopted, meaning moving Torreya to an entirely different location can be conducive to the survival of Terreya. The lecturer, on the other hand, refutes that by affirming that this strategy might have bad consequences to other species. For instance, when humans did the same thing to black locust trees by moving them further north, they spread quickly in these areas and killed most of other plants and trees, which were also endangered. Thus, assisted migration has an unpredicted outcome.

Lastly, in the reading passage, it is believed that seeds and saplings of the trees can be moved

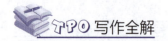

from the wild to a research center, and this research center can ensure the continued survival of the species. In sharp contrast, the lecturer claims that the trees kept in the research center will not resist diseases since the Torreya trees have to be really large and genetically diverse in order to survive certain diseases. However, research centers don't have the capacity to hold diverse populations of trees, so they cannot survive certain diseases.

TPO 19 综合写作

◆ 笔记要点

	Reading	Listening
MP	buzzing should be banned	×
1	buzzers provide incorrect infmtion → mislead custmr	Buzzers = 人 use products really think good → paid to tell true infmtion
2	buzzers pretend customer → consumer less critical	Custmr ask a lot Q about product e.g. price and service
3	meet buzzer → mistrust ↑ → harm social relation	B give good products & 人 try B prodct → have good experience → more trust

◆ 参考范文

The reading passage lists three controversies of the new tactic "buzzing" to advertise a product. However, the student in the listening passage argues against these claims by providing three counter-arguments.

To begin with, in the reading material, it is suggested that consumers don't know whether a person praising a product is paid and the buzzers may well provide incorrect information because of the money incentive. On the contrary, the student argues that this is not true and he uses his experience as a buzzer to show this. He states that buzzing is not an ordinary advertisement and buzzers don't get paid just by reading some lines out loud. Instead, buzzers are those who have used the product and think that it is good, and then they are hired by the company to promote the product.

Additionally, the reading passage claims that consumers are less critical when listening to the endorsements since buzzers pretend they are just individuals. The student, on the other hand, refutes that by affirming that the opposite is true since people ask buzzers a lot of questions like the price, service and even how long the buzzer has been using the product. If the answer the buzzer provides is not good, people will not buy the product. Thus, potential customers can be very critical by asking lots of questions.

Lastly, in the reading passage, it is believed that buzzing might have bad impact on social relationship since it brings about mistrust and dishonesty. In sharp contrast, the lecturer claims that if the product is not good, the company is not able to hire any buzzers to promote it. Moreover, customers will have good experience of using the product because of buzzers. Thus, buzzing facilitates trustworthiness and makes people more open to others.

TPO 20 综合写作

◆ 笔记要点

	Reading	Listening
MP	"let it burn" policy ×	✓
1	tree and other vegetns damaged	火 →space for 小 plants & seeds need high heat to germinate → new plants grow → forest more divers
2	1) 大 animal run 2) 无 habitats & break food chain → animal × return	小 plants → 小 animal e.g. rabbits↑ → predators ↑ → stronger food chain → animal population ↑
3	tourism value ↓ → economy ↓	fire is unusual ← low rainfall, strong wind and undergrowth visitor back

◆ 参考范文

The reading passage believes that three kinds of damages were caused by "let it burn" policy in 1988 Yellowstone forest fire. However, the lecturer argues against this claim by citing three pieces of evidence accordingly.

To begin with, in the reading material, it is suggested that the Yellowstone fire caused tremendous damage to the park's trees and vegetation. On the contrary, the lecturer argues that the scotched areas actually provided a chance for new plants to colonize, and it made vegetation more diverse since the fire created such a condition for certain plants to grow. For instance, small plants can take over the open and shaded areas. Certain seeds that are covered underground are able to

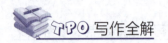

germinate with the exposure to the heat caused by the fire. Thus, fires actually make the park more diverse in plants and vegetation.

Additionally, the reading passage claims that the habitats of wildlife like deer and elks are endangered by the "let it burn" policy. The lecturer, on the other hand, refutes that by affirming that forest fires provide a chance for small plants to grow into a habitat, which is suitable for small animals like rabbits and hares to live in. With enough food source, the predators depending on these small animals can thrive. Thus, forest fires make the food chain much stronger than before.

Lastly, in the reading passage, it is believed that forest fires compromise the value of the park as a tourist destination, which consequently hurt the local business. In sharp contrast, the lecturer claims that the probability that big forest fires happen every year is very small since a combination of factors are needed to make them happen like low level of rainfall, strong wind and dry climate. However, the combination of these factors doesn't happen to be there all the time and there has not been any forest fire since the 1988 forest fire happened in Yellowstone.

TPO 21 综合写作

◆ 笔记要点

	Reading	Listening
MP	种 genetic modifd tree good	×
1	GM tree hardier e.g. papaya tree resist ringspot virus	non GM tree diverse → survive GM tree same gene meet clmt change → all die
2	GM tree econmc benft for farmers ← grow fast & 多 yield & hardier	hidden cost : 1) charge more for seeds 2) pay every time you plant
3	GM tree save native tree	GM compt resource e.g. sunlight, soil with natural trees

◆ 参考范文

　　The reading material and the lecture hold two opposing opinions about the idea of genetically modified trees. The lecturer provides three disadvantages of genetically modified trees as opposed to the benefits provided in the reading material.

To begin with, in the reading material, it is suggested that genetically modified trees are designed to be resistant to certain virus infection. The lecturer, however, believes that even though genetically modified trees can be resistant to some conditions, they tend to be very vulnerable to new challenges in a sense that their genes are uniform and suffer from the lack of diversity. In fact, when there is a challenge posed to the genetically modified trees like climate change or pests, they might be totally wiped out. Non-genetically modified trees, on the other hand, maintain a diversity of genes and some of the species can survive new challenges. Eventually, the whole species get a chance to survive and thrive.

Secondly, the reading material states that genetically modified trees bring more economic benefits to farmers. On the contrary, the lecturer argues that farmers get charged more when they grow genetically modified trees than non-genetically modified trees. To be specific, farmers who grow genetically modified trees get charged when they collect the seeds and plant the trees. Moreover, they need to pay every time they plant genetically modified trees.

Lastly, it is believed in the reading passage that genetically modified trees can prevent overexploitation of wild trees. The lecturer, on the other hand, posits that they actually damage the wild trees. Genetically modified trees are very aggressive and they are planted among the trees that are not genetically modified. To make matters worse, the genetically modified trees compete with the wild trees for water, sunlight, and nutrients in the soil. Consequently, the wild trees will be crowded out.

TPO 22 综合写作

◆ 笔记要点

	Reading	Listening
MP	Ethanl × replace gasoline	×
1	Burn ethanl produc CO_2 → global warming.	ethanl from plants & plant 吸 CO_2 ≈ CO_2 from burn ethanl
2	Produc ethanl → reduce plant for other uses e.g. animl food	ethanl from cellulose: part of cell walls, not eaten by animal → × food ↓
3	无 govenm support → ethanl expens	Buyer ↑ → production ↑ → price ↓ e.g. produc 3 times → price ↓ by 40%

◆ 参考范文

The lecturer and the reading passage hold two competing opinions with regard to ethanol fuel made from plants like sugar cane and corn. The reading passage believes that such fuel is not a good alternative to gasoline. However, the lecturer argues against such a claim by citing three pieces of evidence accordingly.

To begin with, in the reading material, it is suggested that ethanol will not help to solve the problem of global warming because ethanol releases carbon dioxide into the atmosphere when it is burned. On the contrary, the lecturer argues that burning ethanol will not add to global warming since ethanol is produced from corn and sugar cane, which absorb carbon dioxide during their growing process. Consequently, the carbon dioxide absorbed counteracts that which is produced when burning ethanol fuel.

Additionally, the reading passage claims that the production of ethanol would reduce the quantity of plants available for other uses. For example, a substantial source of food for animals would disappear. The lecturer, on the other hand, refutes that by affirming that the scale of ethanol production will reduce food source since only cellulose, a part of the cell wall, is needed for the production of ethanol and obviously animals don't eat cell walls. Thus, it is unconvincing to assume that mass ethanol production decreases food source for animals.

Lastly, in the reading passage, it is believed that ethanol fuel cannot compete with gasoline price wise, and they are currently about the same because of huge government subsidy. The price of ethanol will definitely increase when government stops subsidizing. In sharp contrast, the lecturer claims that ethanol can compete with gasoline price wise in the future even though currently ethanol doesn't have a competitive edge; however, it is not always the case. If more people buy ethanol, there will be more production, which in turn will decrease the price. In fact, it is estimated that the price of ethanol will drop by as much as 40% if the production of ethanol is three times higher than that currently.

TPO 23 综合写作

◆ 笔记要点

	Reading	Listening
MP	Cedar ↓	×

1	insect e.g. beetles ← eat 木	1) healthy cedar have poisonous chemical → more resist 2) beetles attack sick or damaged trees
2	bear ← eat bark for sugar	island 无 bear but cedar ↓
3	climate 变: growing time later → freeze the root	tree die low /warm > high/cold

◆ 参考范文

The reading passage proposes three hypotheses explaining the decline of yellow cedar population. However, the lecturer in the listening material disproves the three possible explanations of yellow cedar population decline by providing three corresponding rebuttals.

To begin with, in the reading passage, it is suggested that insect parasites are responsible for the decline of yellow cedar, especially beetles. The lecturer, on the other hand, argues that healthy yellow cedar can resist insect infestation since it is saturated with a powerful and poisonous chemical that can prevent insects. Those trees that are damaged are mostly likely sick and dead in the first place before the insects' attacks. Eventually, insects like beetles are not responsible for the decline of yellow cedar.

Additionally, the reading passage believes that the brown bear will weaken the yellow cedar in search of sugar content, critically damaging enough trees that result in the decline. The lecturer, on the contrary, affirms that the damage caused by the brown bear cannot be responsible for the overall decline of yellow cedar, citing evidence that yellow cedar population declines dramatically along the coast the North America, including the mainland and islands. Actually, brown bears only reside in the mainland and there are no such animals on the islands. As a result, brown bears are not liable for the cedar population decline.

Lastly, the reading passage argues that climate change, specifically the frost during winter times caused damage to the roots of yellow cedar, gradually killing it. In sharp contrast, the lecturer posits that frost damage cannot explain cedar population decline since the temperature in high elevations is lower. Thus, it is supposed to cause more damage to the cedar population. However, the fact is that more yellow cedar suffered and died in lower elevations, where it is warmer and less yellow cedar died in high elevations, where it is much colder. Thus, frost can't be the cause for the decline of cedar population.

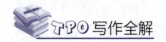

TPO 24 综合写作

◆ 笔记要点

	Reading	Listening
MP	T. rex's fossl has 活 tissues	×
1	blood vessels ← 有 soft organic substnc in channels　小	organic material ← left by bacteria lived in channels
2	blood cell ← sphere 1) iron sphere 2) dark centers 3) same size	1) find sphere in animals not have red cells 2) new origin: reddish mineral
3	collagen ← part of a living bone tissue	1) colagn last not long 100 thousd & fossil 70 milln 2) from researchers' hand

◆ 参考范文

　　The lecturer and the reading passage hold two competing opinions with regard to the identification of the materials in T. rex bones. The reading passage believes that remains of blood vessels, red blood cells and collagen matrix have been found in T. rex bones. However, the lecturer argues that such a claim is very unreliable.

　　To begin with, in the reading material, it is suggested that breaking of the bones revealed small channels inside and the soft substance might well represent the blood vessel of T. rex. On the contrary, the lecturer argues that the soft substance was not the blood vessel, and it might be something else. Long after the T. rex died, bacteria colonized the bones and left organic matters. These soft substances might be the soft residues left by the bacteria colony.

　　Additionally, the reading passage claims that microscopic examination of the various parts of the inner bone revealed the presence of spheres that could be the remains of red blood cells and the size of the red centers were about the size of the red blood cells. The lecturer, on the other hand, refutes that by affirming that the fossil examination of other animals found that even primitive animals that didn't have red blood cells in the sphere mentioned in the reading material. Thus, the sphere was definitely not red blood cells. In fact, the sphere might be different organic materials like reddish minerals.

Lastly, the reading passage states that the test on the dinosaur leg bone showed that it contained collagen, which was expected to be the kind of chemical related to bone tissues. In sharp contrast, the lecturer claims that researchers have never found collagen from animals that are older than 100, 000 years. An animal that lived 70 million years ago couldn't contain collagen since it could not last that long. It might come from a more recent source like the skin of the researchers who handled this fossil.

TPO 25 综合写作

◆ 笔记要点

	Reading	Listening
MP	vessels × batteries	×
1	无 conductor e.g. metal wires	local 人 × archeologists find→ × realize import of metal wires → throw
2	copper cylinders ≈ Seleucia → holding scroll	first for holding scroll, then as batteries ← produce electric by metal rod + liquid
3	无 device use electric	1) magical power ← invisible 2) in medical treatment e.g. relieve pain & stimlt musl

◆ 参考范文

In the reading material, the author states that even though archaeologists believed that the clay jar excavated in Iraq were actually ancient electronic batteries and able to produce electronic current it is unlikely for these vessels to be used as electric batteries. On the contrary, the professor in the lecture provides three specific reasons to dispute the author's statement.

To begin with, the reading material states that if the vessels were used as batteries, there were supposed to be some electric conductors like wire. Since no conductors were found, the vessels were not used as batteries. However, the professor refutes that by saying it was the local people rather than professional archeologists who unearthed these vessels and the people might have not noticed certain wire. Even if they did find something important, they could have overlooked and neglected that.

Additionally, the reading passage posits that the copper cylinders inside of the jar look like the ones discovered in the ruins of Sleucia. Since the cylinders found in Sleucia were used to hold

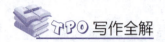

sacred texts, the same might be true of the jar excavated in Iraq. On the contrary, the professor holds the opposite opinion, saying that it cannot prove the point showed in the reading material since the original purpose to hold scrolls doesn't mean it was not used for other purposes. Indeed, they could be adapted for other goals. For example, they could be used as batteries if liquids and some iron rods were used together with them.

Lastly, the reading material believes that there were no devices that depended on electricity to function. Thus, vessels were useless to people. Again, the professor challenges this idea by showing that people could get electric shock and a sense of tingling, which could be demonstrated as a kind of magical power. Also, evidence shows that electric shock can be used to heal patients, stimulate certain parts of the body, and relieve pain.

TPO 26 综合写作

◆ 笔记要点

	Reading	Listening
MP	zebra mussel spread can't stop & cause fish ↓	×
1	ZM survive in ships ballast water →can't stop	1) empty freshwater & refill ocean 水 & out the ocean 2) salt 水 kill the ZM
2	dominate new place ← 无 predator &strong adapt & high reproduction	beginning 无 predator birds find new food =ZM →change to eat & a lot of ZM
3	ZM food compete → overall population ↓	other ↑ ZM 产生 nutrients → bottom fish ↑

◆ 参考范文

The reading passage hypothesizes three major reasons for the unstoppable invasion of the zebra mussel in North America. However, the professor in the lecture refutes all of these three points by providing three approaches to stop the invasion of zebra mussel.

To begin with, the reading passage states that the zebra mussel can attach themselves to the ships' bottom and survive in the ballast water that ships use to balance its cargo. However, the professor explains that such a phenomenon can be avoided by taking some measures. For example, generally ships take on fresh ballast water in Europe and empty the water when they arrive in

America. However, ships can be required to empty the fresh water and refill with ocean water. Then, the zebra mussel will be killed immediately, which helps to prevent the zebra mussel's invasion.

Additionally, the reading passage argues that the zebra mussel can cope with lots of conditions and are able to reproduce fairly quickly in a new habitat. Thus, it will take over the new habitat and pose a threat to native fish population. However, the professor refutes this by saying that fast reproduction can only happen in the beginning. After that, the aquatic birds will switch from original food source to eating this kind of invasive species. So, it is not possible for them to reproduce a lot.

Lastly, the passage states that the zebra mussel eat plankton, which is the major food source for lots of native freshwater fish. Thus, they will compete with the fish for food and colonize the new habitat. Again, the professor doesn't think it will happen since even though mussel have a negative impact on the plankton eating fish, they can have a positive effect on other kinds of fish. The zebra mussel produce lots of nutrients for fish living at the bottom of lakes, rivers and streams. Ultimately, it is unlikely for it to pose a threat to native freshwater fish.

TPO 27 综合写作

◆ 笔记要点

	Reading	Listening
MP	3 reasons → 小 ice age	predation
1	warm → glac. melt → 水 into gulf stream → disrupt current	gulf stream × cause Temp ↓ south area e.g. New Zealand & South Africa
2	火山 → dust → stop sunlight → temp ↓	dust → visual effect e.g. brown snow & colorful sunset but × reports
3	人 ↓ → tree ↑ → CO_2 ↓	time not enough Soon 人 ↑ → tree ↓ → for crops

◆ 参考范文

The reading material hypothesizes three major reasons for the Little Ice Age. However, the professor in the lecture states that the new scientific evidence refutes all of the three-hypothesis in three aspects.

To begin with, the reading material recognizes that melting glaciers' sending a large amount of cold freshwater in the Gulf Stream caused the disruption. The disruption can be accountable for the Little Ice Age. However, the professor in the lecture argues that the Gulf Stream could only decrease the temperature in the regions like Europe and North America, and it was not accountable for the lower temperature in Africa and New Zealand. Hence, it cannot explain the emergence of the Little Ice Age.

Additionally, the reading material posits that volcanic eruption caused the Little Ice Age. The dust created by the volcanic eruption blocked the sunlight, lowering the global temperature. In sharp contrast, the professor in the lecture refutes this by stating that there was not enough dust to make it possible to lower the global temperature. If there had been enough dust, people would have observed the colorful sunset and grey or brown snow, and reported these phenomena. However, there were no reports of that sorts.

Lastly, the reading material explains that the decrease in human population caused trees to grow enormously in the fields that were no longer used for agriculture, and trees absorbed carbon dioxide accordingly, leading to the emergence of the Little Ice Age. On the contrary, the professor disputes that by recognizing the fact that the human population decreased for a short time and quickly bounced back to normal level. It was not long enough for that to happen since the forests were cut down to provide space for human survival.

TPO 28 综合写作

◆ 笔记要点

	Reading	Listening
MP	Peary reach North Pole	×
1	a committee's conclusion	comittee 有 P's friend funded P trip of Peary → × objective two days investgtion → × careful
2	Tom Avry made same trek < 37 days & used same dogsled & dogs	difference of two trips 1) avery: less weight ← airplane transport his food 2) more 好 weather

3	photo: measure shadows → sun's position in photo ≈ its position in N.P.	1) the picture by unfocused camer 2) blurred and faded away over time → × determine Sun's position

参考范文

The reading passage states that Peary's successful expedition to the North Pole can be proved by three pieces of specific evidence even though there are some doubts about it. However, the professor in the lecture refutes these evidence by providing contrary statements.

To begin with, the reading material states that the committee of the National Geographic Society conducted a thorough investigation and the result showed that Peary's accounts were convincing. However, the professor argues that it is not persuasive because the examination was not objective given the fact that the committee members were mostly Peary's friends, and the report was biased and untrustworthy. What's more, it only last two days and Peary himself even said the investigation was not that careful.

Additionally, the reading material posits that a British explorer Avery used the same kind of dogsled and the same number and breed of dogs as Pear had, and if Avery made it to the North Pole, so would Peary. Paradoxically, the professor is not in favor of this position since the conditions of Avery's and Peary's trips to explore the North Pole were totally different. When Avery traveled to the North Pole, the weather was really favorable, and he carried far less food and daily supply than did Peary. In fact, Avery had a helicopter that dropped food along the way. On the contrary, during Peary's trip to the North Pole, the condition was very harsh and hostile. Consequently, it is not justified to compare their expeditions.

Lastly, the reading material argues that judging from the shadow of Peary's photographs, it is possible to calculate that Peary did reach the North Pole. In sharp contrast, the professor, again, disputes that by saying that the shadow of the photos has to be measured precisely in order to determine the position. Unfortunately, the photo was taken by an ancient camera, which was very fuzzy and blurry, making it impossible to determine the position. Ultimately, there is not enough evidence to support the claim that Peary did arrive at the North Pole.

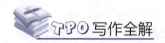

TPO 29 综合写作

◆ 笔记要点

	Reading	Listening
MP	the edmontosaurus migrated	×
1	edmsur eat plants only & no plants in N.S. winter →move temperate zone	100 milln ago, warmer in summer & 24 hrs sunlight → 好 condition for plant → enough food in winter
2	skeletn in same site → live in herds, e.g. buffalo → migratin	live in herds protection from predators, e.g. elks
3	edmsur 有 locomotive power → can migrat long distanc	1) 小 edmsurs not migrat long trek → slow the herds → can't reach the destination 2) 小 edmsurs × surviv alone

◆ 参考范文

The reading passage hypothesizes that edmontosaurus survived the winter by migrating from the North Slope region to the south where it was warmer by providing three specific reasons. However, all the reasons are disputed by the professor in the lecture.

To begin with, the reading passage states that the edmontosaurus fed exclusively on plants but the winter in the North Slope was very inhospitable, making it hard for the plants to grow. Thus, they must have migrated to warmer areas, where it is suitable for the plants to grow. However, the professor refutes that by arguing the temperature in the North Slope was far warmer than today, and there was 24 hours sunlight, which could provide a very suitable condition for the growth of vegetation and plants. Also, even in winter, the dead plants could provide enough nutrition for edmontosaurus to survive.

Additionally, the reading passage posits that moving in herds helps the dinosaurs to migrate. Unfortunately, the professor opposes this idea since migration serves for other kinds of purpose, like providing protection from predators. Also, it is not convincing to argue that they might have migrated due to the fact that they lived in herds. For example, a kind of elk living in the western United States live in herds but they don't migrate.

Lastly, the reading material states that edmontosaurus were able to move long distance given the fact that they had very powerful locomotion. Paradoxically, the professor challenges that by recognizing that it was possible for adult edmontosaurus to move long distance, but it was impossible for juvenile animals to move such a long distance. They could slow the migration and it was never possible for the edmontosaurus to make it since they were very unlikely to leave their little ones behind.

TPO 30 综合写作

◆ 笔记要点

	Reading	Listening
MP	burning mirror is a myth	×
1	tech low → × make 大 copper with parabolic shap	several 小 copper & Greek know parabola
2	set fire take 10 mins & ship × move	ship 有防水 pitch catch fire 快 even ship moving
3	BM not imprv 火 arrow ← same distance	× see rays & just see BM → more surprising

◆ 参考范文

The lecturer and the reading passage hold two competing opinions with regard to the authenticity of an ancient weapon created by the Greeks in order to defend themselves against the Roman navy. The reading passage believes that such an ancient weapon is a myth that the Greeks of Syracuse never really built such a device. However, the lecturer argues against such a claim by citing three pieces of evidence accordingly.

To begin with, in the reading material, it is suggested that the ancient Greeks were not technologically advanced enough to make such a device since it would be several meters wide and would have a very precise parabolic curvature to be effective as a powerful weapon. On the contrary, the lecturer argued that the weapon was not a single piece of copper. Instead, it was put together by using several single pieces of copper. In fact, the ancient Greek mathematicians had the knowledge of the property of parabolic curvature that they could assemble several pieces of small copper to form such a specific shape.

Additionally, the reading passage claims that the burning mirror would have taken a long time to set the ships on fire and an experiment showed that it would take about 10 minutes to set on fire a wooden object 30 metres away, and the Romans would not stay still perfectly in minutes. The

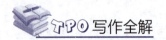

lecturer, on the other hand, refutes that by affirming that the experiment used just wooden material. In fact, there were other materials that were much easier to catch fire than wood like pitch, which was used to seal the ship so that it could be waterproof. Thus, fire could spread and move very quickly.

Lastly, in the reading passage, it is believed that there was no reason for the Greeks to invent the burning mirror since flaming arrows were also very effective. In sharp contrast, the lecturer claims that since the Romans were very familiar with flaming arrows and they would put out the fire caused by such a weapon. However, they would not be suspicious about the mirror. Consequently, the mirror could cause fire in unobservable places surprisingly and the burning mirror was much more effective than flaming arrows.

TPO 31 综合写作

◆ 笔记要点

	Reading	Listening
MP	Sinosaurs' lines not feather	
1	1) lines form after S die 2) skin decomps to fiber→presevr as lines	Same site other fossil no decomps → Sino lines also is well-preserved feather
2	lines is frills not feather	beta protein: feather has & frill 无 Sino fossl 有 protein
3	feather locat along backbone & tail → can't fly & regulat temp → useless for Sino	feather has display function: e.g. peacock has tail feather to attract & Sino structr colorful

◆ 参考范文

The lecturer and the reading passage hold two competing opinions with regard to whether the lines of the fossil skeleton of Sinosauropteryx were feathers. The reading passage believes that Sinosauropteryx was not a feathered dinosaur. However, the lecturer argues against such a claim by citing three pieces of evidence accordingly.

To begin with, in the reading material, it is suggested that the fine lines may not even represent the functional structure of a living dinosaur, and the lines were misinterpreted as an evidence of feathers. On the contrary, the lecturer argues that the lines couldn't be decomposed from the skin since the fossils of other animals from the site showed that their skins were very well preserved under the volcanic ashes. Thus, the lines were not fibers as claimed in the reading material.

Additionally, the reading passage claims that even if the lines are more likely to be fossilized remains of frills than remains of feathers. The lecturer, on the other hand, refutes that by affirming that there is a huge chemical difference between frills and feathers. Feathers contain a certain protein and frills don't have such a specific protein. Chemical examination of the fossil showed that the specific protein was found. Thus, the lines must be the feathers of the dinosaur.

Lastly, in the reading passage, it is believed that the lines in the dinosaur were mostly located along the backbone and the tail of the animal, meaning that the structures were useless for flight and of limited use in thermal regulation. In sharp contrast, the lecturer claims that feathers have other functions other than thermal regulation and flight. For instance, peacocks have colorful feathers, which are used for displaying, and its tails can be used to attract mates. Analysis showed that the feathers of the dinosaur were colorful. They were orange and brown. Thus, the feathers of the dinosaur could be used for display.

TPO 32 综合写作

◆ 笔记要点

	Reading	Listening
MP	where quacker from	×
1	orca attract males	1) orca in surfac & submr deep ocean 2) orca near → detect by sonar
2	大 squid ← × detect by sonar ← soft body & smart	1960–1980 有 sound 1960 till now 有 squid
3	other submarin ← specl tech	1) submr × move quickly 2) sub 有 engine noise

◆ 参考范文

The lecturer and the reading passage hold two competing opinions with regard to the source of the strange sound heard by Russian submarine sailors from the 1960s to the 1980s. The reading passage states three possible sources of the strange sound. However, the lecturer argues against these claims by citing three pieces of evidence accordingly.

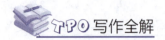

To begin with, in the reading material, it is suggested that the strange sound was actually the calls of male and female orca whales during a courtship ritual. On the contrary, the lecturer argues that it seems plausible but it is highly unlikely that it is the case. It is true there are lots of orca whales living in these areas that Russian submarines used to patrol. However, these whales live in the surface water of the ocean and the submarines are patrolling very deep in the ocean, meaning that it is impossible to hear the sound emitted by the whales. Also, if the strange sound was indeed emitted by the whales, chances were that the sonar system of the Russian submarine would have detected the whales.

Additionally, the reading passage claims that the strange sound might come from giant squid since they have soft bodies with no skeleton. Thus, it was difficult for the sonar system to detect. The lecturer, on the other hand, refutes that by affirming that the Russian submarine detected the sound in the 1960s and it lasted for more than two decades until the 1980s. However, the giant squid have always been there even till today. Obviously, the argument in the reading passage doesn't hold water since one cannot hear the sound one day and suddenly stop hearing it at a later time. Consequently, the strange sound was not likely from the giant squid.

Lastly, in the reading passage, it is believed that the sound might well be from foreign submarines that were secretly patrolling the area. In sharp contrast, the lecturer claims that since the sound traveled very fast and changed direction, it is unlikely that the sound was emitted by a foreign submarine as technology was not so advanced that human beings could invent submarines with silent engines that moved so fast. Thus, the claim that the strange sound was from a foreign submarine doesn't hold water.

TPO 33 综合写作

◆ 笔记要点

	Reading	Listening
MP	use of stone ball	×
1	weapon for hunting ← holes/grooves	× wears/damage on balls & well preserved
2	mearsure weights ← same size	made of different stones with different density → mass diff

3	social markers ← elaborate designs	1) others simple design 2) 无 ball found in tomb high ranking 人

◆ 参考范文

The lecturer and the reading passage hold two competing opinions with regard to the purpose of the carved stone balls in the Neolithic period. The reading passage believes that they might be used as weapons, weights and a measure system and symbols for social status. However, the lecturer argues against this claim by citing three pieces of evidence accordingly.

To begin with, in the reading material, it is suggested that the carved stone balls were weapons used in hunting or fighting. On the contrary, the lecturer argues that the weapons in the Neolithic era showed signs of wear. For instance, they might be cracked or have pieces breaking off. However, the stone balls are very well preserved and they are not damaged. Thus, it is not possible that the stone balls were used as weapons.

Additionally, the reading passage claims that the carved stone balls were used as part of a primitive system of weights and measures to measure things like food or grain. The lecturer, on the other hand, refutes that by affirming that even though they were uniform in size, they were made of different types of stones like green stone or sand stone. They are different in density and some are heavier than others. Thus, it is not possible for them to be used as a standard unit of measure.

Lastly, in the reading passage, it is believed that the carved stone balls served a social purpose to show the important social status of the owners. In sharp contrast, the lecturer claims that some of the stone balls had intricate patterns while others were very simple, which could not have been used for showing social status. Also, in the Neolithic period of Great Britain, high ranking people were usually buried with possessions but stone balls were found in none of these graves and tombs. Thus, stone balls were not possessions to show social status.

TPO 34 综合写作

◆ 笔记要点

	Reading	Listening
MP	why sea cow in Bering ↓	×
1	overhunt by sibr. 人 ← food source	sea cow 大 9m + 10ton & 人少

2	eco changes → kelp = food for cow ↓	other parts × affect: e.g. whale × ↓ kelp fine → × food short
3	eurp. trader ← weapon kill cow & catch the last cow 1768	before Eurp arrive → sea cow 小 other things caused it

◆ 参考范文

The reading passage and the lecturer in the listening material provide opposing opinions about the reasons why Steller's sea cow went extinct. The lecturer refutes the three points made in the reading material by providing three corresponding reasons respectively.

To begin with, the reading material suggests that overhunting is responsible for the extinction of the sea cow since it was considered as a good food source in a harsh environment for Siberian people. The lecturer, on the other hand, argues that since the sea cow was massive and they were generally nine meters long and over ten tons in weight, they could feed a small village for months given its small population. Eventually, Siberian people didn't need a lot of sea cows to survive, So they were not responsible for the extinction of the sea cow.

Additionally, the reading passage states that ecosystem disturbances caused the decline of kelp, the food source of sea cows, which in turn contributed to the extinction of the sea cow. However, the lecturer believes that the hypothetical decline in kelp would have had an impact on the population of other marine animals like whales. Since there was no reported decline of the population of whales and other kinds of sea animals, kelp decline could not be accountable for the distinction of the sea cow. Actually, if it was the case that kelp decline caused extinction of the sea cow, it also would have had a much broader influence on other sea animals.

Lastly, it is suggested that European fur traders possessed weapons that allowed them to hunt countless sea cows. Nonetheless, the lecturer holds the opinion that European settlers migrated to the island after 1700. Actually, the sea cow population before 1700 was quite small. The Europeans could not be regarded as the scapegoat just because they were the last settlers who arrived at the island. Instead, whoever arrived long before should be responsible for sea cow extinction.

TPO 40 综合写作

◆ 笔记要点

	Reading	Listening
MP	keep permanent presence on Venus ✗	build a station 50km above Venus
1	Venus 气压 大 → crush spaceship & anything	50km up Venus atoms pressure = Earth's
2	Venus 无水 & O_2 & supply them from Earth to Venus impractical	Venus 大气 have CO_2 & sulfur → used to produce 水 & O_2
3	clouds reflect & CO_2 layer most sunlights → 少 sunlight reach Venus → can't use solar cell → 无电	1) 50km cloud not thick → lots of sunlight filter 2) cloud below reflect lights

◆ 参考范文

The lecturer and the reading passage hold two competing opinions with regard to whether it is possible to maintain permanent human presence on Venus. The reading passage believes that the harsh climate makes it impossible to achieve this. However, the lecturer argues against this claim by suggesting the possible construction of a permanent station.

To begin with, in the reading material, it is suggested that the high atmospheric pressure will crash anything humans might land on Venus. On the contrary, the lecturer argues that even though it is challenging to set up a permanent station, it is possible. A permanent station can be set up 50 kilometres high in the atmosphere, and it will float in the atmosphere like a balloon. The atmospheric pressure is similar to that of the earth and it will not crash things.

Additionally, the reading passage claims that there is no water on the Venus' surface and it hardly contains any oxygen. Plus, supply of water and oxygen from Earth is highly impossible to provide. The lecturer, on the other hand, suggests that oxygen and water can be produced through chemical process by using compound available on the planet like carbon dioxide and sulfuric gas. Eventually, it is unnecessary to transport oxygen and water from the Earth.

Lastly, in the reading passage, it is believed that given the fact that little sunlight can get through the thick cloud, it is impossible to use solar power cells to get electricity to power their machine and equipment. In sharp contrast, the lecturer claims that it is true cloud is thick near

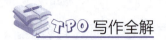

the surface, however, the cloud is not so thick at around 50 kilometres above the surface of the planet. There are plenty of sunlight at that level. Consequently, the solar panel can not only utilize the sunlight above but also absorb the sunlight reflected by the cloud below. Thus, it can generate enough electricity to power the station.

TPO 41 综合写作

◆ 笔记要点

	Reading	Listening
MP	new rules about coal ash not good	×
1	已有 regulations : company use liner in new pond & landfill → 防 leak & pollution	current rules × enough → only new disposal site & old ones cause damage new rules → require old & new disposal sites
2	new rule → customer concern ↑ → not buy products from coal ash → coal ash recycle ↓	mercury 有 strict rules but recycled 50 years
3	new rules → power company cost ↑ → 电 price ↑	company cost ↑ 15 billion but every household ↑ 1%

◆ 参考范文

The lecturer and the reading passage hold two competing opinions with regard to whether it is necessary to implement rules on handling and storing coal ashes. The reading passage believes that imposing these strict rules has three disadvantages. However, the lecturer argues against this claim by citing three pieces of evidence accordingly.

To begin with, in the reading material, it is suggested that there are already very effective environmental regulations, requiring companies to use liners when disposing coal ashes in ponds or landfills. On the contrary, the lecturer argues that just using the liner is not sufficient since liners are only used for newly built landfills and ponds. However, it is not applied in old landfills and ponds, which cause chemical leakage to underground water, contaminating drinking water. Thus, stricter rules and regulations are needed.

Additionally, the reading passage claims that strict rules on storing and handling coal ashes might discourage consumers from buying recycled coal ash products like bricks and concretes. The lecturer, on the other hand, refutes that by affirming that such rules will not stop consumers from buying these recycled coal ash products. For instance, mercury is hazardous, and thus it is handled and stored in accordance with very strict rules and regulations. It has been recycled for 50 years that it has never been a concern for consumers. Thus, strict rules on handling coal ashes will not have negative impact on recycled coal ash products.

Lastly, in the reading passage, it is believed that strict regulations would result in a significant increase in disposing and handling costs for power companies who might increase the price of electricity. In sharp contrast, the lecturer claims that it is well worth the cost. Analysts predict that the cost for these companies will be about 15 billion dollars, meaning there will be only 1% increase in household electricity bills. Thus, it is not a high price to pay for a clean environment.

TPO 42 综合写作

◆ 笔记要点

	Reading	Listening
MP	ways to stop injuries to birds	×
1	one-way glass: birds × see through it → understand as a barrier → × fly through	one-way glass ≈ mirror → reflect sky and trees & birds × understand mirror → think is real → fly into it
2	colorful designs: 人 see through openings & birds see stripes → × fly	1) birds think unpainted openings as holes → fly into it 2) opening is 小 → room is dark
3	magnetic field → emit signal → drive away from building	magnet only in long distance e.g. migrate from cold to warm short e.g. one side of city → another: use eyes and light

◆ 参考范文

The reading passage proposes three possible ways to design glass to prevent injuries to birds. However, the lecturer argues against these strategies by citing three pieces of evidence accordingly.

To begin with, in the reading material, it is suggested that one-way glass can help birds to avoid flying through glass. On the contrary, the lecturer thinks that it is not feasible since when birds are flying outside, glass will serve as a mirror to reflect things like the sky or trees. Birds will fly directly through glass since they think the reflections are really trees or the sky. Thus, one-way

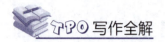

glass is as bad as regular glass.

Additionally, the reading passage claims that colorful designs on regular window glass like thin stripes can help to avoid bird wreckage. Plus, people inside of the building can see through the openings. The lecturer, on the other hand, refutes that by affirming that even though the holes can help people to see through, however, birds also think that they can fly through these open holes. Furthermore, if the open holes are designed to be very small so that birds will not try to fly through them, it will be too dark for people to stay inside.

Lastly, in the reading passage, it is believed that creating a magnetic field helps to guide birds away from buildings. In sharp contrast, the lecturer claims that it will not work out since birds use the magnetic field to navigate only when they are flying a long distance like from a cold country to a warm country. Nonetheless, the magnetic field is not applied when birds are flying short distances. In fact, birds use their eyes and brightness of light to navigate when flying short distances. Consequently, creating a magnetic field will not work out.

TPO 43 综合写作

◆ 笔记要点

	Reading	Listening
MP	3 ways agnostids lived	×
1	other arthropods were swimmers/ predators & sea 有 lots of 小 organisms →free-swimming predators	agnostids eye 小 even blind & 无 other sensory organs → can't chase prey
2	other arthropods dwell on sea floor → agnostids is sea-floor dweller	agnostids spread large distances → move fast from one to another → unusual for sea floor dweller
3	modern arthropods is parasites → agnostids is parasites	find many agnostids fossils → agnostids 多 → kill host

◆ 参考范文

The lecturer and the reading passage hold two competing opinions with regard to how agnostids may have lived. The reading passage proposes three ways that agnostids might have lived. However, the lecturer argues against this claim by citing three pieces of evidence accordingly.

To begin with, in the reading material, it is suggested that the agnostids may have been free-swimming predators that hunted smaller animals. On the contrary, the lecturer argues that there were other arthropods that swam in the ocean, and they had very well-developed eyes and vision. However, agnostids had poor eyes and they were even blind, which suggests that they couldn't have been predators. Moreover, fossil records show that they didn't have other special sensory organs. Thus, agnostids were not free-swimming predators.

Additionally, the reading passage claims that agnostids may have dwelled on the seafloor and survived by scavenging dead organisms and grazing on bacteria. The lecturer, on the other hand, refutes this by affirming that the animals living on the sea floor do not have the ability to move fast and far away. Actually, they move very slowly in localized areas. Nonetheless, agnostids lived in multiple places across a large distance. Consequently, agnostids were not seafloor dwellers.

Lastly, in the reading passage, it is believed that there is possibility that the agnostids were parasites, living on and feeding off larger organisms. In sharp contrast, the lecturer claims that parasites don't have unlimited population. Otherwise, they might kill the host. However, fossil records show that agnostids lived in large numbers, which suggests that agnostids were not parasites.

TPO 44 综合写作

◆ 笔记要点

	Reading	Listening
MP	silver coin in Maine is fake	×
1	maine 1,000 km far from Norse settlement	other objects found in same site from 远方 → the Norse travel 远 bring coin back Maine
2	no other coins found	Norse not permanent settlement → they pack coins & return to Europ
3	native Americans not use silver coin → useless for the Norse	Native Americ value unusual objects e.g. beautiful coins used for necklaces trade with NA 人

◆ 参考范文

The reading passage believes that the coin found in the Maine cannot be considered as genuine historical evidence that it was brought by European travelers to America. Instead, it is suggested that someone placed a coin on that site to mislead the public. However, the lecturer provides

competing explanations about the coin.

First of all, the reading material argues that the Norse settlements have been discovered in far eastern Canada and the Maine site has no real connection with the settlements. The lecturer, however, refutes this by stating that since other objects are found on the same site, not just coins. Thus, it is possible for the Native Americans to travel long distances to reach very distant places and they could have brought coins with them to the Maine site.

Secondly, it is suggested in the reading material that the Norse didn't bring any coin with them since no other coins were found on the site. The lecturer, on the other hand, challenges this statement by arguing that since the settlements in America were not permanent settlements the European travelers could have brought valuable possessions with them and when they traveled back to Europe they could have taken the coin with them. As a result, it is totally reasonable to argue that the coins were brought by the European travelers.

Lastly, the reading material posits that given the fact that the coins were not recognized by native North Americans as money, European travelers understood that the coins were useless to them. The lecturer, on the contrary, thinks that this rationale doesn't hold water since even though Americans back then did not use coins as we do today, the Europeans could have brought the coins with them so that they could trade with Americans because the coins were very attractive and appealing. They could be used on necklaces or even jewelry for ornamentation.

TPO 45 综合写作

◆ 笔记要点

	Reading	Listening
MP	200 milln Y fossil structure × built by bee	×
1	无 200 m fossil of bee & earliest bee fossil 100m	bee fossil 必 preserv tree resin & tree with this resin rare 200m ago → bee not preserv
2	200m 无 flowering plant & bee feed flower→ 无 bee	early bee feed non-flower e.g. pine tree later 有 flower →bee feed it
3	1) structr 无 caps & modern hive 有 caps 2) structr by other insects e.g. beetles	chemical evidence: modern bee 有 waterproof substance & fossil chamber have the same material

◆ 参考范文

The reading passage and the lecturer provide two competing opinions on whether a recently discovered fossil was created by bees. The reading passage believes that it was not created by bees; however, the lecturer cites three reasons to refute the reading passage.

First of all, in the reading passage, it is suggested that no bee fossils were found that dated to 200 million years ago and that specific fossil could have not been created by bees. The lecturer, on the other hand, contends that it is possible for bees to create the fossil since the fossil of bees could not have been preserved for 200 million years. Actually, bees could be preserved by the resin produced by a very rare tree. The fact that no bee fossils were found does not necessarily mean that bees didn't exist 200 million years ago since there was no tree producing the right resin.

Secondly, the reading passage holds that the absence of flowering plants 200 million years ago means that bees did not exist at that time since bees depend on flowering plants to survive. The lecturer, on the contrary, challenges this statement by arguing that it was possible for bees to feed on nonflowering plants back then like pine trees or even ferns. Bees could gradually evolve and feed on flowering plants later. Eventually, their feeding pattern gets stable.

Lastly, the reading passage maintains that the fossil lacks certain detailed structures of bee hives like spiral caps and it was made by other insects. The lecturer refutes this argument by stating that even though the fossil lacks detailed structure of the spiral caps, a distinctive chemical composition was found in the fossil. The same kind of chemical could also be found in the substance that modern bees use to protect themselves against water. Consequently, chemical analysis of the fossil shows that it is highly possible that bees created the fossil 200 million years ago.

TPO 46 综合写作

◆ 笔记要点

	Reading	Listening
MP	electr medical records > paper	×
1	cost ↓ 1) no store space 2) transfer easily	paper recrd for emergcy backup & signature on paper for legal → still need storage spac

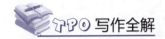

2	error ↓: 1) paper poor handwriting 2) electr: standard form & fonts	doctor use paper examin patients & prescription → later office staff interpret poor writing & type into electr → errors ↑
3	aid research ← easy get informtn of patients	privacy law: follow procedures & get patients permission →Diffclt access informtn

◆ 参考范文

The reading passage and the lecturer hold two competing attitudes toward the electronic documentation of patients' medical information. The reading passage maintains that electronic documentation has several advantages while the lecturer believes otherwise.

Firstly, in the reading material it is suggested that electronic records can help to save money on storage and transference of medical records. The lecturer, however, believes that the cost efficiency of using electronic documentation is not so significant since doctors who use electronics to store information still have to keep the paper documents as a kind of back-up. Actually, they need signatures for legal reasons. Doctors still need to pay electronic storage cost. Consequently, it is not very cost effective to adopt the electronic form of information.

Secondly, the reading material suggests that electronic documentation can help to reduce errors. The lecturer, on the other hand, argues that electronic forms of documents cannot avoid errors since when doctors write prescriptions they use paper, thus poor handwriting can still cause problems because it is the staff members who are supposed to enter the records in the electronic system, not the doctors.

Lastly, the reading material contends that electronic medical systems can aid research given the fact that the databases are already formatted for data collection. The lecturer, however, refutes this statement by arguing that medical information is not accessible because it is subject to privacy law and the hospital has to keep the medical information private. If researchers need to collect electronic data they have to follow certain procedures and permissions by patients. Patients grant them permission when it has something to do with their medical conditions but they block the use of their medical information for any other purpose.

TPO 47 综合写作

◆ 笔记要点

	Reading	Listening
MP	pterosaurs × powered flight	×
1	cold-blood → slow metabolism → energy 少 → × fly warm → fly	fossil → pte have hair-like covering/fur → typical of warm-blooded to keep high temp ∴ metabolism of pte more like warm
2	pte 大 & heavy → × flap fast → airborne	pte have hollow bones → weight 小
3	birds → legs to jump/ run fast → take off pte back leg 小 /weak → × run fast	diffrt 1) birds use hind legs to launch 2) pte four limbs → run fast/jump to launch e.g. modern flying animals, bats

◆ 参考范文

The reading passage and the lecturer hold two competing opinions about whether pterosaurs were capable of powered flight. The reading passage maintains that it is no possible for them to fly by flapping their wings by providing three arguments while the lecturer believes pterosaurs were capable of powered flight by citing three pieces of evidence accordingly.

Firstly, in the reading material, it is suggested that ancient reptiles were probably cold-blooded and they have a slow metabolism, meaning that they are unable to produce enough energy. The lecturer, however, believes that recent fossil records show that pterosaurs had dense hair and fur, which is an indicator of warm blooded animals since they need hair and fur to keep a high body temperature. So, the special body feature means that the pterosaurs could supply enough energy for powered flight.

Secondly, the reading material suggests that there is a limit to the weight of animals that can be kept airborne by powered flight. Pterosaurs were just too large to be able to flap their wings fast enough to stay aloft. The lecturer, on the other hand, argues that anatomical analysis of pterosaurs shows that their bones were not solid instead of hallow. Thus, even though they have a very big frame, their didn't weigh so much. Eventually, it is totally possible for them to be airborne.

Lastly, the reading material contends that large pterosaurs, back-leg muscles were too small to allow them to run fast enough to launch themselves into the air. The lecturer, however, states that there is a huge difference between birds and pterosaurs. Pterosaurs could use four limbs to run fast enough to launch themselves into the air. They are like bats, which can also use four limbs to take off. However, birds only use two limbs to launch.

TPO 48 综合写作

◆ 笔记要点

	Reading	Listening
MP	solve frog ↓	×
1	law 禁 pesticides → harm from pestcd ↓	stop pesticd →farmers close to frog lose crops → × economical practical & fair
2	antifungal treatment → kill fungs	Prblm: 1) treatment to each frog → use in large scale hard 2) not prevent passing fungus to offspring
3	habitat protct : 人 excessive 水 / wetland 干 → habitat ↓	not water use but global warming → wetlands ↓

◆ 参考范文

The reading passage provides three ways to protect frog species while the lecturer believes these approaches are not practical.

Firstly, in the reading material, it is suggested that laws can be put forward to prohibit the use of harmful pesticides, which will reduce the harm that pesticides cause to frogs. The lecturer, however, believes that stopping the use of pesticides is not practical and fair to farmers who plant crops in places with threatened frog population. If farmers have to follow strict rules not to pesticide, they will not stay competitive in the market since they will have lower crop yields compared with their competitors.

Secondly, the reading material suggests that antifungal medication and treatment can be applied so that frogs' skin will not be harmed, thus they can absorb water. The lecturer, on the other hand, argues that treatment of frogs has to be done individually. Such a large scale operation can be very complicated since people need to capture frogs and treat them one by one. Plus, such a method cannot prevent the frogs from passing the disease to their offspring, meaning that every generation of frogs needs to be treated. Thus, such an approach is not practical.

Lastly, the reading material contends that water habitats can be protected from excessive water use so that frog species can recover. The lecturer, however, refutes this statement by arguing that water conservation cannot help to save the frog population. The real reason that caused the disappearance of habitats and the extinction of different species is global warming. So, protecting water cannot help to preserve frog species.

TPO 49 综合写作

◆ 笔记要点

	Reading	Listening
MP	evidence humpback navigate by star	×
1	intelgc enough → use night sky for orient	birds e.g. duck with averg intellgc use star navigt → instinct × intellgc
2	whale in ocean rely on stars → move in straight line	whale has biomagnetite → sensitive to earth magnt field → orient by mag × star
3	use spy-hopping look at star	1) sharks spy hop → look for food 2) whale spyhop in the day → can't see stars

◆ 参考范文

The reading passage provides three pieces of evidence proving that humpback whales use stars to navigate. However, each of them is confronted by the listening material.

First, the reading passage contends that humpback whales are intelligent enough to navigate by stars. However, the professor in the lecture argues that there is no connection between them. Some birds like ducks, can use stars for orientation, but their intelligence is average. So in the case of humpback whales, this ability of navigation by stars has nothing to do with intelligence. Using stars to navigate is just a natural instinct.

Secondly, according to the reading passage, humpback whales in the open ocean rely on stars so that they can maintain their movement in a straight line. Nevertheless, the listening material challenges this idea by saying that the brain of whales has biomagnetite, a substance sensitive to the

Earth's magnetic field. This fact proves that they use magnetic field instead of stars for orientation.

Finally, the reading passage says that humpback whales use spy-hopping to look at stars and then navigate by them. On the contrary, the listening material points out that the above claim does not hold water. Other animals also display the spy-hopping behaviors. For example, sharks do this to hunt animals. Moreover, whales often spy hop during the day when there is no stars which can be seen. Thus, it is speculative to say that humpback whales spy hop in order to navigate by stars.

TPO 50 综合写作

◆ 笔记要点

	Reading	Listening
MP	problm on send 人 to Mars	×
1	a round trip take 2 yrs & limited capcty → 水 /O_2/ food not enough	1) hydroponics to grow plants for food 2) plants waste 水 →fresh 水 & CO_2→O_2
2	0 gravity harm health	1) exercise to muscle ↑ 2) take vitamins bone dense ↑
3	1) harm from radiation 2) install a shield too heavy	1) high level radioation unusual 2) install 小 shield to prevent radiotn

◆ 参考范文

The reading passage points out that there are three problems which make it impossible to send humans to Mars. However, the listening material gives the solutions to the above problems in the reading passage.

Firstly, the author claims that a round trip to Mars takes two years but the cargo capacity of a spaceship is limited so that a Mars mission is impossible. Nevertheless, the lecturer directly refutes this argument by pointing out that astronauts can use hydroponics, a technique for growing plants in water to cultivate food in spacecraft. This technique can also transform waste water into clean water. Meanwhile, these growing plants can absorb carbon dioxide and release oxygen. In this case, astronauts will have enough food, drinkable water, and oxygen.

Secondly, in the reading part, it is suggested that spending long time in zero gravity will decrease muscle mass and lower bone density, meaning that people will experience grave medical problems. On the contrary, the lecturer argues that such a reasoning process does not bear further analysis. Astronauts have learned to use several techniques to deal with the negative effect caused by zero-gravity. For example, they can do regular exercise to improve the muscle mass or take vitamins, especially calcium, to increase the bone density.

Thirdly, the author of the reading passage asserts that humans on a mission to Mars would be exposed to dangerous levels of space radiation, since a spacecraft traveling in interplanetary space can't be protected by earth's magnetic field and installing a shield will add too much weight to the ship. But according to the lecture, the above claim does not hold water. She says that the dangerous level of radiation is occasional so we can build special instruments to monitor the radiation level and install a small shelter. When the radiation is strong, astronauts car stay in the shelter until the radiation is gone.

独立写作

独立写作技巧讲解

独立写作简介

本项写作任务会给出一个题目，要求考生对题目表达个人观点，并使用理由和具体的例子来佐证自己的观点。

具体要求如下图：

	出题形式	文体	写作时间
任务二	1) Do you agree or disagree with the following statement? 2) Some people believe X. Other people believe Y. Which of these two positions do you prefer or agree with?	议论文	30 mins

为便于考生理解，笔者在此处给出了几个例题：

Sample questions:

1) Do you agree or disagree with the following statement? A teacher's ability to relate well with students is more important than excellent knowledge of the subject being taught.

2) Some people like to travel with a companion. Others prefer to travel alone. Which do you prefer?

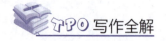

答题具体步骤

写作任务类型	任务步骤描述
任务二 独立写作 基于知识和经验的写作	● 审题 ● 30 分钟内构思，写作和修改文章 ● 用具体的例子和理由来证明主观点，全篇最少 300 单词，没有上限

独立写作各部分写作技巧

<h3 style="text-align:center">一、开头段</h3>

俗话说，万事开头难。很多考生在写独立写作时，也会觉得开头段无从下笔，耗费过多时间。在讲解开头段写作方法之前，我们先来看一篇满分作文的开头段。

例题：Do you agree or disagree with the following statement? Young people today are more likely to help others than the young were in the past.

Nowadays, with the interaction between individuals becoming increasingly frequent, social relationship has been brought under the spotlight of the mass media.【背景】Sociologists are strong believers of the claim that young people today are more likely to help others than the young were in the past, while old people view the issue from a different angle.【双方观点引出题目】In my eyes, helping others becomes less likely for young people today for the following reasons.【表明个人观点】

从上述考生满分文章来看，我们会发现，开头段通常可以分成三部分，即背景＋题目引出＋个人观点。如下图所示：

	背景
开头段	题目引出
	个人观点

要想快速高效地写出开头段，模板套路是必不可少的。笔者给大家推荐的开头段汉语模板如下：

现在，随着……（原因），上义词成为公众热议的焦点。一类人认为＋题目，然而，另一类人持有相反的观点。在我看来，个人观点，理由如下。

下面笔者将具体讲解开头段每个部分写作的方式，将上面的汉语模板变成英文。

◆ 1. 背景

关于背景，笔者首先要强调的是背景写作<u>两大原则：一是不能与题目无关，二是不能和题目完全重复。</u>不管使用何种背景写作方式，只要能够满足以上两个原则，都是可以接受的背景。

但是在考场上时间有限，最好用的方法应该是能够以不变应万变的写法。笔者下面介绍一种简单易操作的<u>背景写作方法——上义词背景法</u>，可以适用于所有的题目。背景句的句套如下：

时间状语，原因，<u>上义词成为公众热议的焦点</u>。

笔者在下面一一讲解背景句句套中的每个成分如何写成英文。

1.1 时间状语

特点：较为固定，<u>记住下面给出的表达方式任意一个即可。</u>

nowadays, at present, currently, in contemporary society, in this day and age

1.2 原因

特点：通常是一种<u>社会趋势类</u>，需根据<u>后面的上义词自行编写。</u>下面表达仅供参考：

随着科技的进步：with the advances of technology

随着社会的发展：with the development of society

随着时代的变迁：with the change of times

随着竞争越来越激烈：with the competition becoming increasingly fierce

随着物质财富的丰富：with the affluence of material wealth

随着自然环境的恶化：with the deterioration of natural environment

1.3 上义词成为公众关注的焦点

特点：作为背景句的核心，需要学会上义词背景法。

英文表达如下：

上义词 has become one of the most controversial topics among the general public.

上义词 has never failed to attract wide attention from the masses.

上义词 has been brought under the spotlight of the mass media.

A growing number of people attach importance to 上义词 .

要学会这种方法，需要两步走：

<u>Step 1: 提取题目核心意思。</u>

<u>Step 2: 找到题目核心意思的上义词。</u>

下面先来介绍第一步：

Step 1: 如何提取题目核心意思？

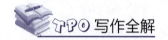

题目核心意思顾名思义，是指源自题目，体现题目讨论的核心事件。托福写作题型不同，提取的方法也有差异，具体如下：

A. 非对比类题目，直接提取题目中的核心事件。

例题演示：

Do you agree or disagree with the following statement? Always telling the truth is the most important consideration in any relationship between people. (TPO 2)

题目类型：非对比类

题目核心意思：人际关系中诚实的重要性

B. 对比类题目，需提取对比的对象。

例题演示：

(1) Do you agree or disagree with the following statement? Young people today are more likely to help others than the young were in the past. (2016/12/3)

题目类型：对比类

题目核心意思：现在和过去年轻人帮助他人

(2) Do you agree or disagree with the following statement? It is more important to keep your old friends than it is to make new friends. (TPO 3)

题目类型：对比类

题目核心意思：交新朋友和维护老朋友的重要性

(3) Do you agree or disagree with the following statement? In twenty years there will be fewer cars in use than there are today. (TPO 4)

题目类型：对比类

题目核心意思：现在和二十年后汽车的数量

Step 2: 如何找到题目核心意思的上义词？

首先，要理解上义词这个概念，上义词是指对事物更加概括和抽象的说明。比如，蔬菜就是茄子、白菜和芹菜的上义词。

上义词如下图所示：

其次，要学会提取上义词的方法，具体如下：

A. 找到题目核心意思更加概括和抽象的名词性表达。

B. 用特殊疑问词 (what/how/why 等) 对题目核心意思进行提问。

例题演示：

(1) Do you agree or disagree with the following statement? Always telling the truth is the most important consideration in any relationship between people. (TPO 2)

题目类型：非对比类

题目核心意思：人际关系中诚实的重要性

上义词：

a）找到题目核心意思更加概括和抽象的名词性表达。

人际交往中的重要因素成为公众热议的焦点。

b）用特殊疑问词 (what/how/why) 对题目核心意思进行提问。

人际交往中什么最重要成为公众热议的焦点。

(2) Do you agree or disagree with the following statement? Young people today are more likely to help others than the young were in the past. (2016/12/3)

题目类型：对比类

题目核心意思：现在和过去年轻人帮助他人

上义词：

a）找到题目核心意思更加概括和抽象的名词性表达。

年轻人的行为成为公众热议的焦点。

b）用特殊疑问词 (what/how/why) 对题目核心意思进行提问。

年轻人如何对待他人成为公众热议的焦点。

(3) Do you agree or disagree with the following statement? It is more important to keep your old friends than it is to make new friends. (TPO 3)

题目类型：对比类

题目核心意思：交新朋友和维护老朋友的重要性

上义词：

a）找到题目核心意思更加概括和抽象的名词性表达。

交友的重要性成为公众热议的焦点。

b）用特殊疑问词 (what/how/why) 对题目核心意思进行提问。

交什么样的朋友成为公众热议的焦点。

(4) Do you agree or disagree with the following statement? In twenty years there will be fewer cars in use than there are today. (TPO 4)

题目类型：对比类

题目核心意思：现在和二十年后汽车的数量

上义词：

a）找到题目核心意思更加概括和抽象的名词性表达。

未来的交通工具成为公众热议的焦点。

b）用特殊疑问词 (what/how/why) 对题目核心意思进行提问。

未来交通方式会怎样成为公众热议的焦点。

将上述背景的组成部分整合起来，组成完整的背景句，句套如下：

时间状语，原因，背景词 has been one of the most intensively discussed topics among the general public.

例题展示：

(1) Do you agree or disagree with the following statement? Always telling the truth is the most important consideration in any relationship between people. (TPO 2)

背景：

a）现在，随着人际交往越发频繁，人际交往中的重要因素成为公众热议的焦点。

b）在当今社会，随着交际圈的扩大，交往中什么最重要成为公众热议的焦点。

(2) Do you agree or disagree with the following statement? Young people today are more likely to help others than the young were in the past. (2016/12/3)

背景：

a）如今，随着人际交往越来越密切，人际关系成为公众热议的焦点。

b）现在，随着时代的变化，年轻人如何对待他人成为公众热议的焦点。

(3) Do you agree or disagree with the following statement? It is more important to keep your old friends than it is to make new friends. (TPO 3)

背景：

a）在当今时代，随着竞争越来越激烈，交友的重要性成为公众热议的焦点。

b）如今，随着社会的发展，交什么样的朋友成为公众热议的焦点。

(4) Do you agree or disagree with the following statement? In twenty years there will be fewer cars in use than there are today. (TPO 4)

背景：

a）现在，随着科技的进步，未来的交通工具成为公众热议的焦点。

b）如今，随着社会的发展，未来交通方式会怎样成为公众热议的焦点。

◆ 2. 题目引出

特点：句套相对固定，题目直接照抄即可。

题目引出的句套如下：

a）一类人 are strong believers of the claim that + 题目 while 另一类人 hold the opposite opinion.

b）一类人 are firmly in favor of the statement that + 题目 while 另一类人 view the issue from the opposite angle.

◆ 3. 表明个人观点

特点：观点要明确清晰，注意题目同义改写。

句套有以下两种表达方式：

第一种：

From my perspective, I side with/subscribe to the former/latter viewpoint for the following reasons.

第二种：

From my standpoint/position, + 题目改写 with the reasons as follows.

As far as I am concerned, + 题目改写. Here are the two reasons to support my viewpoint.

In my eyes, + 题目改写 for the following reasons.

小贴士：题目同义改写

定义：

用不同的语言表达转述相同的意思。

改写方式：

（1）通过变换主语改变句子结构（人→物→ doing → it）。

（2）替换同义词或短语。

例题演示：Teachers should assign homework to students every day.

（1）改变句子结构

Homework should be assigned to students every day by teachers.

Assigning homework to students every day is necessary.

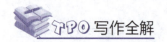

It is necessary for teachers to assign homework to students every day.

（2）替换同义词

原句：Teachers should assign homework to students every day.

同义句：Professors/Teaching staff are supposed to arrange/give daily assignments to school-age children.

二、主体段

开头段完成后，就要进入全文最重要的部分——主体段。在介绍主体段之前，笔者先要明确一下独立写作的全文结构。全文结构种类很多，但是笔者本书中推荐结构为：<u>一边倒总分总</u>，即<u>想出两个或三个分论点来完全同意或不同意所给出的题目</u>。推荐原因是：<u>这种结构适用于所有题目</u>。

下面正式进入主体段的讲解，先来看一个主体段的示范：

Do you agree or disagree with the following statement? Young people today are more likely to help others than the young were in the past.

题目大意：与过去的年轻人相比，现在的年轻人更有可能去帮助他人。

主观点：不同意

主体段一：

1) Furthermore, the more fierce competition nowadays is another factor which makes young people less likely to help others. 【主题句】2) One defining character of people is the degree to which they tend to care more about their own interests in a competition. 【正向解释】3) Job hunting is a good case in point. 4) Just imagine that there are 10 candidates competing for one position, which means that the winner has to outcompete the others. 5) Obviously, each candidate would regard others as his enemies instead of friends, thus providing no help for the other one. 【3~5 句举例论证】6) However, in the past, the competition was not so fierce as it is today, so that the youngsters treated others more friendly in old days. 【反向解释】7) Hence, the possibility that young people provide others with assistance is smaller, due to the more competitive environment. 【小结】

1）此外，现在更激烈的竞争是另一个使得年轻人不太可能帮助别人的因素。【主题句】2）人的一个决定性特征就是他们在竞争中更关心自己的利益。【正向解释】3）找工作是一个很好的例子。4）想象一下，有 10 名候选人竞争一个职位，这意味着获胜者必须战胜别人。5）很明显，每个候选人都将别人视为敌人而不是朋友，因此不会对另一个人提供任何帮助。【3~5 句举例论证】6）然而，在过去，竞争不像今天这么很激烈，所以以前的年轻人对待他

人更友好。【反向解释】7）因此，由于更加激烈的竞争环境，年轻人为别人提供援助的可能性比较小。【小结】

我们从上面的范文段落可以总结出主体段的基本结构。主体段 = 主题句 + 解释 + 举例，如下图：

主题句
解释
举例

下面笔者将一一介绍上面每个部分的写作技巧。

（一）主体段主题句写作

主体段主题句位于主体段的第一句话，是本段的核心。先来看两个主题句示范：

Firstly, the less free time owned by the young people【分论点】will reduce the likelihood that they help others.【主观点】

Furthermore, the more fierce competition nowadays【分论点】is another factor which makes young people less likely to help others.【主观点】

从上面两个主题句，可以看出主题句的基本构成如下：

主题句 = 逻辑词 + 主观点 + 分论点

◆ 1. 逻辑词

特点：只需记住固定表达即可。

首先：first and foremost, to begin with, for starters, in the first place/ instance

其次：in addition, besides that, what's more, in the second place

再次：thirdly, furthermore, finally

◆ 2. 主观点

主题句中体现主观点的原因：明确观点倾向，避免展开跑题。

主题句中体现主观点的方式：对题目进行同义改写。

◆ 3. 分论点

3.1 分论点的思考原则

原则 1：分论点之间要互斥，不能重合。

（1）不能互为因果。

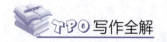

（2）不能相互包含。

（3）不能过度概括。

原则2：不能过于具体，目的是减小展开中词汇难度。

3.2 分论点的思考方法

为符合以上原则，需要掌握分论点的思考方法。不过在讲解方法之前，笔者先要讲清楚独立写作题目中的两种题型，因为题型不同，思考分论点的方式也有所差异。

独立写作题型分类如下：

a）价值判断类题目：讨论一个事情"好或坏"或者"应该与否"的问题。

b）现象证明类题目：讨论一件事情"是否存在"，无关利弊好坏。

为便于理解，来看以下的几个说法，尝试思考一下是否同意以及想到的分论点：

1) People should exercise.

2) It is important to do exercise every day.

3) Today people do more exercise than people 10 years ago.

思考后会发现，第一和第二两种说法思考分论点的方向有些相似，都是想做锻炼的利弊。但是第三种说法却不能直接罗列锻炼的好处，应该要去想现在和过去人的差异，比如健康意识提升和工作压力加大等原因。为什么会出现以上的差异呢？原因在于题型的不同。第一和第二两种说法为价值判断类题目，第三种说法为现象证明类题目。

基于上述的差异，笔者下面来介绍相应的分论点思考方法，具体如下：

a）价值判断类题目：想利弊，多以题目中有 should/ be important 等词为特点。

b）现象证明类题目：想原因，多以古今对比类题目为主。

以上两种思考分论点的方向可以帮助我们解决大部分题目分论点的思考，但是还是有少数题目无法通过上述题目想到分论点，此时，就可以使用第三种思考分论点的方向——拆分。

3.3 分论点的拆分

（1）拆现成：题目中有 and/or 连接的两个关键词，拆分开来，每个主体段只展开其中一个关键词即可。

TPO 1

Do you agree or disagree with the following statement? At universities and colleges, sports and social activities are just as important as classes and libraries and should receive equal financial support.

题目分析：主观点无论同意与否，都可以将题目中两个关键词 sports 和 social activities

分开来写，各成一段。

（2）生拆：找题目中的抽象 / 概括名词的下义词。下义词如图所示：

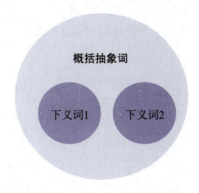

生拆的步骤：

Step 1: 找到题目中的抽象或概括性名词。

Step 2: 从中选取一个抽象或概括性名词，找到其下义词。

TPO 11

Some people say that the Internet provides people with a lot of valuable information. Other people think access to much information creates problems. Which view do you agree with?

题目分析：

主观点：互联网给人们提供了很多有价值信息。

Step 1: 找到题目中的抽象或概括性名词。

people & valuable information

Step 2: 选取一个抽象或概括性名词，找到其下义词。

people: 学生 & 员工

valuable information：学习材料 & 日常信息

（二）主体段展开方式

写出主题句之后，下面最重要也是最有难度的部分就来了。那就是如何展开主题句，换句话说，就是如何把一个 10 来个单词的主题句变成一个 130 单词以上的主体段。我们来看看《官方指南》上的评分标准：

5 分	...is well developed, using clearly appropriate explanations, exemplifications, and/ or details

从满分 5 分评分标准来看，段落展开的方式有三种，分别是：解释 (explanations)、例证 (exemplification)、细节 (details)。而且三者之间的连词是 and/ or，也就是说，三种方式可

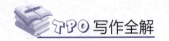

以单独使用，也可随机混用。另外，例证和细节其实本质都是信息具体化，只是呈现形式略微不同，所以笔者此处都归类为举例。

◆ **1. 主体段展开方式之解释法**

定义：运用相对抽象的因果逻辑证明主题句成立的方法。

解释法分类：

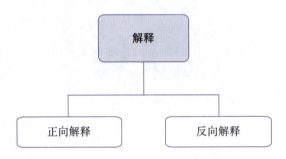

1.1 正向解释

沿着主题句的方向来证明主题句成立。

例题演示：

Do you agree or disagree with the following statement? Young people today are more likely to help others than the young were in the past.

主观点：现在年轻人帮助别人的可能性变小了。

主题句：Furthermore, the more fierce competition nowadays is another factor which makes young people less likely to help others.

越发激烈的竞争使得现在年轻人不太可能帮助他人了。

正向解释：就是要直接回答越发激烈的竞争为什么使得现在年轻人不太可能帮助他人了。

范文中给出的正向解释如下：

One defining character of people is the degree to which they tend to care more about their own interests in a competition. （人们在竞争中更加关注自身利益）

将主题句和解释合二为一，形成如下思路：

愈发激烈的竞争→（人们在竞争中更加关注自身利益）→年轻人不太可能帮助他人

另外，笔者要提醒考生，在进行正向解释时，要注意不同的主题句解释的重点不同：

a）对于主论点和分论点区别明显的主题句，重点解释的是搭建主论点和分论点之间的逻辑关系：

分论点→（正向解释：搭建因果）→总论点

例题展示：

Do you agree or disagree with the following statement? It is important to wear the same clothes in school or at work.

主观点：Agree

主题句：To begin with, wearing the same clothes in school or at work can make people improve efficiency.

穿相同的衣服 → 提升效率

正向解释：

穿相同的衣服→减少工作学习中的干扰→投入更多的时间到工作学习中→减少犯错→提高效率

b）对于主论点和分论点混为一体的主题句，重点解释的是整个主题句的前因或者后果：

（正向解释：拓展前因）→主题句→（正向解释：拓展后果）

例题展示：

Do you agree or disagree with the following statement? The rules that the whole society expects young people to follow are too strict.

主观点：Agree

主题句：Firstly, consider the strict rules from school.

学校的规则很严厉

正向解释：

为了规范学生的行为，方便学校的管理→学校给学生制定了很严厉的规则→学生感到巨大压力→出现厌学情绪。

小贴士：解释中因果逻辑词的使用

在进行汉英转换中，因果逻辑词使用非常高频，但是笔者要求遵循两个原则：

● 要准确

● 要多样

因为：

主句，because/ since/ for/ in that/ as/ for the reason that... + 句子.

主句，in that + 句子.

主句，because of/ due to/ owing to/ on account of + *n.* /doing... + 句子.

所以：

句子 A so that/ and thus/ with the result that 句子 B.

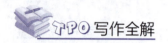

句子 1. As a result/ therefore/ thereof/ accordingly/ consequently/ in this way/ in that case, + 句子 2.

1.2 反向解释

定义：与正向解释方向相反，解释重点与正向解释一致。

分类：

a）A 正负比较：A vs 负 A

适用题目：题目本身仅在讨论一件事情

例题展示：

Do you agree or disagree with the following statement? Parents should express their disagreement when they think that teachers' teaching method is wrong.

主观点：Agree

主题句：表达不同观点会让学生受到更好的教育。

正向解释：

表达不同观点 → 老师会改变原先的教学方法→更加适合学生→学生得到更多的知识→受到更高质量的教育。

反向解释：

不表达不同观点→老师继续使用错误的教学方法→学生丧失对学习的兴趣→学生课上出现走神→无法受到更高质量的教育。

b）AB 型比较：A vs B

适用题目：题目本身在对比两件事情

例题展示：

Do you agree or disagree with the following statement? Strict teachers are better than humorous ones.

主观点：Disagree

主题句：幽默的老师能更好地保障教学效果。

正向解释：

幽默的老师→授课语言更加风趣→课堂更有趣→引起学生的兴趣→学生能够更加专注于课上内容→提升教学效果

反向解释：

严厉的老师→课堂形式单一无趣→学生很难集中注意力→出现走神或者犯困→教学效果难以保证

正向和反向解释使用时的注意事项：

1）正反向解释可单独使用，可同时使用。

2）若同时使用注意语言要进行同义改写，避免语言重复；逻辑词使用要正确多样。

转折逻辑词的使用：

● 正向解释 . By/In contrast/ On the contrary, 反向解释 .

● 正向解释，while/whereas 反向解释 .

3）在不跑题和不重复的前提下，尽可能多写。

◆ 2. 主体段展开方式之举例法

定义：运用细节信息对主题句或解释进行具体化的过程。

举例方式如下图：

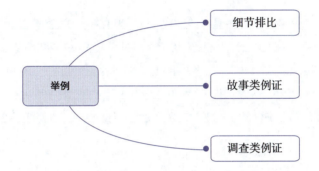

2.1 细节排比

定义：对主题句或解释中的概括词，加入两个及以上的下义词进行定点具体化。

应用步骤：

Step 1: 找主题句或解释中的概括词。

Step 2: 对概括词找下义词。

下义词的呈现形式：

a) 名词性短语：*n* such as/ like +*n*1 and *n*2.

b) 完整句：概括性句子 . To be specific, / Specifically speaking, / In details, /In other words/ Put it in another way/ That is to say, + 具体化句子 .

例题演示：

Do you agree or disagree with the following statement? At universities and colleges, sports and social activities are just as important as classes and libraries and should receive equal financial support. (TPO 1)

主观点：同意

主题句：Secondly, social activities play a vital role in cultivating students' practical abilities,

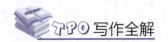

contributing to the all-round development of college students.

社会活动有助于培养学生的实践能力，从而有助于全面发展。

Step 1: 找主题句或解释中的概括词。

Social activities（社会活动）

Practical abilities（实践能力）

Step 2: 对概括词找下义词。

Social activities: international exchange programs & participation in social welfare activities

Practical abilities: become familiar with multicultural environments and develop an international perspective & organizational skills, team building abilities and leadership

细节排比：

To be specific, through the international exchange programs sponsored by the school, students have the opportunities to study for a short term in universities of foreign countries, like the United States and Canada. In-depth exposure to foreign culture and customs helps them become familiar with multicultural environments and develop an international perspective. Also participation in social welfare activities can foster students' organizational skills, team building abilities and leadership.

2.2 故事类例证

特点：易于编写，几乎适合所有题目类型。

a）以人为核心的故事逻辑：某人（名人/身边人）做了某事，结果如何。

b）以事为核心的故事逻辑：某个事物出现了，对某一群人产生了某种影响。

例题展示：

(1) Do you agree or disagree with the following statement? Technology has made children less creative than they were in the past. (TPO 9)

主观点：科技让孩子更加有创造力

主题句：First of all, advanced technology can better stimulate young people's curiosity and make it easier for students to explore the world.【从激发兴趣的角度来论证】

科技更好地激发孩子兴趣，探索未知。

举例：以人为核心的故事

For instance, when I was in middle school, my zoology teacher played us a video about "safari on the African prairie".【举例：引入例子之教学视频】The audio and visual effects were so intriguing that for the first time I found biology so interesting to learn.【举例：详述视频如何激发兴趣】From then on, I never stopped my inquiry in zoology and chose zoology as my major in university, which paved my way to make breakthroughs in the future research.【举例：详述兴趣对于创新的作用】

(2) Do you agree or disagree with the following statement? It is more important for students to understand ideas and concepts than it is for them to learn facts. (TPO 7)

主观点：理解概念更重要

主 题 句：Additionally, understanding ideas facilitates industrial development and improves people's living standards.

理解概念有助于工业的发展和提升生活水平。

举例：以事为核心的故事

For example, the invention of the steam engine helped to improve human productivity and efficiency and facilitated Industrial Revolution.【举例：引入蒸汽机】It was first used for mining and gradually, with a deeper understanding of the idea behind it, it was applied to mills, factories, breweries and it was also accredited for the development in agriculture and transportation.【举例：详述概念理解对蒸汽机发展的影响过程】However, without the application of the steam power in different aspects of people's life, we could have lived in brutal poverty.【举例：总结蒸汽机对人们生活的影响】

2.3 调查类例证

特点：较为官方，模板套路性强

编写逻辑：

a）某一机构在某年在某些人中做了一个关于 ×× 调查，该调查表明……

b）根据某机构做的一项调查，我们可以发现……

例题展示：

Do you agree or disagree with the following statement? In order to become financially responsible adults, children should learn to manage their own money at young age. (TPO 15)

主观点：应该学会从小理财

主题句：Another obvious benefit of allowing kids to start managing money early is that they will acquire financial knowledge and skills, essential to become financially responsible.

从小理财有助于学会理财知识和技能。

举例：调查类例证

According to a recent bank report, the average young adult amasses $45,000 in debt by the time they turn 29.【举例：引入调查，说明目前年轻人的财政状况】Further scrutiny shows that 90% of the young people in debt grew up in the family where parents seldom left allowance to kids.【举例：引用调查探究年轻人负债的原因】

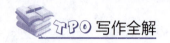

三、结尾段

特点：

（1）结构简单：主要重述立场和概括分论点，注意对上述信息的同义改写。

（2）模板相对固定，自我修改形成个性化模板。

结尾段句套汇总如下：

Taking what has been discussed above into account, we can reach the conclusion that 主观点 , because + 分论点一 and 分论点二 .

Factoring the above evidence, it is safe to conclude that 主观点 , because + 分论点一 and 分论点二 .

Taking what has been mentioned into account, we can reach the conclusion that 主观点 , since + 分论点一 and 分论点二 .

In a nutshell, I am convinced that 主观点 , for + 分论点一 and 分论点二 .

独立写作范文 & 精析

TPO 1 独立写作

◆ 1. 题目

Do you agree or disagree with the following statement? At universities and colleges, sports and social activities are just as important as classes and libraries and should receive equal financial support.

◆ 2. 思路大纲

主观点：社会活动和体育一样重要

分论点一：社会活动方面：实践能力，全面发展

分论点二：体育活动方面：身心健康，高效学习

◆ 3. 高分范文和思维导图

1) Currently, with the popularization of higher education, the allocation of university's financial resources has never failed to attract attention from the masses. 2) Consequently, some educators and professors argue that sports and social activities are as important as classes and libraries and such activities should receive equal financial support. 3) As for me, I totally side with the above statement.

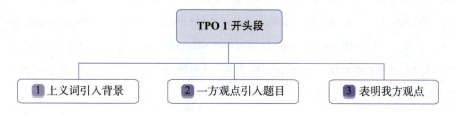

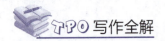

1) First of all, sports contribute to students' mental and physical health, which lays a solid foundation for their study efficiency in classes and libraries. 2) For one thing, overwhelmed by tons of assignments and tasks from academic study, students have to sit nearly around the clock, thus leading to a sedentary lifestyle. 3) Working out regularly in the gym can prevent them from suffering from near-sightedness and backache. 4) For another, negative emotions such as frustration and pressure from the heavy academic work need to be released. 5) Doing sports is a good vent to empty out all these destructive feelings. 6) Just imagine that if you have failed a mathematics test, you can just play basketball with your friends for a whole afternoon and totally forget about the disaster. 7) Whatever sports you want to engage in, sports facilities including gym, playground, and tennis court are indispensable so that the fund from the university is in great need.

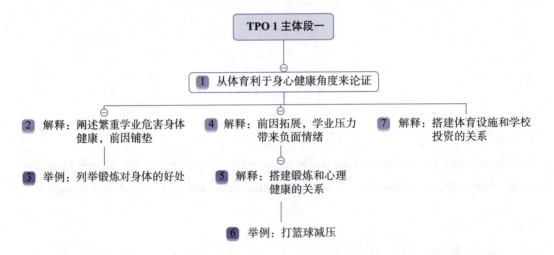

1) Secondly, social activities play a vital role in cultivating students' practical skills, contributing to the all-round development of college students. 2) To be specific, by joining in international exchange programs sponsored by the school, students have the opportunities to study for a short term in universities of foreign countries like the United States and Canada. 3) In-depth exposure to foreign culture and customs helps them become familiar with multicultural environments and develop an international perspective. 4) Also, participation in social welfare activities can foster students' organizational skills, team building abilities and leadership. 5) All the above qualities and skills are of equal importance with expertise acquired in class. 6) As we all know, in such a society full of fierce competitions, the job market is becoming more and more selective, which means that a good command of theoretical and professional knowledge is no longer adequate. 7) Well-rounded students, the ones equipped with practical skills and abundant expertise, enjoy more popularity in the job market. 8) Given this situation, equal importance should be attached to social activities held by the school.

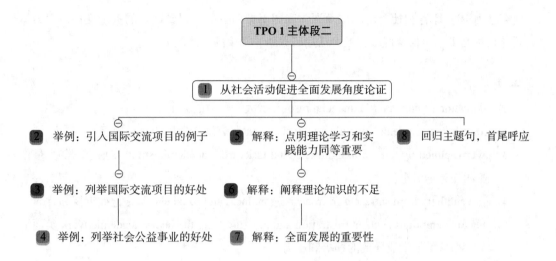

To sum up, equal financial supports should be given to the following two areas: sports and social activities as well as classes and libraries, because sports facilities can help students keep fit and social activities can equip students with practical skills.

◆ 4. 范文译文

1）目前，随着高等教育大众化的推进，高校财力资源的配置问题始终受到大众的关注。2）因此，一些教育工作者和教授认为，体育和社会活动与课堂和图书馆一样重要，这种活动应得到同等的财政支持。3）至于我，我完全赞同上述说法。

1）首先，体育运动对学生的身心健康有着重要的促进作用，为学生在课堂和图书馆的学习效率奠定了坚实的基础。2）一方面，专业学习的作业和任务不堪重负，学生不得不几乎全天坐着，从而导致久坐不动的生活方式。3）定期在健身房锻炼可以防止近视和背痛。4）另一方面，需要释放负面情绪，如繁重的学业导致的挫折和压力。5）做运动是清除所有这些破坏性情绪的好机会。6）试想一下，如果你没有通过数学考试，你可以和朋友一起一整个下午打篮球，完全忘记这场灾难。7）无论您想从事什么运动，健身房、操场和网球场等体育设施都是不可或缺的，因此大学的资金需求非常大。

1）其次，社会活动在培养学生实践能力、促进大学生全面发展方面发挥着重要作用。2）具体而言，通过学校主办的国际交流项目，学生有机会短期到美国、加拿大等国外大学学习。3）深入接触外国文化和习俗有助于他们熟悉多元文化环境，拓展国际视野。4）参加社会公益活动可以培养学生的组织能力、团队建设能力和领导能力。5）以上所有的素质和技能与课堂上所获得的专业知识同等重要。6）众所周知，在这样一个充满激烈竞争的社会，就业市场越来越挑剔，这就意味着理论专业知识的掌握已经不够。7）具有实践能力和丰富专业知识的全面发展的学生在就业市场上更受欢迎。8）在这种情况下，学校举办的社会活动应该受到同等重视。

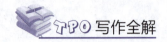

综上所述，体育和社会活动以及课堂和图书馆两方面应得到同等的资金支持，因为体育设施可以帮助学生保持健康，社会活动可以培养学生的实践能力。

◆ 5. 重点场景表达

1) allocation of university's financial resources 大学财力的分配

2) contribute to students' mental and physical health 有助于学生的身心健康

3) overwhelmed by tons of assignments and tasks from academic study 专业学习的大量作业和任务不堪重负

4) prevent them from suffering from near-sightedness and backache 防止他们近视和背痛

5) negative emotions such as frustration and pressure from the heavy academic work 负面情绪，如繁重的学业导致的挫折和压力

6) a good vent to empty out all these destructive feelings 发泄所有这些破坏性情绪的好机会

7) fail a mathematics test 数学考试不及格

8) sports facilities including gym, playground, and tennis court 体育设施，包括健身房、操场和网球场

9) become familiar with multicultural environments and develop an international perspective 熟悉多元文化环境，培养国际视野

10) participation in social welfare activities 参与社会福利活动

11) foster students' organizational skills, team building abilities and leadership 培养学生的组织能力、团队建设能力和领导能力

12) a good command of theoretical professional knowledge 掌握理论专业知识

TPO 2 独立写作

◆ 1. 题目

Do you agree or disagree with the following statement? Always telling the truth is the most important consideration in any relationship between people.

◆ 2. 思路大纲

主观点：说真话在维持人际关系上并不总是重要的
分论点一：偶尔不吐露真言可以保护私人空间
分论点二：善意的谎言可以维护各种关系

◆ 3. 高分范文思维导图

1) It is undisputed that honesty is a very important factor in all kinds of relationships. 2) People tend to establish friendship with someone who is decent, congenial and honest, because nobody is willing to deal with a cheater. 3) However, when it comes to the question of whether telling the truth is the most important factor in relationships, I, personally, am of the opinion that it is not possible to be completely honest with others based on the following reasons.

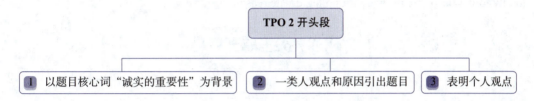

1) First of all, to maintain a quality friendship, one needs to keep a certain distance and have their own private space. 2) Sometimes, one might have awkward and embarrassing moments that they don't want to share with others, and for me, it is totally understandable to keep these moments to themselves. 3) For example, I was a disobedient kid back in high school, and I was not my teachers' favorite student since I would ditch classes. 4) I used to have a hard time getting along with others and my parents were desperate at that time. 5) However, these bad experiences didn't lead me astray for a long time and as time went by, I gradually gained confidence and became motivated to do the things that I liked. 6) Frankly, I feel really uncomfortable to unveil these experiences in front of my friends, being afraid that they might be judgmental and I might get alienated from my close friends.

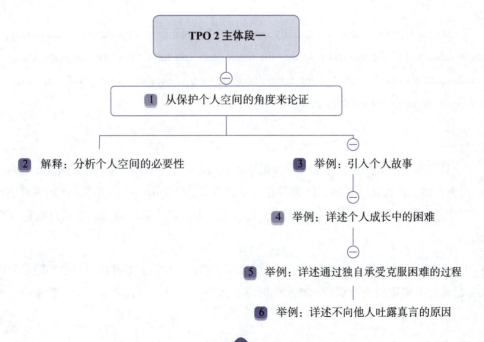

1) Additionally, sometimes a little white lie can be very helpful to maintain an intimate relationship whether one is dealing with family members, friends or girlfriends and boyfriends. 2) For example, if you forgot one of your best friends' birthday, he or she might get really upset about it. 3) Any person with a little bit of emotional intelligence would not tell him or her the true story. 4) It is okay for you to say that you had been working all day long and it just slipped your mind. 5) This can keep your friend from getting hurt as much as they would if they just thought you totally forgot his or her birthday for no legitimate reason.

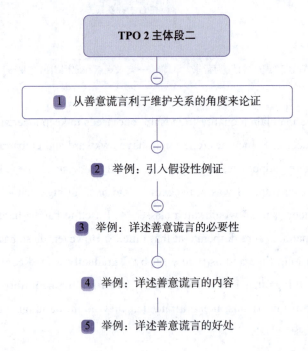

To conclude, to maintain a mutually beneficial friendship or any kind of relationship, it is indispensable to leave some room so that the other party can have their private space. Plus, some white lies can also be lubricant to the relationship as long as they are for a good cause instead of being based on one's personal interest.

◆ 4. 范文译文

1）诚实是各种关系中一个非常重要的因素，这是毫无争议的。2）人们倾向于与一个正派、友善和诚实的人建立友谊，因为没有人愿意与骗子打交道。3）然而，谈到说真话是否是人际关系中最重要的因素这个问题时，我个人认为，基于以下原因，不可能对他人完全诚实。

1）首先，为了保持高质量的友谊，人们需要保持一定的距离，并拥有自己的隐私空间。2）有时候，人们可能会有尴尬和难堪的时刻，他们不想与其他人分享，而对我来说，把这些时刻留给他们自己是完全可以理解的。3）例如，我在高中时是一个不听话的孩子，我不是我老师最喜欢的学生，因为我有时会翘课。4）我曾经很难与他人相处，当时我的父母对此很绝望。5）然而，这些不好的经历并没有让我误入歧途，随着时间的推移，我逐渐获得了信心，并且变得有动力去做我喜欢的事情。6）坦率地说，我觉得在朋友面前透露这些经历真的很不舒服，担心他们可能会说三道四，我可能会被我的亲密朋友疏远。

1）另外，无论是与家庭成员、朋友还是男女朋友打交道，有时一个善意的谎言可能对维持亲密关系非常有帮助。2）例如，如果你忘记了你最好的朋友的生日，他或她可能真的很难过。3）任何具有一点情商的人都不会告诉他或她事情的真相。4）你可以说你一整天都在工作，而且这件事只是不小心忘记了。5）这可以让你的朋友免受伤害，尤其是如果他们认为你没有任何正当理由而完全忘了他或她的生日。

总而言之，为了保持互利的友谊或任何形式的关系，留下一些余地以使他人可以拥有他们的私人空间是不可或缺的。此外，一些善意的谎言也可以成为这种关系的润滑剂，只要它们是为了一个好的目的而不是为了个人的利益。

◆ 5. 重点场景表达

1) keep a certain distance and have their own private space 保持一定的距离并且拥有自己的隐私空间

2) have a hard time getting along with others 很难与他人相处

3) lead sb. astray 让某人误入歧途

4) unveil these experiences in front of friends 在朋友面前透露这些经历

5) emotional intelligence 情商

6) sth. slips one's mind 某人遗忘某事

7) for no legitimate reason 没有任何正当理由

8) be lubricant to the relationship 成为关系的润滑剂

TPO 3 独立写作

◆ 1. 题目

Do you agree or disagree with the following statement? It is more important to keep your old friends than it is to make new friends.

◆ 2. 思路大纲

主观点：维系老朋友更重要

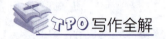

分论点一：更好地保证友谊的质量

分论点二：获得更多私人空间

◆ 3. 高分范文和思维导图

1) Friends are a big part of our lives. 2) Sometimes it is our friends who give us timely support and encouragement so that we can hang in there in face of hardships and barriers in our life. 3) Some people argue making new friends is more important than keeping old friends while others believe otherwise. 4) I, personally, think that keeping old friends is more important than establishing new friends hips.

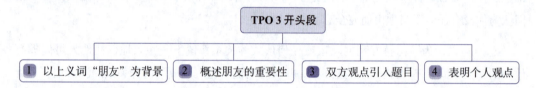

1) First of all, having fewer friends guarantees quality friendship, which in turn makes people happier. 2) It is common sense that if a person constantly makes new friends, he or she is cooler and more popular than others who don't. 3) However, establishing new friendships can be a long and hard process. 4) That someone has your number doesn't mean he or she is a friend of yours. 5) It doesn't mean someone is your friend now or in the future just because he or she was your friend at some point. 6) In fact, just keeping old friends means that we can spend quality time together and be committed to our friendship. 7) Given the fact that we have just a few old friends, we have enough time to hang out together, grab some food together, watch a game, and even go to a concert together.

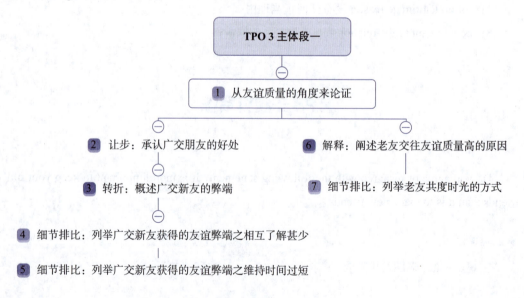

1) Additionally, maintaining close relationship with old friends means that we can have time to enjoy our personal space, which in turn brings more happiness to our life. 2) Maintaining a quality friendship takes time because we have to comfort our friends when things go wrong, listen to our friends when they complain about their work, and even empathize with our friends when they are in bad mood. 3) If we have too many friendships to maintain, we might be overwhelmed and stressed out since life is not all about pleasing others. 4) Instead, it is more important to learn to enjoy personal space which can be gained by keeping old friends. 5) When we are alone, we can read a book, watch a movie and even take a walk, all of which can help us to relax and reflect.

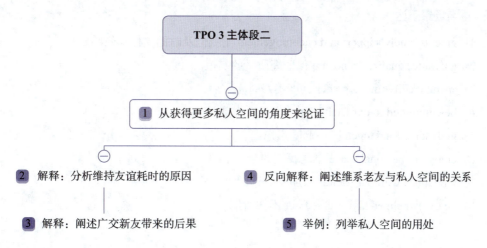

In all, keeping old friends is more important since it ensures high quality friendship and leaves more time for us to enjoy our personal space, which in turn makes us happier.

◆ 4. 范文译文

1）朋友是我们生活中很重要的一部分。2）有时候，我们的朋友会给我们及时的支持和鼓励，以便我们能够在生活中面对困难和障碍时坚持住。3）有些人认为结交新朋友比保持老朋友更重要，而另一些人则认为不然。4）我个人认为拥有老朋友比建立新友情更重要。

1）首先，拥有较少的朋友可以保证高质量的友谊，这反过来会让人更快乐。2）一般人认为，如果一个人不断结交新朋友，那么他或她会比其他人更酷、更受欢迎。3）然而，建立新的友谊可能是一个漫长而艰难的过程。4）别人有你的号码并不意味着他或她是你的朋友。5）某个时候某人是你的朋友并不意味着他或她现在或将来都是你的朋友。6）实际上，只留老朋友意味着我们可以共度美好时光，更专注于我们的友谊。7）如果我们只有几个老朋友，我们可以花时间聚在一起闲逛，一起吃点东西、看比赛，甚至一起去听音乐会。

1）另外，与老朋友保持密切的关系意味着我们有时间享受我们的个人空间，这反过来

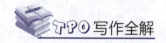

为我们的生活带来更多的快乐。2）保持高质量的友谊需要时间，因为当有事时，我们必须安慰我们的朋友，听朋友抱怨他们的工作，甚至在他们心情不好时表达同情。3）如果我们有太多的友谊需要维护，就可能会不知所措，因为生活并不是讨好别人。4）相反，学会享受通过维系几个老朋友获得的个人空间更重要。5）我们可以看书、看电影，甚至散步，所有这些都可以帮助我们放松和反思。

总而言之，保持老朋友更重要，因为它确保了高质量的友谊，让我们有更多时间享受我们的个人空间，这反过来使我们更快乐。

◆ 5. 重点场景表达

1) give us timely support and encouragement 给我们及时的支持和鼓励

2) guarantee quality friendship 保证高质量的友谊

3) spend quality time together 共度美好时光

4) be committed to our friendship 专注于我们的友谊

5) grab some food together 一起吃点东西

6) enjoy our personal space 享受我们的个人空间

7) empathize with our friends 对朋友表达同情

8) be overwhelmed and stressed out 不知所措

TPO 4 独立写作

◆ 1. 题目

Do you agree or disagree with the following statement? In twenty years there will be fewer cars in use than there are today.

◆ 2. 思路大纲

主观点：未来车辆会越来越少

分论点一：实现减缓交通拥堵和污染

分论点二：政府管理越来越严苛

◆ 3. 高分范文和思维导图

1) With the ever-increasing affluence of the masses, people tend to commute by car because cars do bring convenience and privacy to them. 2) However, when it comes to the question of whether there will be fewer cars in twenty years, people tend to give distinctive answers. 3) I, personally, am in favor of the statement that the number of cars will be in decline based on the

following reasons.

1) First of all, too many private vehicles cause traffic jams and serious environment pollution. 2) Nowadays, people with average salary and payment can afford a car. 3) Thus, there are more and more private vehicles than ever before, which in turn increases the likelihood of traffic congestions. 4) Such inconvenience is getting very serious in major cities around the world. 5) For instance, according to the report issued by Garmin, a pioneering company in producing GPS, it takes approximately an hour to travel 10 kilometres during rush hours in Beijing, as opposed to only 20 minutes during off-peak hours. 6) Also, too many cars tend to produce enormous amounts of poisonous exhaust in the air, which leads to air-borne issues like asthma, lung problems and even cancer. 7) In fact, people who have environmental awareness have already abandoned cars and chosen other forms of transport.

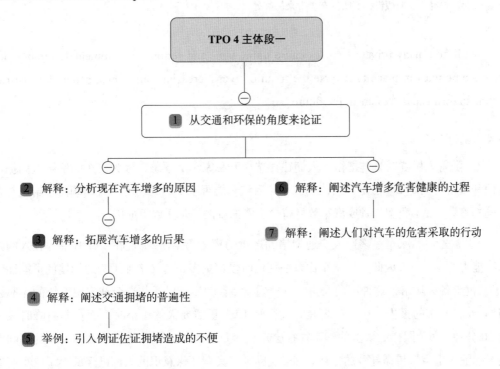

1) Additionally, governments around the globe start to realize the consequence of increasing car ownership and begin to regulate the number of vehicles in urban areas. 2) Indeed, too many

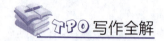

cars cause noise in urban places, which is very disturbing and disruptive to people. 3) Also, too many private vehicles put pressure on limited space available in urban places. 4) Thousands of parking spaces could have been used for other purposes, like building libraries, gardens, parks or playgrounds for kids. 5) Currently, governments have put forward a series of policies to limit the number of vehicles like increasing registration fee, gasoline price, parking fees, insurance and even maintenance cost. 6) Consequently, these measures will discourage people from buying more cars.

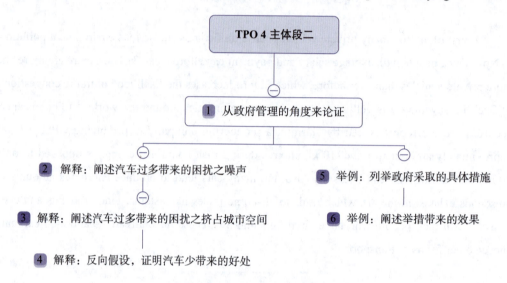

In all, too many private vehicles cause traffic jams and serious environmental pollution and there are policies in place to reverse the trend of ever increasing cars. Thus, people will be less willing to own and drive cars in the future.

◆ 4. 范文译文

1）随着人民群众日益富裕，人们往往选择开私家车上下班，因为汽车的确给人们提供方便和私密空间。2）但是，当谈到二十年后汽车能否减少的问题时，人们倾向于给出与众不同的答案。3）我本人赞成汽车数量将会下降的说法，基于以下原因。

1）首先，私家车过多造成交通拥堵和严重的环境污染。2）现在，拥有中等收入的人都有能力买车。3）因此，私家车比以往任何时候都更多，这又增加了交通拥堵的可能性。4）在世界各大城市，这种不便变得非常严重。5）例如，根据制造全球定位系统的先驱公司 Garmin 发布的报告，在北京高峰时段行驶 10 公里需要大约 1 小时，而在非高峰时段只有 20 分钟。6）同样，太多的汽车往往会产生大量有毒的废气，这会导致哮喘、肺部问题甚至癌症等由空气传播导致的疾病。7）实际上，具有环保意识的人们已经放弃了汽车而选择其他形式的交通工具。

1）此外，全球各国政府开始意识到增加汽车保有量的后果，并开始控制城市车辆的数量。2）确实，太多的汽车在城市地区造成噪声，这是非常令人不安且极具破坏性。3）同样，太多的私人车辆对城市有限的空间施加了巨大压力。4）数千个停车位本可用于其他目的，比如为孩子们建造图书馆、花园、公园或体育场。5）目前，各国政府提出了一系列限制汽车数量的政策，比如增加注册费、汽油价格、停车费、保险甚至维护成本等。6）因此，这些措施将阻止人们购买更多的汽车。

总而言之，太多的私人车辆造成交通拥堵和严重的环境污染，各国政府已经制定了扭转汽车日益增长趋势的政策，因此未来人们不愿意拥有和驾驶汽车。

◆ 5. 重点场景表达

1) With the ever-increasing affluence the masses 随着人民群众日益富裕

2) people with average salary and payment 拥有中等收入的人们

3) produce enormous amounts of poisonous exhaust in the air 会产生大量有毒的废气

4) environmental awareness 环保意识

5) regulate the number of vehicles 控制城市车辆的数量

6) put pressure on 对……施加压力

7) registration fee, gasoline price, parking fees, insurance and even maintenance cost 注册费、汽油价格、停车费、保险甚至维护成本

8) discourage people from buying more cars 阻止人们购买更多的汽车

TPO 5 独立写作

◆ 1. 题目

Do you agree or disagree with the following statement? People today spend too much time on personal enjoyment, doing things they like to do rather than doing things they should do.

◆ 2. 思路大纲

主观点：现在人们将更多时间花在应该做的事情上

分论点一：人们现在工作压力很大

分论点二：人们现在日常开销很大

◆ 3. 高分范文和思维导图

1) Increasing affluence makes it possible for people to experience all sorts of entertainments ranging from watching movies at home to traveling around the globe. 2) However, some people argue that people are so obsessed with entertainment activities instead of focusing on things they

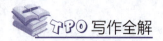
should do. 3) I, personally, don't agree with the claim based on the following reasons.

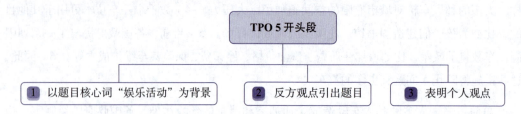

1) First of all, the truth is that people in modern society have so great responsibilities to assume in their intensely competitive careers. 2) Indeed, people, especially urban dwellers, live a hectic life, barely having time to entertain themselves or spend quality time with their families. 3) To be more specific, employees are overwhelmed with an enormous amount of workload like attending business meetings, submitting reports to their supervisors, going on business trips, or even addressing customers' problems. 4) Also, so competitive is the professional environment that employees are under enormous pressure from their coworkers and immediate supervisors. 5) Any negligence or dereliction of duty will cost them a promising career and possibly they will be fired by their managers.

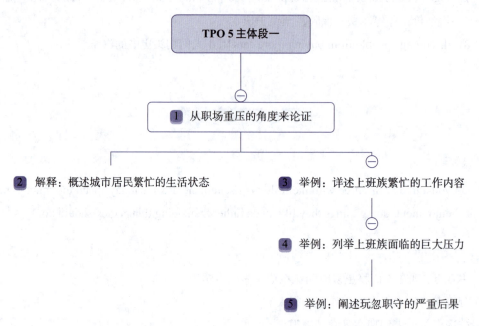

1) Additionally, they experience pressure in their private life. 2) This pressure can be broken down into two separate categories. 3) One reason why people are stressful is that they might have a tight budget, making them struggle to make ends meet. 4) For instance, adults have to pay mortgage, kids' tuition, and medical bills. 5) All the above cost will make it difficult for people to

have a leisurely lifestyle. 6) The other contributing factor to the pressure comes from competition and jealousy. 7) When a close friend purchased a bigger house or a fancy sedan, people tend to be jealous of this friend and aspire to have the same property, which in turn makes them stressed out.

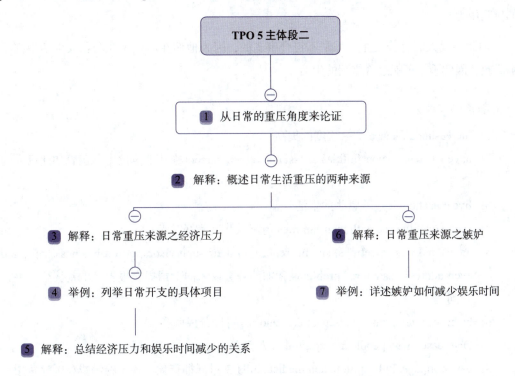

Thus, it is not true to say that people focus too much on entertainment since they are overwhelmed in both career and private life, making it less likely to lead a leisurely life.

◆ 4. 范文译文

1）富裕程度的提高使人们可以体验从在家看电影到环游世界等各种娱乐活动。2）然而，有些人认为人们对娱乐活动如此痴迷，而不是专注于他们应该做的事情。3）基于以下原因，我个人不同意这种说法。

1）首先，事实是，现代社会的人们在职业生涯中承担着如此巨大的责任，因为这些职业竞争激烈。2）事实上，人们，尤其是城市居民，过着紧张的生活，几乎没有时间娱乐自己或与家人共度美好时光。3）更具体地说，作为员工，人们会因为参加商务会议、向上司提交报告、出差甚至解决客户问题等工作而不堪重负。4）职场内部竞争同样激烈，员工时刻受到来自同事和直接主管的巨大压力。5）任何疏忽或失职都会使他们失去光明的职业前途，甚至他们可能会被经理解雇。

1）另外，人们在他们的私人生活中承受重大压力。2）这种压力可以分成两类。3）人们有压力的一个原因是他们的预算紧张，使他们难以维持生计。4）例如，成年人必

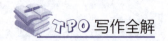

须支付抵押贷款、孩子的学费和医疗费用。5）所有上述开销将使人们难以拥有悠闲的生活方式。6）压力的另一个促成因素来自竞争和嫉妒。7）当一位好友购买了一幢更大的房子或一辆昂贵的轿车时，人们往往会嫉妒这位朋友，并渴望拥有同样的财产，这反过来又使他们感到压力。

因此，说人们过分关注娱乐是不符合事实的，因为他们在职业生涯和私人生活中都不堪重负，因此不太可能过着悠闲的生活。

◆ 5. 重点场景表达

1) increasing affluence 富裕程度的提高

2) have so great responsibilities to assume in their careers 在职业生涯中承担着如此巨大的责任

3) live a hectic life 过着紧张的生活

4) spend quality time with their families 与家人共度美好时光

5) attend business meetings, submit reports to their supervisors, go on business trips, and even address customers' problems 参加商务会议、向上司提交报告、出差甚至解决客户问题

6) be broken down into two separate categories 可以分成两类

7) One reason why people are stressful is 人们有压力的一个原因是

8) pay mortgage, kids' tuition, and medical bills 支付抵押贷款、孩子的学费和医疗费用

9) The other contributing factor to the pressure comes from 压力的另一个促成因素来自

TPO 6 独立写作

◆ 1. 题目

Do you agree or disagree with the following statement? Life today is easier and more comfortable than it was when your grandparents were children.

◆ 2. 思路大纲

主观点：现在的生活更加轻松

分论点一：从社会福利的角度来论证

分论点二：从收入角度来论证

◆ 3. 高分范文和思维导图

1) Taking a panoramic picture of human evolution, people's life has improved significantly

despite twists and turns. 2) Even though pessimists argue that problems like environment deterioration, resource depletion and population explosion make the world a worse place to live, I reckon that people's life has been far better than it was when our grandparents were children.

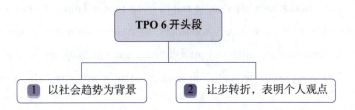

1) First of all, most of the countries around the world have their own social welfare systems, which significantly improve people's living standard. 2) As long as an individual is a legal citizen of a certain country, he or she is entitled to enjoy a series of social welfares like food stamps, unemployment benefit, and even medicare. 3) To be more specific, food stamps are aimed to help those low income people to get food; unemployment assistance is offered to workers who have lost their jobs; medicare intends to cover people's health and medical costs. 4) These social programs help millions of families get out of poverty and live a decent life. 5) For example, when my brother was laid off two years ago, he was entitled to apply for the unemployment benefit and some housing subsidy. 6) With these two benefits, he was able to live a decent life. 7) Had these social programs not been in place, he could have led a low quality life.

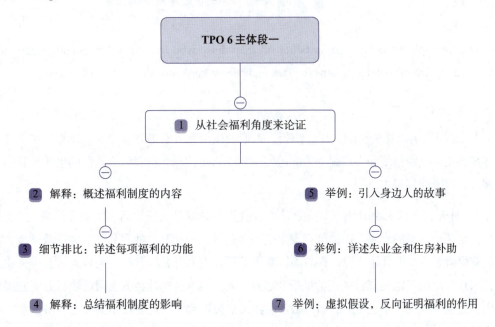

1) Secondly, ever-increasing salary is another contributing factor to the higher living standard. 2) With a strong economy, employees especially those in developed countries are getting

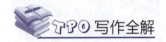

better payment and salary. 3) More disposable income makes it possible for people to invest in themselves, their children and their community. 4) For instance, they can buy a bigger house, a luxurious car, and finance their kids' college education so that kids will not suffer from the financial pressure of getting a student loan. 5) People might even plan a family trip to a foreign country and spend quality time with their family members. 6) Also, with more money in their pocket, people will be more involved in philanthropic activities and reaching out to the unlucky ones in their community. 7) Rising salary leads to ripple effects that eventually help to improve people's livelihood.

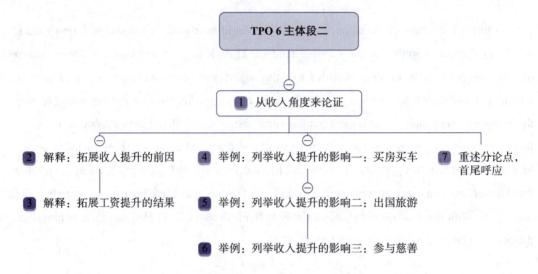

In all, people nowadays are far better off than those who lived decades ago since currently there are a myriad of social programs in place and people generally have been better paid.

◆ **4. 范文译文**

1）纵观人类进化的全貌，尽管曲折，人们的生活却大有改观。2）尽管悲观主义者认为环境恶化、资源枯竭和人口爆炸等问题使世界变得更糟糕，但我认为人们的生活比我们的祖父母是孩子时好得多。

1）首先，全球大部分国家都有自己的社会福利制度，人民生活水平明显提高。2）只要个人是某个国家的合法公民，就有权享受一系列的社会福利，如食品券、失业救济金，甚至医疗保险。3）更具体地说，食品券旨在帮助低收入人群获得食品；失业人员获得失业援助；医疗保险的目的是支付人们的健康和医疗开销。4）这些社会方案帮助数百万家庭摆脱贫困，过上体面的生活。5）例如，两年前我弟弟被解雇时，他有权申请失业救济金和一些住房补贴。6）有了这两种福利，他能够过上体面的生活。7）如果这些社会方案没有到位，他可能会过着低质量的生活。

1）其次，不断提高的工资是人民生活水平提高的另一个促进因素。 2）经济强劲，特别是发达国家的员工薪酬和待遇都有所提高。 3）更多的可支配收入使人们有可能投资自己、他们的孩子和社区。 4）例如，他们可以买一个更大的房子，一辆豪华的汽车，并为孩子的大学教育提供资金，这样孩子们就可以使他们免除学生贷款的经济压力。 5）人们甚至可以全家去国外旅行，与家人共度美好时光。 6）人们口袋里还有更多的钱，会更多地参与慈善活动，愿意帮助社区里不幸的人。 7）工资上涨导致涟漪效应，最终有利于改善民生。

总的来说，现在的人们比几十年前的人们生活得更好，因为现在有大量的社会福利方案，人们的薪酬也变得更高。

◆ 5. 重点场景表达

1) social welfare system 社会福利制度

2) improve people's living standard 提高人民生活水平

3) food stamps, unemployment benefit, and even medicare 食品券、失业救济金，甚至医疗保险

4) unemployment assistance 失业援助

5) health and medical costs 健康和医疗开销

6) lay off 使下岗

7) lead a low quality life 过着低质量的生活

8) contributing factor 促进因素

9) a luxurious car 一辆豪华汽车

10) suffer from the financial pressure 遭受经济压力

11) involved in philanthropic activities 参与慈善活动

12) lead to ripple effects 导致涟漪效应

TPO 7 独立写作

◆ 1. 题目

Do you agree or disagree with the following statement? It is more important for students to understand ideas and concepts than it is for them to learn facts.

◆ 2. 思路大纲

主观点：理解概念更重要

分论点一：有助于我们更好地理解世界

分论点二：有助于工业的发展

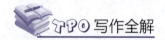

◆ 3. 高分范文和思维导图

1) Facts are based on experience and observation while most ideas and concepts are derived and generalized from thousands of facts. 2) When it comes to the question of whether it is more important to understand ideas and concepts than it is to learn facts, I, personally, reckon that understanding ideas and concepts are more important than learning facts based on the following reasons.

1) First of all, understanding concepts and ideas can promote better understanding of the world we are living in even though it is more demanding than just learning facts. 2) Indeed, concepts and ideas are complicated and fairly abstract to understand since they involve intense thinking process. 3) However, the understanding of a concept or an idea can be used in different areas, helping people to explore more academic subjects and disciplines. 4) For example, not everybody can conceptualize the great implication of an apple falling from a tree. 5) However, Isaac Newton, a great physicist, came up with his famous universal gravitation theory based on this incident. 6) The law, in other words, concept formulated by Newton helps people to understand the reason behind natural phenomena like the motion of the Moon around the Earth, the tides and falling objects.

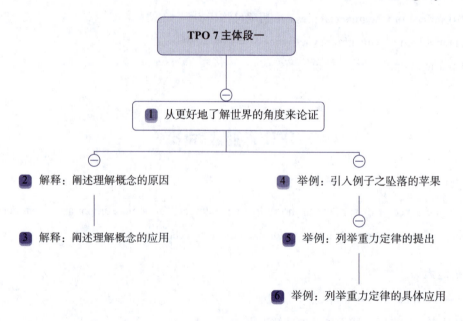

1) Additionally, understanding ideas facilitates industrial development and improves people's

lives. 2) Understanding the rationale and logic of an idea can be very beneficial to people in that the idea or concept might be applied in different areas in people's lives, which eventually helps people to improve their livelihood in general. 3) For example, the invention of the steam engine helped to improve human productivity and efficiency and facilitated Industrial Revolution. 4) It was first used for mining, and gradually with deeper understanding of the idea behind the steam engine, it was applied to mills, factories, breweries and it was also accredited for the development in agriculture and transportation. 5) However, without the application of the steam engine in different aspects of people's life, we could have lived in brutal poverty.

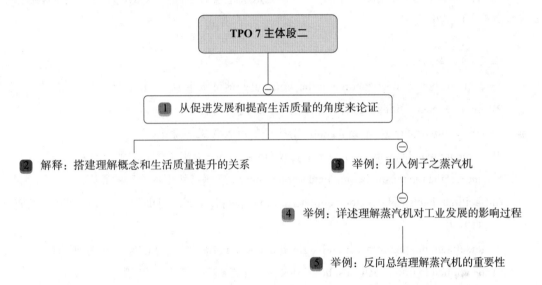

To conclude, understanding concepts and ideas is more important than just learning facts since ideas help human race understand the world better and improve people's livelihood.

◆ 4. 范文译文

1）事实基于经验和观察，而大多数想法和概念是根据成千上万的事实推导和概括的。2）当谈到理解概念比了解事实更重要的问题时，我个人认为理解概念确实要比学习事实更重要，基于以下原因。

1）首先，理解概念和想法可以更好地理解我们所生活的世界，即使它比仅仅学习事实要求更严格。2）的确，概念和想法复杂且相当抽象，因为它们涉及认真的思考过程。3）然而，对一个概念或理念的理解可以用在不同的领域，帮助人们探索更多的学科。4）例如，不是每个人都可以将从苹果树上掉下来的苹果概念化。5）然而，伟大的物理学家艾萨克·牛顿基于这件事情提出了他著名的万有引力理论。6）牛顿制定的法则，换言之，概念有助于人们理解自然现象背后的原因，如月球围绕地球的运动、潮汐和落物等。

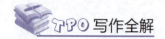

1）另外，理解理念有助于工业发展和改善人们的生活。2）理解一个想法的理论基础和逻辑可能对人们非常有益，因为这个想法或概念可能适用于人们生活中不同的领域，最终帮助人们改善他们的生活。3）例如，蒸汽机的发明显著地提高了人类生产力和效率，促进了工业革命。4）蒸汽机首次用于采矿，但是后来随着逐渐更加深入地了解蒸汽机的理念，它又被应用于纺织厂、工厂、酿酒厂，甚至对农业和交通运输领域的发展功不可没。5）然而，如果没有在人们生活的不同方面应用蒸汽动力，我们很有可能还过着难以忍受的贫困生活。

总之，理解概念和想法比仅仅学习事实更重要，因为想法可以帮助人类更好地理解世界并改善人们的生活。

◆ 5. 重点场景表达

1) promote better understanding of the world 更好地理解世界

2) involve intense thinking process 涉及认真的思考过程

3) conceptualize the great implication 对……的巨大含义概念化

4) come up with his famous universal gravitation theory 提出了他著名的万有引力理论

5) understand the reason behind natural phenomena 理解自然现象背后的原因

6) facilitate industrial development and improve people's lives 有助于工业发展和改善人们的生活

7) understanding the rationale and logic of one idea 理解一个想法的理论基础和逻辑

8) be applied to mills, factories, breweries 应用于纺织厂、工厂、酿酒厂

9) be accredited for the development in agriculture and transportation 对农业和交通运输领域的发展功不可没

10) live in brutal poverty 过着难以忍受的贫困生活

TPO 8 独立写作

◆ 1. 题目

Do you agree or disagree with the following statement? Television advertising directed towards young children (aged two to five) should not be allowed.

◆ 2. 思路大纲

主观点：应该禁播针对年幼孩子的广告

分论点一：为了减少父母和孩子间的矛盾

分论点二：为了提升孩子的身体健康

◆ 3. 高分范文和思维导图

1) Mentally mature adults know the inherent bias of advertising since it intends to promote products' sales and image. 2) However, when it comes to the question of whether television advertising directed toward young children should be allowed, there is much debate. 3) I, personally, would say such advertisements should be strictly banned based on the following reasons.

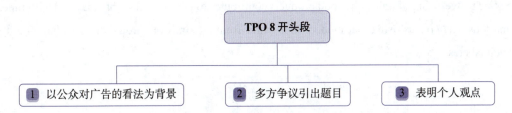

1) First of all, these advertisements mislead kids to buy too many products that they don't need, which might cause confrontation between parents and kids. 2) Young kids do not understand the persuasive intent of advertising so that they are easy targets for commercial persuasion. 3) Business research confirms that advertising does typically persuade young consumers to buy their products. 4) This is particularly true of advertisements for toys, because kids have an insatiable appetite for a wide range of toys like LEGOS, car models and *Action Hero* figures. 5) Whenever they see interesting toy advertisements, they will urge their parents to buy the products for them. 6) In most cases, since kids already have tons of toys and it is actually insane to buy more, parents might turn them down, which instigates parent-kid conflicts.

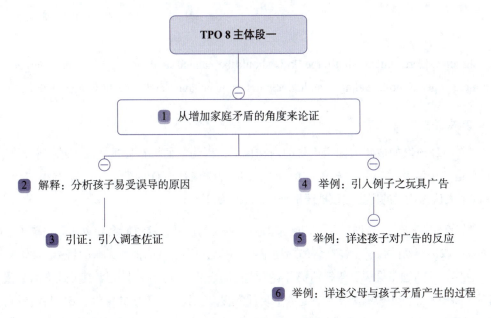

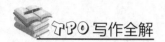

1) Additionally, kids exposed to lots of advertisements form bad eating habits, which will have a negative impact on their health. 2) With the advancement of their visual and sound effects, food and beverage advertisements make kids easy targets for commercial persuasion. 3) Lots of advertisements are about food and snacks that contain high calories like sugared cereals, candies, and different kinds of flavored sodas. 4) Generally, these TV commercials are very colorful and vivid, showing the kids having a good time eating these candies or drinking the flavored sodas. 5) Such advertising of unhealthy food products contributes to poor nutrition that may last a lifetime, and thus it is no surprising that modern kids suffer from all kinds of chronic diseases like obesity and diabetes.

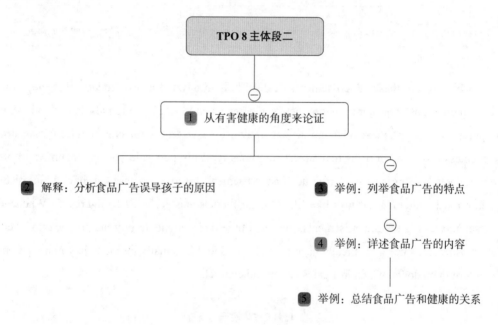

In all, advertisements that target kids should be banned as they make kids easy targets for commercial persuasion, leading to addictive purchasing behavior and unhealthy eating habits.

◆ 4. 范文译文

1）心理成熟的成年人知道广告的内在偏见，因为它们旨在促进产品的销售和形象。2）但是，在涉及针对年幼孩子的电视广告是否应该被允许的问题上，还有很多争议。3）我个人认为这样的广告应该被严格禁止，原因如下。

1）首先，这些广告误导孩子们购买太多不需要的产品，这可能会导致父母与孩子之间的对抗。2）年幼的孩子不懂广告的劝导意图，因此很容易成为商业说服的目标。3）商业研究证实，广告通常会说服年轻消费者购买它们的产品。4）玩具广告尤其如此，因为孩子们对乐高积木、汽车模型和《动感超人》玩偶等很多玩具有着无尽的胃口。5）每当看到有趣的玩具广告时，孩子们都会催促父母为他们购买产品。6）在大多数情况下，由于孩子已经有了大量的玩具，再购买更多就不正常了，父母可能会拒绝他们，从而挑起父母与孩子之间的冲突。

1）另外，孩子接触大量的广告会形成不良的饮食习惯，这会对他们的健康产生负面影响。2）随着视觉和声音效果的进步，食品和饮料广告使孩子容易成为商业说服的目标。3）大量的广告是关于含有高热量的食物和零食，如糖类麦片、糖果和不同种类的风味汽水。4）一般来说，这些电视广告很丰富多彩、生动活泼，展示孩子们正在吃这些糖果或风味汽水的好心情。5）这种不健康食品的广告导致可能持续一生的营养不良，因此，现代的孩子患有各种慢性疾病，如肥胖和糖尿病等，这种现象毫不奇怪。

总之，针对孩子的广告应该被禁止，因为它们使孩子容易成为商业说服的目标，导致上瘾的购买行为和不健康的饮食习惯。

◆ 5. 重点场景表达

1) mentally mature adults 心理成熟的成年人

2) inherent bias of advertisement 广告固有的偏见

3) television advertising directed toward young children 针对年幼孩子的电视广告

4) cause confrontation between parents and kids 导致父母和孩子之间的对抗

5) persuasive intent in advertising 广告的说服意图

6) have an insatiable appetite for a 对……有贪得无厌的胃口

7) turn them down 拒绝他们

8) instigate parent-kid conflicts 煽动父母和孩子的冲突

9) advancement of visual and sound effects 视觉和音效的进步

10) contribute to poor nutrition 导致营养不良

11) chronic diseases like obesity and diabetes 慢性疾病，如肥胖和糖尿病

TPO 9 独立写作

◆ 1. 题目

Do you agree or disagree with the following statement? Technology has made children less creative than they were in the past.

◆ 2. 思路大纲

主观点：科技让孩子更加有创造力

分论点一：更好地激发孩子兴趣，探索未知

分论点二：为孩子提供更多自由

◆ 3. 高分范文和思维导图

1) Despite the convenience brought by advanced technologies, some people argue that there are certain drawbacks that can be hardly ignored. 2) There is a heated debate over whether technology has made children less creative than they were in the past. 3) However, I tend to disagree with this idea based on the following reasons.

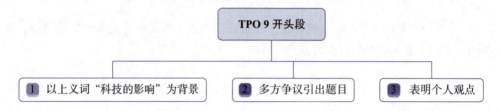

1) First of all, advanced technologies can better stimulate young people's curiosity and make it easier for students to explore the world. 2) Indeed, teachers apply advanced technologies in their teaching like multi-media, projector, and multi-functional blackboard with which they can draw pictures, write and even play videos. 3) The involvement of technology helps to provide materials for students in a more vivid, colorful and intuitive way and thus better stimulate students' interest in a certain subject. 4) Under the drive of interest, they are more likely to delve deeper into certain areas, which serves as a foundation of creativity. 5) For instance, when I was in middle school, my zoology teacher played a video about "safari on the African prairie" to us. 6) The audio and visual effects were so intriguing that for the first time I found biology so interesting to learn. 7) From then on, I never stopped my inquiry in zoology and chose zoology as my major in university, which paved my way to make breakthroughs in the future research.

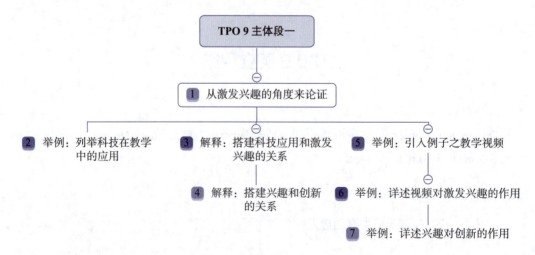

1) Secondly, technology provides kids with more platforms to express their own innovative thoughts freely. 2) As we all know, the traditional school system shackles children by setting up various rules and restrictions, contributing to the deterioration of their creativity. 3) However, the utilization of high technology can keep their creativity intact and flowing by offering more freedom to exercise their imagination. 4) The blog is a good case in point. 5) Students can volunteer to organize and manage a common class blog, which will act as a common source of expression for the entire class. 6) This platform provides freedom for students to post whatever they want and comment upon or share each other's material. 7) They can openly write on topics that intrigue them and give vent to their ideas without having to worry about grading or grammatical errors. 8) Under such a relatively free circumstance offered by advanced technology, students' creativity can definitely be enhanced.

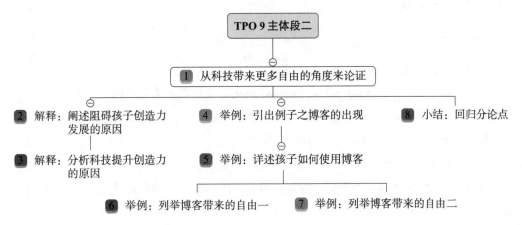

In all, instead of suffocating kids' creativity, technology inspires kids to learn more and explore deeper about the world in a fun and effective way.

◆ 4. 范文译文

1）尽管先进技术带来了便利，但有人认为存在一些不容忽视的缺陷。2）技术是否使孩子的创造力比过去低，这引发了激烈的争论。3）但是，我倾向于不同意这个看法，基于以下原因。

1）首先，先进的技术能够更好地激发年轻人的好奇心，使学生更容易探索世界。2）的确，老师将多媒体、投影仪和多功能黑板等先进技术应用于教学中，这样教师可以绘画、写作甚至播放视频。3）技术的参与有助于以更生动、丰富多彩和直观的方式为学生提供素材，从而更好地激发学生对某个科目的兴趣。4）在兴趣的驱动下，他们更有可能深入研究某些领域，这是创造力的基础。5）例如，当我在初中的时候，我的动物学老师给我们播放了一段关于"非洲草原上的野生动物园"的视频。6）音频和视觉效果非常吸引人，以至于我第

一次发现生物学的学习非常有趣。 7）从此，我从未停止过动物学研究，选择动物学作为我的大学专业，为未来的研究取得突破铺平了道路。

1）其次，技术为孩子们提供了更多平台来自由表达自己的创新思想。 2）众所周知，传统的学校制度通过制定各种规则和限制来束缚儿童，从而导致他们创造力的恶化。3）然而，高科技的运用可以通过提供更多的自由来发挥想象力，使他们的创造力保持完整和流畅。 4）博客就是一个很好的例子。 5）学生可以自愿组织和管理一个班级博客，这将成为整个班级的常见表达途径。 6）该平台允许学生自由发布任何他们想要的内容并评论或分享彼此的材料。 7）他们可以公开记述有趣的话题，发表自己的想法，而不必担心评分或语法错误。 8）在先进技术提供的这种相对自由的环境下，学生的创造力一定可以提高。

总而言之，技术不是窒息孩子的创造力，而是鼓励孩子们学习更多，并以有趣而有效的方式深入探索世界。

◆ 5. 重点场景表达

1) stimulate young people's curiosity 激发年轻人的好奇心

2) apply advanced technologies in their teaching 将先进技术应用于教学

3) in a more vivid, colorful and intuitive way 以更生动、丰富多彩和直观的方式

4) under the drive of interest 在利益驱动下

5) delve deeper into certain areas 深入研究某些领域

6) make breakthroughs in the future research 在未来的研究中取得突破

7) provide kids with more platforms to express their own innovative thoughts freely 为孩子们提供了更多平台来自由表达自己的创新思想

8) shackle children by setting up various rules and restrictions 通过制定各种规则和限制来束缚儿童

9) the deterioration of their creativity 创造力的恶化

10) keep their creativity intact and flowing 使他们的创造力保持完整和流畅

11) act as a common source of expression for the entire class 成为整个班级的常见表达方式

TPO 10 独立写作

◆ 1. 题目

Do you agree or disagree with the following statement? Playing computer games is a waste of time. Children should not be allowed to play them.

◆ 2. 思路大纲

主观点：玩游戏不浪费时间

分论点一：玩游戏可以促进合作

分论点二：玩游戏可以激发学生的学习兴趣

◆ 3. 高分范文和思维导图

1) Increasing mass affluence and advancement of digital devices in the past few decades has brought much convenience to people's life and work. 2) At the same time, however, some educators argue that young students are so addicted to playing videos, and totally neglect its potential harm. 3) I, personally, believe that playing video games benefits kids and it should be made accessible to kids based on the following reasons.

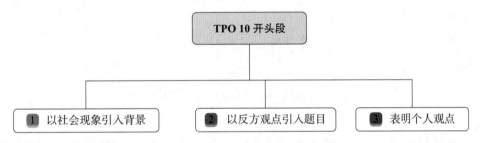

1) First of all, playing video games facilitates cooperation between students. 2) Lots of non-violent video games give students a chance to work together and carry out a certain strategy in order to win the game. 3) For instance, the game NBA2K, a basketball simulation video game, is a very good case in point. 4) Even though it is a video game, in essence there is no big difference between playing the real basketball and playing NBA2K since the video game also involves lots of interactions and cooperation. 5) During the game playing, different offensive and defensive strategies have to be executed together in order to win the game. 6) Specifically, gamers are required to execute their own movements and actions to match their teammates' expectation. 7) Thus, the importance of collaboration will gradually take roots in kids. 8) Their early experience of cooperation will definitely serve as very valuable and intangible assets for one's future.

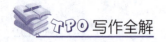

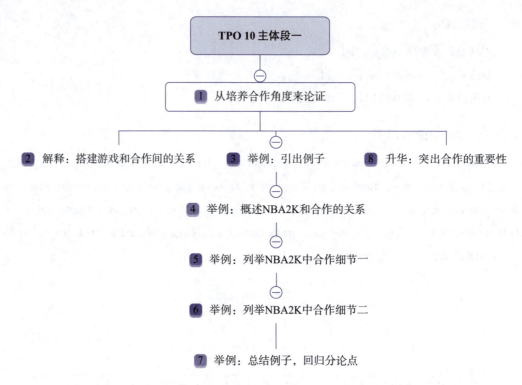

1) Additionally, video games are very conducive to stirring students' interest and helping students to acquire certain knowledge. 2) It is common sense that video games are more interactive and vivid, and kids are easily hooked once they are applied for their learning. 3) The old saying "Interest is the best teacher." is still relevant today. 4) Once the students are interested in learning something, they will spare no effort in a certain subject and eventually they can acquire more knowledge. 5) For instance, video games such as *Civilization*, *Age of Empires* and *The Story of Three Kingdoms* may spark a child's interest in world history, geography, and ancient cultures. 6) The sound and visual effects make it more fun for students to play these games and they will be very mesmerized by these ancient anecdotes and myths. 7) What's more, these games often allow children to design and exchange maps or other customized contents. 8) It is like a catalyst that motivates students to explore more in mythology, cultures and geography. 9) Children pick up a wide range of complex languages and contents that serve as preparation for future learning.

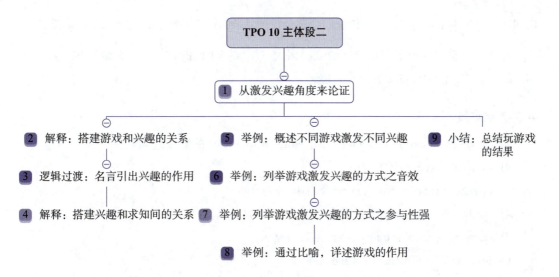

In conclusion, kids should be allowed to play video games since it enhances kids' cooperation awareness, stir students' curiosity of acquiring new knowledge, and makes learning more effective and interesting.

◆ 4. 范文译文

1）过去几十年来，人们物质生活的富足和数字设备的进步为人们的生活和工作带来了许多方便。2）然而，与此同时，一些教育工作者认为年轻学生对玩游戏过于沉迷而完全忽视了其潜在的危害。3）我本人认为，玩电子游戏有利于孩子，应该让他们接触，基于以下原因。

1）首先，玩电子游戏有利于学生之间的合作。2）许多非暴力电子游戏让学生有机会彼此合作并执行某种策略以赢得比赛。3）例如，篮球模拟电子游戏 NBA2K 就是一个很好的例子。4）尽管这是一款电子游戏，但实质上，打真正的篮球和玩 NBA2K 之间没有太大的区别，因为电子游戏还涉及很多互动和合作。5）在比赛中，不同的进攻和防守策略必须一起执行才能赢得比赛。6）具体而言，玩家需要执行自己的动作和行动以配合队友的期望。7）因此，合作的重要性将逐渐植根于儿童。8）他们早期的合作意识肯定会成为未来宝贵的无形资产。

1）此外，电子游戏非常有助于激发学生的兴趣，并帮助学生获得一定的知识。2）众所周知，电子游戏更具互动性和生动性，因此孩子们在应用到学习后很容易被吸引。3）老话说"兴趣是最好的老师"，这句话今天仍然有用。4）一旦学生有兴趣学习某些东西，他们将不遗余力地研究某个学科，并最终获得更多的知识。5）例如，《文明》《帝国时代》和《三国故事》等电子游戏可能会触发孩子对世界历史、地理、古代文化的兴趣。6）声音和视觉效果使学生玩这些游戏更有趣，他们会被这些古老的轶事和神话所迷住。7）更重要的是，这些游戏通常允许儿童设计和交换地图或其他个性化内容。8）它激励学生在神话、文

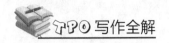
化和地理中探索更多东西。9）孩子们会学会各种复杂的语言和内容作为未来学习的准备。

总之，应该允许孩子们玩电子游戏，因为它增强孩子们的合作意识，激发学生获得新知识的好奇心，使学习更加有效和有趣。

◆ 5. 重点场景表达

1) the potential harm of playing video games 玩电子游戏的潜在危害

2) mass affluence 大众的富裕

3) advancement of digital devices 数字设备的进步

4) facilitate cooperation 促进合作

5) carry out a certain strategy 执行某种策略

6) involve lots of interactions and cooperation 涉及很多互动与合作

7) valuable and intangible assets 有价值的无形资产

8) acquire certain knowledge 获得一定的知识

9) spare no effort in a certain subject 在某个学科上不遗余力

10) interactive, vivid 互动，生动

11) be very mesmerized by these ancient anecdotes and myths 被这些古老的轶事和神话所吸引

12) motivate students to explore more in mythology, cultures and geography 激励学生更多地探索神话、文化和地理学

13) acquire creative and technical skills　获得创造和技术技能

TPO 11 独立写作

◆ 1. 题目

Do you agree or disagree with the following statement? Some people say that the Internet provides people with a lot of valuable information. Others think access to too much information creates problems.

◆ 2. 思路大纲

主观点：网络提供了有价值的信息

分论点一：了解多元文化

分论点二：信息获取更迅速

◆ 3. 高分范文和思维导图

1) Nowadays people are inundated with all sorts of information, which is fueled by the

invention of the Internet and people's access to the Internet. 2) When it comes to the question of whether the Internet provides valuable information or creates problems, people tend to give different answers. 3) Personally, I would say the Internet does provide people with a wide range of valuable information as long as people treat the information selectively.

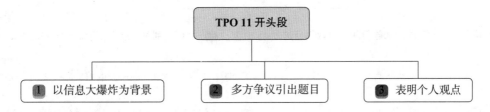

1) Indeed, it is not unusual to see negative information online. 2) For instance, reports about celebrities' private life might contain such information as sex scandals, drug abuse, random hookups, or getting rehabilitation. 3) Young people, who are in their formative years, are not immune to these negative influence so it might be catastrophic for the younger generation's future development. 4) However, with certain level of regulation and management, such bad influence can be avoided. 5) Moreover, the Internet does provide valuable information for people, which makes people's life better.

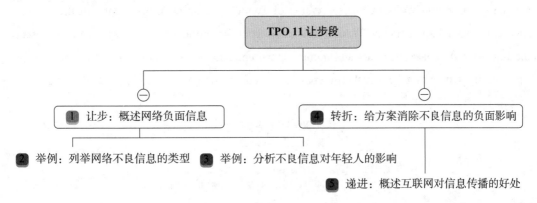

1) First of all, one can easily find relevant information about other cultures and get to know more about different ways of life. 2) One can learn the mindsets of people from other countries without suffering from the boredom of long journeys as long as one is willing to make some effort to do the research online. 3) With the Internet access and the invention of cutting-edge technological gadgets like tablets, laptops, and even smart phones, one can look up webpages that are dedicated to introducing specific parts of a foreign culture and the local people's ways of living. 4) Moreover, one can find people from cultures all around the world on Facebook, Twitter, Instagram. 5) By befriending them through these on-line social networks, one can communicate with them directly like sending messages or even facetiming with them, which is more interactive and thrilling.

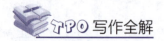

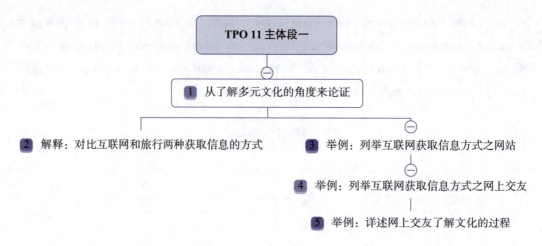

1) Additionally, the Internet provides people with different kinds of news sources in a very convenient and fast way. 2) Traditionally, people watch TV programs or read newspapers to get to know what is happening at home and abroad. 3) However, these kinds of news sources are not instant, meaning that one can only get to know certain news in a few hours or a day. 4) Fortunately, it is much more effective and faster to spread information online. 5) For instance, the catastrophic earthquake devastated Wenchuan city on May 12, 2008. 6) With such breaking news spreading around on Weibo, Chinese version of Twitter, people from other parts of the country started to respond immediately. 7) Just a few hours after the earthquake, they volunteered to rescue the injured and donate materials and money to the epicenter, saving hundreds of people's lives. 8) Evidently, without the help of the Internet, more people would have died in the earthquake.

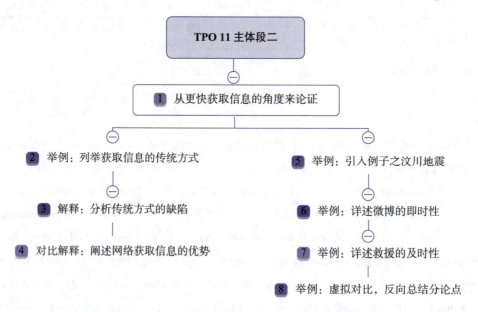

To conclude, despite some negative information provided by the Internet, people can gain useful information and spread news more quickly than ever before.

◆ 4. 范文译文

1）现在人们被各种信息淹没，这是因为互联网的发明和人们对互联网的接入。2）谈到互联网提供有价值的信息还是产生问题，人们往往会给出不同的答案。3）就我个人而言，只要人们有选择地对待信息，互联网的确提供广泛的有价值的信息。

1）事实上，在网上看到负面信息并不罕见。2）例如，关于名人私生活的报道可能包含诸如性丑闻、吸毒、一夜情和接受改造等信息。3）处于成长年代的年轻人，对这些负面影响没有免疫力，因此这对年轻一代的未来发展可能是灾难性的。4）但是，在一定程度的控制和管理下，可以避免这种不良影响。而且互联网确实为人们提供了有价值的信息，使人们的生活越来越好。

1）首先，可以很容易地找到有关其他文化的信息，并更多地了解不同的生活方式。2）只要愿意努力在网上进行查阅而不会遭受长途旅行之无聊乏味，就可以了解来自其他国家的人们的思维方式。3）互联网接入、平板电脑、笔记本电脑甚至智能手机等尖端科技产品的发明，可以使人们查阅专门介绍外来文化的特定部分和当地人民生活方式的网页。4）此外，人们可以在 Facebook、Twitter、Instagram 上找到来自世界各地文化的人。5）通过这些在线社交网络与他们交往，可以直接与他们交流，如发送消息甚至与他们视频聊天，这更具互动性，也很刺激。

1）另外，互联网非常便捷地为人们提供不同种类的新闻来源。2）过去，人们通过看电视节目或阅读报纸来了解国内外发生的事情。3）然而，这些新闻来源并不是即时的，也就是说，几个小时或一天之后才能知道某些新闻。4）幸运的是，在线传播信息非常有效、快速。5）2008 年 5 月 12 日，汶川特大地震摧毁了这个地区。6）这种突发新闻在微博，也就是中文版的 Twitter 上面全面扩散，中国各地人民立即作出了回应。7）地震发生几个小时后，他们自愿抢救伤员，向震中捐资赠物，挽救了数百人的生命。8）很明显，没有互联网的帮助，地震期间可能会有更多的人死亡。

总而言之，尽管互联网提供一些负面信息，人们可以比以前更快地获得有用的信息和传播新闻。

◆ 5. 重点场景表达

1) access to the Internet 访问互联网

2) valuable information 宝贵的信息

3) sex scandals, drug abuse, random hookups, and getting rehabilitation 性丑闻、吸毒、一夜情和接受改造

4) be not immune to 不能免疫于

5) certain level of regulation and management 一定程度的控制和管理

6) cutting-edge technological gadget 尖端的技术工具

7) facetime with them 跟他们视频聊天

8) what is happening home and abroad 本国和国际新闻

9) breaking news 突发新闻

TPO 12 独立写作

◆ 1. 题目

Do you agree or disagree with the following statement? It is better to have broad knowledge of many academic subjects than to specialize in one specific subject. Use specific reasons and examples to support your answer.

◆ 2. 思路大纲

主观点：掌握多门学科知识更好

分论点一：促进科研创新

分论点二：促进人际交往

◆ 3. 高分范文和思维导图

1) Knowledge of different subjects serves as a basis for people to explore the unknown. 2) When it comes to the question of whether it is better to specialize in one subject or have broad knowledge of different academic disciplines, people tend to give different answers. 3) I, personally, reckon that it is in the best interest of society and individuals to have comprehensive knowledge of different subjects.

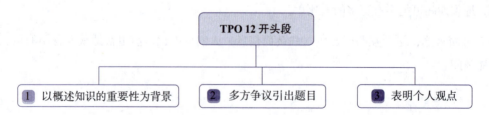

1) First of all, both scientific search and technological innovation require multidisciplinary knowledge. 2) Scientific research on medical treatments might involve experts in different areas. 3) For example, in order to come up with methods to deal with chronic pain, physical massage,

acupuncture, and even psychological counseling might be needed since it can be a complex and complicated syndrome. 4) The same is true for technological inventions. 5) For instance, GPS is a very useful tool for people to find out the best route to get to their destination. 6) However, such a genius gadget cannot be invented without comprehensive knowledge of multiple disciplines like geography, physics and language programming. 7) Consequently, without well-rounded knowledge in different fields, scientific breakthroughs and technological advancements cannot be made possible.

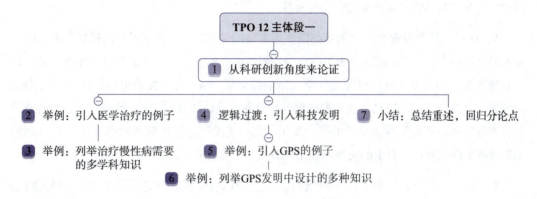

1) Additionally, on a personally level, a broad range of knowledge of different fields can serve as a catalyst to socialize and interact with others. 2) Even though one doesn't have to be expert in order to break the ice, certain basic knowledge and information from a variety of fields can help one to avoid awkwardness, thus carrying out a great conversation. 3) For example, last month, I attended a house party, where lots of graduate students from different majors showed up like economics, psychology, and mechanical engineering. 4) As a student majoring in linguistics, I had no knowledge of these fields, which gave me a hard time socializing with other students in the party. 5) However, had I had some basic knowledge of these disciplines, I would have connected with others on a deeper level.

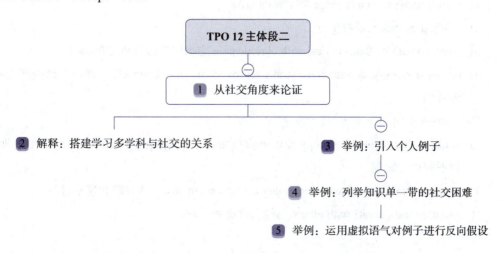

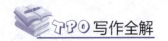

To conclude, comprehensive knowledge of various disciplines facilitates scientific breakthroughs and technological advancements. It also serves as an effective tool to socialize with others.

◆ 4. 范文译文

1）不同学科的知识可以作为人们探索未知的基础。2）当谈到专门研究一个学科或者在不同学科有广泛的知识哪个更好时，人们往往会给出不同的答案。3）我个人认为，对不同学科有全面的知识符合社会和个人的利益。

1）首先，科学探索和技术创新都需要多学科的知识。2）关于医疗的科学研究可能涉及不同领域的专长。3）例如，为了提出治疗慢性疼痛的方法，可能需要身体按摩、针灸甚至心理咨询，因为慢性疼痛可能是一个复杂的综合征。4）技术发明也是如此。5）例如，GPS 是一个非常有用的工具，让人们找到到达目的地的最佳路线。6）然而，如果没有地理学、物理学和语言编程等多学科的综合知识，就不能发明这样的精巧的小工具。7）因此，如果没有全面的知识，科学的突破和技术的进步是不可能达到的。

1）另外，在个人层面上，不同领域的广泛知识可以作为促进社交和互动的催化剂。2）尽管一个人没必要成为专家才能打破沉默，但是有不同领域的基本知识和信息可以帮助人们避免尴尬，从而进行一次很好的交谈。3）例如上个月，我参加了一个家庭聚会，有来自不同专业的许多研究生，比如经济学、心理学和机械工程学。4）作为一个语言专业的学生，我对这些领域一无所知，这让我很难与其他同学交往。5）但是，如果我对这些学科有一些基本的了解，那么我就可以更深层次地与其他人交流。

总之，各门学科的综合知识有利于科学的突破和技术进步，也是与他人交往的有效工具。

◆ 5. 重点场景表达

1) multidisciplinary knowledge 多学科的知识

2) medical treatment 药物治疗

3) come up with methods to deal with chronic pain 想出解决慢性疼痛的办法

4) physical therapy, acupuncture, and even psychological counseling 理疗、针灸甚至心理咨询

5) technological inventions 技术发明

6) multiple disciplines like geography, physics and language programming 多学科如地理、物理和语言编程

7) scientific breakthroughs and technological advancements 科学突破和技术进步

8) socialize and interact with others 与他人社交和互动

9) carry out a great conversation 进行一次好的谈话

10) give me a hard time to socialize with other students 让我跟其他学生交流很难

11) basic knowledge of these disciplines 这些学科的基本知识

TPO 13 独立写作

◆ 1. 题目

Do you agree or disagree with the following statement? The extended family (grandparents, cousins, aunts, and uncles) is less important now than it was in the past.

◆ 2. 思路大纲

主观点：大家庭不如过去重要

分论点一：社会转型导致重要性下降

分论点二：生活节奏加快导致重要性下降

◆ 3. 高分范文和思维导图

1) Social and economic advancements result in tremendous changes in family structure and dynamics. 2) When it comes to the question of whether the extended family is less important than it was in the past, people tend to give different answers. 3) I, personally, reckon that the extended family is less significant than it was yesterday based on the following reasons.

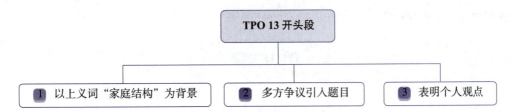

1) First of all, social transformation has depreciated the importance of extended families. 2) In an extended family, the dominant family unit in the past, grandparents, parents, uncles, aunts and cousins lived under the same roof. 3) In such a joint family, the workload could be shared among the family members, which was especially important in the ancient agricultural society. 4) To be specific, they had to work together and assume different responsibilities such as planting crops and raising cattle so that they could have enough food to feed themselves. 5) However, nowadays after entering the electrical age, every immediate family can live a comfortable life more easily, thus leading to the appearance of diversified family structures. 6) For instance, nuclear family, single

parent family, remarried family, etc. constantly emerge in our life.

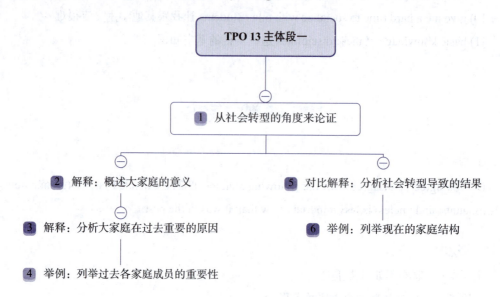

1) Additionally, the extended family is of less importance due to the acceleration of life rhythm. 2) Nowadays the rapid life pace has reduced the amount of time that people spend staying with their parents, let alone their aunts, uncles and grandparents. 3) In this case, chances are that these relatives have little knowledge about the current situation of other family members, which means that people have to rely on themselves when confronted with troubles. 4) Nevertheless, in the past, people had more spare time for family reunion and regular gathering and more opportunities for family members in the extended family to deepen their mutual understanding. 5) As a result, when younger children asked for help, they could give more appropriate suggestions.

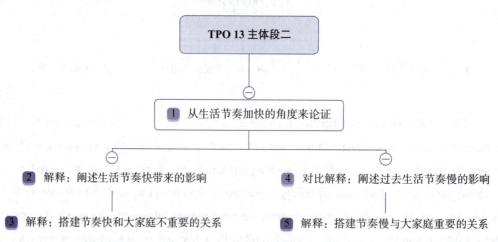

In all, with the change of family value and family structures and the acceleration of life rhythm, people tend to be less dependent on a large extended family. Thus, an extended family is less important than ever before.

◆ 4. 范文译文

1）社会和经济发展导致家庭结构和动力的巨大变化。2）谈到大家庭是否比过去重要的问题，人们往往会给出不同的答案。3）我个人认为，由于以下原因，大家庭没有过去重要。

1）首先，社会转型降低了大家庭的重要性。2）在一个大家庭中，过去占主导地位的家庭单位，祖父母、父母、叔叔、姑姑和堂亲生活在同一个屋檐下。3）在这样一个共同的家庭中，家庭成员之间共担工作，这在古代农业社会中尤为重要。4）具体来说，他们必须一起工作，承担不同的责任，如种植农作物、养牛，以便有足够的食物来养活自己。5）但是，现在进入电器时代后，每个直系亲属都可以更轻松地过上舒适的生活，从而形成多元化的家庭结构。6）例如，核心家庭、单亲家庭、再婚家庭等在我们的生活中不断出现。

1）另外，由于生活节奏的加速，大家庭的重要性降低。2）如今快节奏的生活减少了人们与父母待在一起的时间，更不用说他们的姑姑、叔叔和祖父母了。3）在这种情况下，这些亲属很可能对其他家庭成员的现状知之甚少，这就意味着人们在遇到麻烦时要依靠自己。4）但是，过去人们有更多的闲暇时间用于家庭团聚和定期聚会，大家庭中的家庭成员有更多的机会加深相互了解。5）因此，年青的孩子求助时，他们可以给予更合适的建议。

总的来说，随着家庭价值和家庭结构的变化，人们往往不太依赖于一个大家庭。因此，大家庭比以往任何时候都没有那么重要。

◆ 5. 重点场景表达

change in family structure and dynamics 家庭结构和动力的变化

workload can be shared among the family members 家庭成员可以分担工作

work together and assume different responsibilities 一起工作，承担不同的责任

diversified family structures 多元化的家庭结构

remarried family 再婚家庭

rapid life pace 快速的生活节奏

confronted with troubles 面临麻烦

family reunion 家庭团聚

deepen their mutual understanding 加深相互了解

give more appropriate suggestions 给出更合适的建议

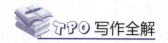

TPO 14 独立写作

◆ 1. 题目

Do you agree or disagree with the following statement? People benefit more from traveling in their own country than from traveling in foreign countries.

◆ 2. 思路大纲

主观点：出国游比国内游好

分论点一：欣赏不同的风景，品尝不同的美食

分论点二：感受不同的文化

◆ 3. 高分范文和思维导图

1) As the saying goes: "the world is a book; those who do not travel read only a page." 2) People like to travel to places at home or abroad. 3) However, some people argue that it is better to travel within their own country than traveling abroad. 4) I, however, tend to disagree with this claim based on the following reasons.

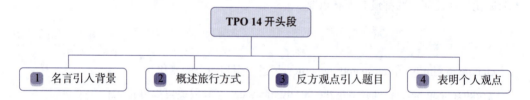

1) First of all, one can appreciate distinctive views and taste various sorts of authentic food when traveling globally. 2) For example, when traveling in the Philippines, a tropical country, one can appreciate the beautiful sunrise and sunset while lying on the beach. 3) The sparkling blue ocean together with the tropical trees like palm trees, banana trees and coconut trees along the seashore are just breathtaking. 4) If you travel in Japan, its delicate gardens and grandiose temples are hard to miss out. 5) Also, one can explore the local cuisines when traveling in other countries like the Thai Pad Thai, Italian pizza and Belgian macaroons. 6) Cuisine culture is also a big part of a country and the flavor of the Pad Thai is definitely not the same from the one you tried in your home country. 7) Obviously, it tastes more genuine in its place of origin.

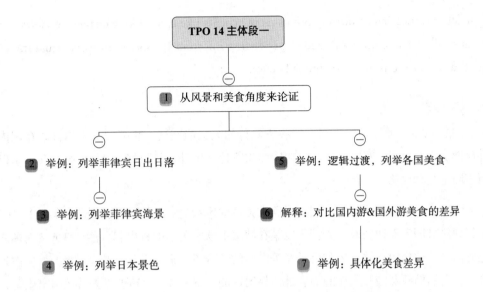

1) Additionally, traveling globally gives someone more exposure to distinctive cultures, customs and ways of living. 2) Those who do travel abroad might find it easy to adapt to new environments and are more likely to respect and thus learn from other cultures. 3) For instance, in China, the elderly and young children have priority on the bus and giving your seats to seniors will be appreciated. 4) However, giving seats to old people while on the train in Japan might be regarded as an offence since the old people think they are not that old yet. 5) Also, interacting with the Muslims and witnessing their ways of life makes one have a better understanding and appreciation of different religions and beliefs, which can serve as a great source of reminiscence. 6) However, people who have never traveled abroad sometimes are bound by the limited perspectives and may not become well-rounded people.

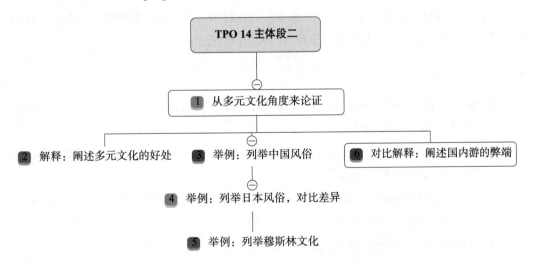

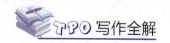

In all, traveling internationally brings more benefits like appreciating distinctive views tasting various sorts of authentic food, and experiencing different lifestyles. However, just traveling domestically makes one bound by limited views.

◆ 4. 范文译文

1）俗话说："世界是一本书，那些不旅行的人只能阅读一页。" 2）人们喜欢在国内或国外旅游。 3）然而，有些人认为，在国内旅行比在国外旅行更好。 4）但是，我基于以下原因不同意这种说法。

1）首先，在全球旅行时，人们可以欣赏独特的风景，并品尝各种地道的美食。 2）例如，当旅行到热带国家菲律宾时，人们可以躺在沙滩上欣赏美丽的日出和日落。 3）波光粼粼的蓝色海洋以及棕榈树、香蕉树和椰子树等沿岸的热带树木都令人叹为观止。 4）如果你到日本旅行，它的精致花园和宏伟的寺庙是不易错过的。 5）另外，还可以去其他国家旅游，探索当地的美食，比如泰式米粉、意大利比萨饼和比利时蛋白杏仁饼干等。6）烹饪文化也是一个国家的重要组成部分，泰式米粉与你在本国尝试过的那个绝对不一样。7）很明显，它在发源地更加正宗。

1）此外，全球旅行让更多人接触到独特的文化、习俗和生活方式。2）那些出国旅游的人可能会发现很容易适应新的环境，更有可能尊重并从其他文化中学习。3）例如在中国，老年人和幼儿在公交车上有优先权，把你的座位让给老年人将受人尊重。4）但是，在日本，由于老年人认为他们还没有那么老，所以乘坐火车时给老年人礼让座位可能会被视为冒犯。5）同时，与穆斯林交流并见证他们的生活方式，使人们对不同宗教和信仰有更好的理解，这可以成为回忆的重要来源。6）然而，从来没有去过国外的人有时受到有限的观点约束，可能不会成为全面的人。

总之，国际旅行带来更多的好处，比如欣赏独特的风景，品尝各种正宗的食品，体验不同的生活方式。然而，只是在国内旅行会使人的视野受到限制。

◆ 5. 重点场景表达

1) travel to places at home or abroad：在国内或国外的地方旅行

2) travel abroad：出国旅游

3) can appreciate distinctive views and taste various sorts of authentic food：可以欣赏独特的风景，品尝各种地道的美食

4) appreciate the beautiful sunrise and sunset：欣赏美丽的日出和日落

5) lie on the beach：躺在沙滩上

6) sparkling blue ocean：波光粼粼的蓝色海洋

7) tropical trees like palm trees, banana trees and coconut trees along the seashore：沿岸的

热带树木如棕榈树、香蕉树和椰子树

8) delicate gardens and grandiose temples：精致的花园和宏伟的庙宇

9) Thai Pad Thai, Italian pizza and Belgian macaroons：泰式米粉、意大利比萨饼和比利时蛋白杏仁饼干

10) give someone more exposure to distinctive cultures, customs and ways of living：接触到独特的文化、习俗和生活方式

11) interact with：与……交往

12) be bound by the limited perspectives：受限于狭隘的视角

13) become well-rounded people：成为全面的人

TPO 15 独立写作

◆ 1. 题目

Do you agree or disagree with the following statement? In order to become financially responsible adults, children should learn to manage their own money at a young age.

◆ 2. 思路大纲

主观点：从小管钱

分论点一：有助于养成良好的消费习惯

分论点二：有助于学会理财知识和技能

◆ 3. 高分范文和思维导图

1) Parents tend to have different approaches to educate the kids to be financially responsible in the future. 2) One approach is to let kids manage their own money at a young age. 3) Some argue against this idea by saying that kids are not mature enough to make the right decision, while others favor this method since kids will know better about their choices and budget by managing their own money. 4) I, personally, am in favor of this approach based on the following reasons.

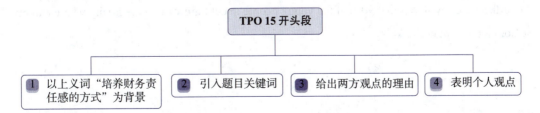

1) First of all, leaving kids' allowance to themselves can help them get into a rational spending

habit and thus live within their means. 2) To illustrate, if parents always help their kids to manage money, the kids will find it hard to understand the value of money. 3) After making the transition to adulthood, most of them tend to be clueless about how to properly spend their income and end up being impulse buyers who purchase whatever they want. 4) However, children who have the privilege to keep their own money at a young age are likely to learn how to buy smart through trials and errors, which is the first step to become financially responsible people. 5) For instance, while shopping around, these kids have the habit of clipping some coupons, checking grocery store's weekly specials and keeping an eye on promotions.

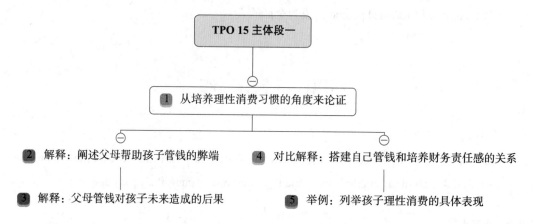

1) Another obvious benefit of allowing kids to start managing money early is that they will acquire financial knowledge and skills, essential to becoming financially responsible. 2) Just as an old proverb goes, "Experience is the best teacher.", which remains relevant today. 3) Managing personal finance means that children can make their financial decisions independently instead of relying on others and they will undertake any consequence accompanying these decisions. 4) In this process, kids will learn about certain financial concepts and management skills from balancing a checkbook to understanding what bank or interest means, serving as the precondition of assuming financial obligation in the future. 5) However, if kids had no experience of managing money in childhood, they tend to "bite off more than they can chew" in the future. 6) According to a recent World Bank report, the average young adult amasses $45,000 in debt by the time they turn 29. 7) Further scrutiny shows that 90% of the young people in debt grew up in the family where parents seldom left allowance to kids.

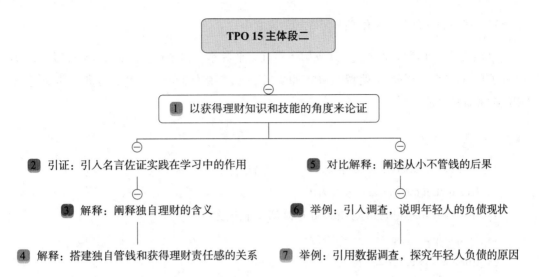

In conclusion, although helping kids build up financial responsibility is no easy job, from the above careful analysis, we do find that it is advisable and rational to give the kids the freedom to manage their own money since it enables them to form a rational consumption habit and grasp useful financial management skills.

◆ 4. 范文译文

1）家长往往有不同的方法来教育孩子将来对自己的财务负责。2）一种方法是让孩子在年轻时管理自己的钱。3）有些人反对这个观点，认为孩子们不够成熟，无法做出正确的决定，而另一些人赞成这种方法，因为孩子们通过管理自己的钱会更好地了解他们的选择和预算。4）基于以下原因，我个人赞成采用这种方法。

1）首先，给孩子留下零花钱可以帮助他们养成理性的消费习惯，从而做到量入为出。2）比如说，如果父母总是帮助他们的孩子管理金钱，孩子们会很难理解金钱的价值。3）到成年后，他们中的大多数人往往对如何合理安排他们的收入一无所知，最终成为购买任何他们想要的冲动型买家。4）然而，年轻时有权保留自己的钱的孩子可能会通过试错学会如何来买得更聪明，这是成为有财务责任感的人的第一步。5）例如，在购物的同时，这些孩子有习惯收集一些优惠券，检查杂货店的每周特价，并留意促销活动。

1）允许孩子尽早开始管理钱的另一个显而易见的好处是，他们将获得财务知识和技能，这对于财务负责至关重要。2）正如一句古老的谚语所说，"经验是最好的老师"，今天仍然有用。3）管理个人财务意味着孩子可以独立做出财务决策，而不是依赖他人并对这些决策产生的任何后果负责。4）在这个过程中，孩子们将学习一些财务概念和管理技巧，比如平衡收支或了解银行利息的意义，这对未来财务负责尤为重要。5）但是，如果孩子没有在儿童时期管理金钱，他们在未来往往会"自不量力"。6）根据世行最近的一份报告，普通年轻成年人在他们满29岁时累积的债务达到45 000美元。7）进一步审查表明，90% 负债的

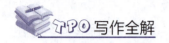

的年轻人成长在父母很少留给孩子零花钱的家庭中。

总而言之，虽然要帮助孩子建立财务责任并非易事，但通过上述仔细分析，我们发现让孩子自由管理自己的钱是明智的和合理的，因为此举使他们养成理性的消费习惯和掌握有用的财务管理技能。

◆ 5. 重点场景表达

1) leave kids' allowance to 给孩子留下零花钱

2) live within their means 量入为出

3) make the transition to adulthood 过渡到成年阶段

4) be clueless about 对……不清楚

5) impulse buyers 冲动型买家

6) have the privilege to 有权利做……

7) through trials and errors 通过试错

8) clip some coupons 收集一些优惠券

9) check grocery store's weekly specials 检查杂货店的每周特价

10) keep an eye on promotions 留意促销活动

11) undertake any consequence accompanying these decisions 承担决策带来的后果

12) balance a checkbook 平衡收支

13) bite off more than one can chew 自不量力

TPO 16 独立写作

◆ 1. 题目

Do you agree or disagree with the following statement? The best way to travel is in a group led by a tour guide.

◆ 2. 思路大纲

主观点：个人出游比团队游要好

分论点一：日程安排更加灵活

分论点二：更有利于自我的提升

◆ 3. 高分范文和思维导图

1) The increasing affluence of the masses makes traveling more accessible to basically everyone, and nowadays it is not uncommon for people to travel domestically and globally.

2) However, when it comes to the question of whether joining a tour group is the best way to travel, people tend to give different answers. 3) I, personally believe that traveling alone is a better way based on the following reasons.

1) Firstly, traveling alone means a more flexible schedule and more freedom, which guarantees a more satisfying traveling experience. 2) Indeed, when traveling solo, one can customize his own itinerary and change his travel plan whenever he wants. 3) For instance, one can explore the local food whether it is Pad Thai, Italian pizza, or Belgian macaroons. 4) One can live in a hostel, interact with local people and team up with other travelers without having to adjusting his schedule to meet others' satisfaction and expectation. 5) However, when traveling with a group, the destinations and the time one can spend in each of these scenic spots are fixed, meaning that one has no choice but to follow even though one has concerns and disagreements. 6) These drawbacks of traveling with a tour group will lead to a bad traveling experience.

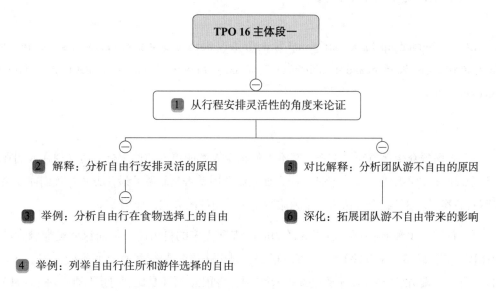

1) Additionally, traveling alone provides one with a chance to discover oneself and face challenges alone, which can make someone a stronger and more well-rounded person. 2) When traveling solo, one gets a chance to rediscover him self—things one is uncomfortable with or things one is afraid of, and face challenges alone. 3) As the saying goes："What doesn't kill you

makes you stronger." 4) It is so true that the more you travel alone, the more confident you are. 5) These qualities that one develops through traveling alone can be transferred to one's life and career. 6) However, during guided tours, everything has been arranged well by the guide so that tourists are deprived of the chances to hone their abilities.

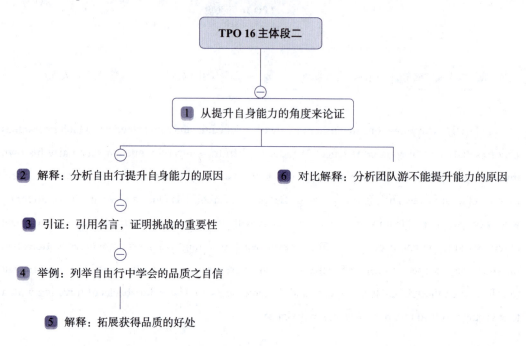

In all, signing up for a tour group is definitely not the best way to travel since traveling alone offers more freedom and flexibility, and also helps to build up character that is essential for a successful life.

◆ 4. 范文译文

1）人民群众变得越来越富裕，基本上使每个人都能更方便地旅行，而且现在人们在国内和全球旅行并不罕见。 2）但是，谈到加入旅游团是否是旅游的最佳方式，人们往往会给出不同的答案。 3）我个人认为，单独旅行是一种更好的方式，原因如下。

1）首先，单独旅行意味着更灵活的时间表和更多的自由度，从而保证更加满意的旅行体验。 2）确实，单独旅行时，可以根据自己的需要定制行程并改变旅行计划。 3）例如，你可以探索当地的食物，不管是泰式米粉、意大利比萨饼还是比利时蛋白杏仁饼干。 4）人们可以住招待所，与当地居民互动，并与其他旅行者同游，无须调整时间表来满足他人和期望。 5）然而，随团旅行时，每个景点的目的地和时间是固定的，这意味着即使人们有疑虑和分歧，也别无选择。 6）随团旅游的弊端将导致旅游体验不好。

1）另外，单独旅行提供了一个发现自己、面对挑战的机会，可以使一个人变得更强壮、更全面。2）单独旅行时，人们有机会重新发现自己——一个人不舒服或害怕的事情，或独自面临挑战。3）俗话说："没有杀死你的东西会让你更强大。"4）你单独旅行越多，你就越自信。5）通过单独旅行培养的这些品质可以转移到自己的生活和事业上。6）然而，在有导游的游览中，导游安排得很好，游客被剥夺了磨炼自己能力的机会。

总之，报名参加旅游团绝对不是旅行的最佳方式，因为单独旅行提供了更多的自由和灵活性，也有助于培养对成功生活至关重要的品格。

◆ 5. 重点场景表达

1) travel domestically and globally 在国内和全球旅行

2) join a tour group 加入一个旅游团

3) travel solo 单独旅行

4) meet others' satisfaction and expectation 满足他人和期望

5) a stronger and more well-rounded person 一个更强大和更全面的人

6) guided tour 有导游的旅行

7) offer more freedom and flexibility 提供更多的自由和灵活性

8) build up character that is essential for a successful life 培养对成功生活至关重要的品格

TPO 17 独立写作

◆ 1. 题目

Do you agree or disagree with the following statement? Most advertisements make products seem much better than they really are. Use specific reasons and examples to support your answer.

◆ 2. 思路大纲

主观点：广告美化了产品

分论点一：修图技术的进步

分论点二：为了满足广告本身的目的

◆ 3. 高分范文和思维导图

1) It is more than common for the public to skip the annoying advertisements during one episode of their favorite popular TV series, and we do it so often that sometimes we just ignore the presence of advertisements and their following effects, because we know for sure that nothing can be that good. 2) To promote their products, companies take the measure of broadcasting fancy

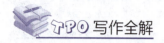

advertisements to attract more customers. 3) I agree with the statement that in most cases, products advertised seem much better than they really are.

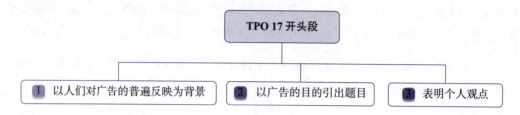

1) For one thing, with the development of technology, it is becoming easier and easier for companies to use modern ways to achieve the goal of largely enhancing the presentation or the appearance of their products. 2) For example, every time I pass the bus station with huge billboards advertising burgers of the season, I just cannot help but drool without even noticing. 3) With the help of Photoshop, a software used for beautifying images, all I can see is the juicy patty, the refreshing lettuce, and the spongy buns on top of everything; also, the sauce covers the meat perfectly and you can imagine smelling the fragrance of the roasted beef. 4) However, that is not the whole story. 5) What welcomes me at most times when actually stepping into the burger store, is the overwhelming disappointment. 6) Layers stack together, greasy mayonnaise drips on the side, and the buns are completely soaked wet. 7) I'm sure not many people would enjoy experiencing the breaking up of their anticipations, myself included.

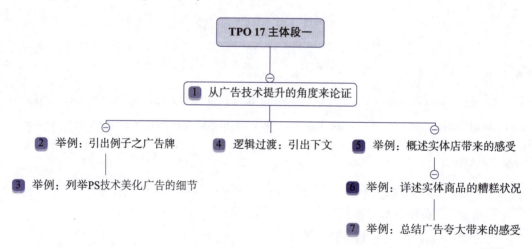

1) Also, it is in the nature of advertising to serve the purpose of promoting products. 2) To exaggerate them in a subtle way is to help companies reach their potential customers which will in turn, help them grow in the long run. 3) As long as it is the same product with the same function, there is no harm in drawing people's attention by using visual aids. 4) Without a reasonable range of exaggeration, the whole advertisement would be a total waste of resources, money, and energy.

138

5) Therefore, commercials presented in an exaggerated way conform to their basic function of attracting customers and boosting sales.

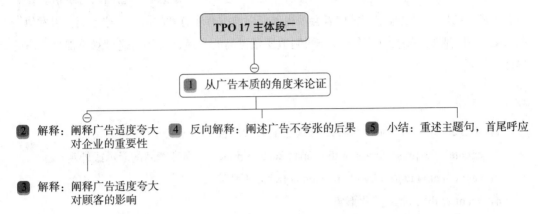

In conclusion, advertisements cannot fully represent real products. However, it doesn't necessarily mean that there is no value in them. In the process of watching advertisements of all forms, consumers may acquire some information that they have not noticed before and that would trigger their interest in purchasing and using the products, which would encourage companies to manufacture products of even higher quality, and I consider it a win-win situation for both parties.

◆ 4. 范文译文

1）在观看喜爱的热门电视连续剧剧集时，公众常常跳过恼人的广告，而且我们经常这样做，以至于有时我们会忽略广告的存在及其后续的效果，因为我们确实知道没有什么会像广告中描述的那么好。2）为了推广产品，公司会采取播放花式广告的措施来吸引更多的顾客。3）我同意这样的观点：在大多数情况下，广告中的产品看起来比实际情况要好得多。

1）首先，随着技术的发展，公司采用现代化的方式实现大幅提升产品展示或外观的目标变得越来越容易和简单。2）例如，每次我经过公共汽车站时都会看到广告宣传本季汉堡包的巨大广告牌，我不禁流口水。3）在一款用于美化图像的软件 Photoshop 的帮助下我所能看到的只有多汁的小馅饼、清爽的生菜和海绵状面包；此外，酱汁完美地覆盖了肉，你可以想象闻到烤牛肉的香味。4）然而，那不是全部。5）在真正踏入汉堡包店时，大多数时候迎接我的都令人非常失望。6）各层食材层叠在一起，油腻的蛋黄酱滴在一边，面包完全湿透。7）我相信没有多少人会喜欢经历他们期望的破灭，包括我自己在内。

1）另外，广告的本质应该是促销产品。2）以微妙的方式夸大产品是为了帮助公司接触他们的潜在客户，从而帮助公司长期发展。3）只要是具有相同功能的同一产品，使用视觉辅助工具吸引人们的注意力并没有什么坏处。4）如果没有合理的夸大，整个广告就会浪

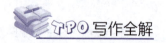

费资源、资金和精力。5）因此，夸张的商业广告符合其吸引顾客和促进销售的基本功能。

总之，广告不能完全代表真实的产品，但是，这并不一定意味着它们没有价值。在观看各种形式的广告的过程中，消费者会获得他们以前没有注意到的信息，这可能会引发他们购买和使用产品的兴趣，从而鼓励公司制造质量更高的产品，我认为这对双方都是双赢的局面。

◆ 5. 重点场景表达

1) skip the annoying advertisements 跳过恼人的广告

2) enhance the presentation or the appearance of products 提升产品的展示或外观

3) cannot help but drool without even noticing 不禁流口水

4) beautify the image 美化形象

5) the breaking up of their anticipations 期望的破灭

6) serve the purpose of promoting products 实现促销产品的目的

7) exaggerate the products in a subtle way 以微妙的方式夸大产品

8) conform to their basic function of attracting customers and boosting sales 符合其吸引顾客和促进销售的基本功能

9) a win-win situation for both parties 双赢的局面

TPO 18 独立写作

◆ 1. 题目

Do you agree or disagree with the following statement? Students are more influenced by their teachers than by their friends.

◆ 2. 思路大纲

主观点：学生更多受朋友的影响
分论点一：相处时间更长
分论点二：朋友之间没有代沟

◆ 3. 高分范文和思维导图

1) People around us have inherent influence on our beliefs, values and even behaviors. 2) However, when it comes to the question of whether students are more influenced by their teachers or by their friends, people tend to give different answers. 3) I, personally, reckon that students are more influenced by their peers than by teachers based on the following reasons.

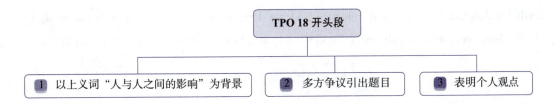

TPO 18 开头段

1 以上义词"人与人之间的影响"为背景　　2 多方争议引出题目　　3 表明个人观点

1) On the one hand, students spend a significant amount of time with their peers, who tend to influence students' thinking and behaviors. 2) As is known to all, kids spend time with their peers on and off campus. 3) In school, they take classes, do group projects, and carry out experiments together. 4) After school, they might also hang out with their peers and friends, going to a concert, watching a movie or playing sports. 5) It is during these moments that students are inherently influenced by their peers and friends. 6) For example, my little cousin is a nine grade student who has recently found that a number of his classmates are so mesmerized by the design and function of the latest iPhone X. 7) Thus, many of his friends and classmates ask their parents to buy them the newest version of iPhone. 8) Feeling the pressure from his peers and friends, my cousin also asks his Dad to purchase him the phone.

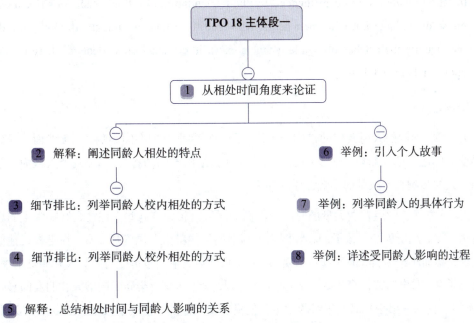

TPO 18 主体段一

1 从相处时间角度来论证

2 解释：阐述同龄人相处的特点

3 细节排比：列举同龄人校内相处的方式

4 细节排比：列举同龄人校外相处的方式

5 解释：总结相处时间与同龄人影响的关系

6 举例：引入个人故事

7 举例：列举同龄人的具体行为

8 举例：详述受同龄人影响的过程

1) On the other hand, students are less likely to be influenced by their teachers since there is a huge generation gap existing between them. 2) Indeed, young students and teachers especially those who entered the profession decades ago tend to have different values, beliefs, and lifestyles. 3) For instance, students prefer to incorporate modern technologies even video games into their learning experience while some teachers might oppose such teaching approaches because they believe rote memory and lecture are better ways for students to gain knowledge. 4）Such a division

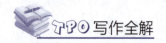

makes it difficult for teachers to influence students' learning or motivate them to focus on study. 5）Furthermore, teachers' influence on students outside of the classroom is even more negligible.

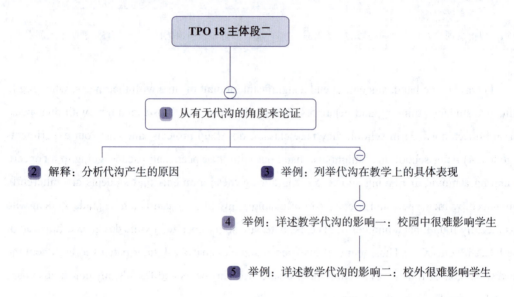

In all, students are more influenced by their friends than by their teachers since most of the time students hang out with their peers, who tend to influence students' thinking, mindsets and consequently their behaviors while teachers exert little impact on students as there is a huge generation gap between them.

◆ 4. 范文译文

1）我们周围的人对我们的信仰、价值观乃至行为都有内在的影响。 2）然而，谈到学生是受老师还是朋友影响较大的问题，人们往往会给出不同的答案。3）我个人认为，学生受同龄人的影响大于教师的影响，原因如下。

1）一方面，学生花费大量的时间与他们的同龄人相处，这些人往往会影响学生的思维和行为。 2）众所周知，孩子们在校园内外与他们的同龄人共同度过。 3）在学校，他们一起上课，参加小组项目，并一起进行实验。4）放学后，他们也可能与同龄人和朋友出去玩、去听音乐会、看电影或体育比赛。5）在这些时刻，学生本身就会受到同龄人和朋友的影响。6）例如，我的表弟是一名九年级的学生，他最近发现他的一些同学被最新的 iPhone X 的设计和功能所迷住。7）因此，他的很多朋友和同学都要求他们的父母给他们购买最新版本的 iPhone。 8）感觉到来自同龄人和朋友的压力，我的表弟也要求他的父亲给他购买这款手机。

1）另一方面，由于师生之间存在巨大的代沟，学生受到教师影响的可能较小。2）事实上，年轻学生和教师，尤其是那些几十年前进入这个行业的教师，往往有着不同的价值观、信念和生活方式。3）例如，学生喜欢将现代技术甚至电子游戏融入学习体验中，而一些教师可能会反对，因为他们认为死记硬背和讲座是学生获取知识的更好方式。4）这种观念的差异让教师很难影响学生的学习或激励他们专注于学习。5）此外，教师对课堂以外的学生的影响甚至可以忽略不计。

总的来说，学生受到朋友的影响比受教师的影响更大，因为大多数时间学生与同龄人在一起，他们倾向于影响学生的想法、思维以及他们的行为。而教师对学生的影响很小，因为他们之间存在巨大的代沟。

◆ 5. 重点场景表达

1) on and off campus 校内外

2) hang out with their peers and friends 与同龄人和朋友出去玩

3) be so mesmerized by the design and function of the latest iPhone X 被最新的 iPhone X 的设计和功能所迷住

4) the pressure from peers 来自同龄人的压力

5) generation gap 代沟

6) incorporate modern technologies even video games into their learning experience 将现代技术甚至电子游戏融入学习体验中

7) rote memory and lecture 死记硬背和讲座

8) motivate them to focus on study 激励他们专注于学习

TPO 19 独立写作

◆ 1. 题目

Do you agree or disagree with the following statement? In order to be well-informed, a person must get information from many different news resources.

◆ 2. 思路大纲

主观点：应该从多种信息源获取信息

分论点一：可以获取更全面的信息

分论点二：可以培养批判性思维能力

◆ 3. 高分范文和思维导图

1) With the advent of new technological gadgets, such as laptops, tablets and smart phones, people now have access to all sorts of news sources. 2) In face of the overwhelming news sources, some people tend to watch news from a single source while others prefer to do so from

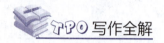

different sources. 3) I, personally, think it is far better to watch news from distinctive sources based on the following reasons.

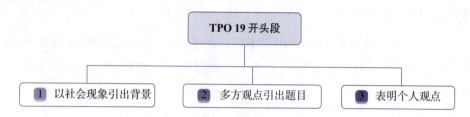

1) First of all, news from various sources is biased and it is quite irrational to read or watch news from a single source, and actually it makes better sense to be exposed to news that provides different kinds of ideas. 2) Even though it is very essential for news media to be fair and unbiased, most of the news media are biased and prejudiced in reality. 3) One of the reasons is that the news sources serve different purposes such as the government, independent institutions and think tanks. 4) Many of the media or news agencies take advantage of such vague phrases as "experts believe", "most people agree" or "observers argue that", all of which are quite biased since "most people" is a slippery expression. 5) Those people might not represent the majority of the people and lack diversity in terms of race, gender and other demographic factors.

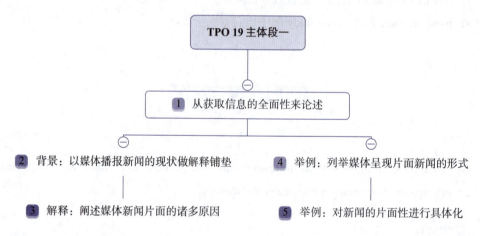

1) Additionally, being exposed to news from different sources can help people develop critical thinking abilities and thus have a fairer and more justified stance on certain issues. 2) Restricted by his past experiences, education backgrounds and economic conditions, a person tends to hold a fixed view of some issues. 3) However, having access to different ideas reported by various media can broaden people's horizons and enrich their experience, thus improving their critical thinking skills. 4) For instance, I took it for granted that every child at an appropriate age had the chance to go to primary school until I watched a documentary about the astonishing low

elementary school enrolment in the poverty-stricken regions in my country. 5) The families can barely feed their children and the local government has little educational resources to provide proper education for them. 6) This documentary totally changed my perspective on the primary school enrollment in hinterland.

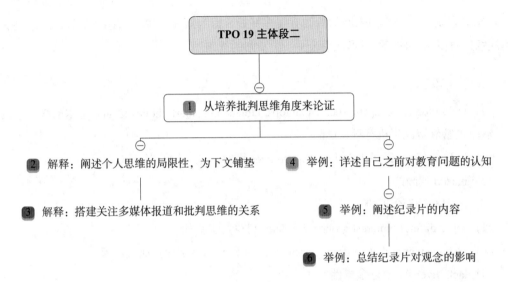

In all, exposure to news from different sources has many benefits since news sources are generally biased, and by watching news with different opinions，we can form a much fairer and clearer view.

◆ 4. 范文译文

1）随着笔记本电脑、平板电脑和智能手机等新技术的出现，人们现在可以接触各种新闻来源。2）面对五花八门的新闻来源，有的人倾向于通过单一来源观看新闻，有些则倾向于从不同来源收看新闻。3）我个人认为从不同来源获取信息要好很多。

1）首先，来自各方的消息是有偏见的，从单一来源读取或观看新闻是非常不合理的，而实际上接触到提供不同想法的新闻更为合理。2）虽然对新闻媒体来说公平、公正是非常重要的，但是大多数新闻媒体在现实中都存在偏见。3）其中一个原因是新闻媒体服务于不同的利益团体，如政府、独立机构和智库。4）许多媒体或新闻机构利用"专家认定""大多数人同意"或"观察者争辩"等含糊的词语，所有这些都是有偏见的，因为"大多数人"是一个不靠谱的表达。5）这些人并不一定代表大多数人，在种族、性别等人口因素方面缺乏多样性。

1）另外，接触不同来源的新闻可以帮助人们培养批判性思维能力，从而在某些问题上有一个更公正、更合理的立场。2）由于不同的生活经历、教育背景和经济条件等，人们在某些问题上有固定的观点。3）然而，接触不同媒体报道的不同的想法可以拓宽人们的视野，

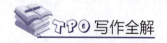
丰富他们的经验，促进批判性思维能力。4）例如，我曾认为每个适龄孩子都有机会上小学，直到我看了一部关于我国贫困地区低得惊人的小学入学率的纪录片。5）家庭几乎不能让孩子吃饱，地方政府教育资源很少，无法提供适当的教育。6）这部纪录片彻底改变了我对贫困地区小学入学的看法。

总的来说，接触不同来源的新闻有很多好处，因为新闻来源普遍存在偏见，通过观看不同意见的新闻，我们可以形成更公平、更清晰的视角。

◆ 5. 重点场景表达

1) technological gadgets, such as laptops, tablets and smart phones 诸如笔记本电脑、平板电脑和智能手机等科技产品

2) in face of the overwhelming news sources 面对五花八门的消息来源

3) biased 偏颇的

4) irrational 不合理的

5) serve different interest groups 为不同的利益集团服务

6) race, gender and other demographic factors 种族、性别和其他人口因素

7) lack diversity 缺乏多样性

8) an appropriate age 适当的年龄

9) poverty-stricken regions 贫困地区

10) educational resources 教育资源

11) primary school enrolment 小学入学

TPO 20 独立写作

◆ 1. 题目

Do you agree or disagree with the following statement? Successful people try new things and take risks rather than only doing what they know how to do well.

◆ 2. 思路大纲

主观点：成功人士会更爱尝试新事物和冒险

分论点一：成功的商人是这样的

分论点二：顶级的运动员也是这样的

◆ 3. 高分范文和思维导图

1) Successful people share distinctive features like hardworking, perseverant, capable, and

dedicated. 2) When it comes to the question of whether successful people try new things and take challenges rather than staying in their comfort zone, people tend to give different answers. 3) I, personally, reckon that taking challenges rather than just doing comfortable things is a common feature shared among successful individuals.

1) First of all, highly successful and established businesspeople take risks so that they can outstrip their competitors and stay alive in the market. 2) In fact, taking risks and spotting opportunities are the basic and quintessential character of an entrepreneur since once a businessman lets go an opportunity, it is gone forever. 3) For example, my uncle runs a real estate company. 4) He decided to purchase some deserted industrial workshops and transform these disused industrial space into a modern housing complex. 5) Once he brought up this groundbreaking and bold idea, most of his senior managers thought he was insane given the fact that such a big project could be very costly, ending up losing huge amounts of money. 6) However, my uncle took the risk, hired first class interior design professionals and installed modern appliances in these buildings, and eventually he converted these rundown workshops into fashionable and comfortable lofts. 7) It turned out to be a big success, making huge profit for the company.

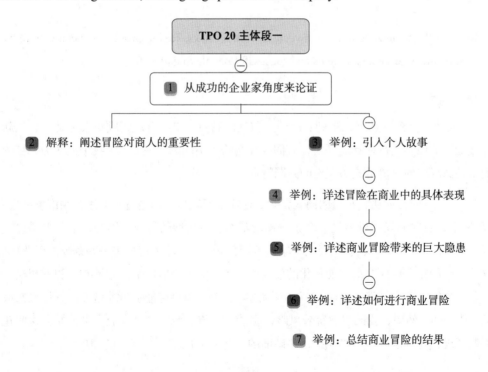

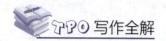

1) Additionally, first class athletes have to constantly take risks and face challenges on and off court to bring home the championships. 2) Staying competitive, pushing the limits, and confronting failures are required to become top athletes. 3) For example, part of the reason why Michael Jordan is the most respected NBA player of all time is that he was always the one who played the role of "Mr. Clutch", a nickname for players who take the most decisive shot and help to win the game. 4) In these critical moments, Michael was aware of the risks involved since if he missed the shot, his team would have lost the game. 5) However, he was fully prepared and confident that taking risks also meant increasing the likelihood of success. 6) Clearly, if he played safe in these critical moments, chances were that he would not have been remembered as such a great basketball player.

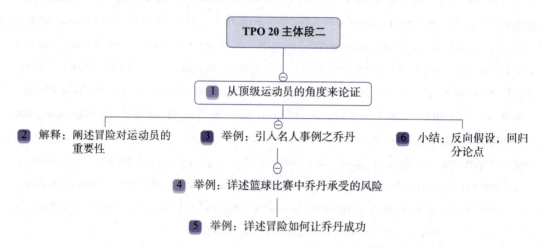

In all, both life and career are not vacuum without risks. Taking proper risks can help to make great businessmen, respected athletes and successful people in daily life.

◆ 4. 范文译文

1）成功人士具有勤奋、坚韧、能干、敬业的特点。 2）当谈到成功人士是否尝试新事物并接受挑战而不是待在舒适区时，人们往往会给出不同的答案。 3）我个人认为，接受挑战而不是做舒适的事情是成功人士的共同特点。

1）首先，非常成功和知名的商人冒险，这样他们就可以超越竞争对手，在市场上生存。 2）事实上，冒险和发现机会是一个企业家最基本、最典型的特征，因为机会一旦错过，就永远消失了。 3）例如，我叔叔经营一家房地产公司。 4）他决定购买一些荒废的工业厂房，把这些废弃的工业空间改造成现代化的住宅区。 5）他一提出这个开创性和大胆的想法，他的大部分高级管理人员就认为他疯了，因为这样一个大项目可能造价非常高昂，结果造成巨额的损失。 6）然而，我的叔叔冒着风险，聘请了一流的室内设计专业人员，并在这些建筑中安装了现代化的家电，最终他把这些破旧的厂房改造成了时尚舒适的楼房。 7）这是一个巨大的成功，为公司创造了巨大的利润。

1）另外，一流的运动员要不断冒险，面对场内外的挑战，带回总冠军。2）保持竞争力、突破极限、面对失败是成为顶尖运动员的要求。3）例如，乔丹之所以成为 NBA 历史上最受尊敬的球员之一，是因为他始终扮演着"关键先生"的角色。这是给那些做出决定性的一击并帮助赢得比赛的球员的一个绰号。4）在这些关键时刻，迈克尔意识到了风险，因为如果他投篮不中，他的球队一定会输掉比赛。5）但是，他做好充分准备并深信，冒险也意味着增加成功的可能性。6）很显然，如果他在这个关键时刻打法保守的话，那么很有可能他不会作为这样一个伟大的篮球运动员被人们记住。

总之，生活和事业都不是没有风险的真空。冒险可以让人成为伟大的商人、尊敬的运动员和日常生活中的成功人士。

◆ 5. 重点场景表达

1) stay in their comfort zone 待在他们的舒适区

2) take challenges 接受挑战

3) highly successful and established businesspeople 非常成功和知名的商人

4) outstrip their competitors 超过他们的竞争对手

5) stay alive in the market 在市场上存活

6) most quintessential character of an entrepreneur 企业家的最典型特征

7) run a real estate company 经营房地产公司

8) transform these disused industrial space into modern housing complex 将这些废弃的工业空间改造成现代化的住宅区

9) install modern appliance 安装现代家电

10) bring home the championships 把冠军带回家

11) in these critical moments 在这些关键时刻

12) be fully prepared 做好充分准备

TPO 21 独立写作

◆ 1. 题目

Do you agree or disagree with the following statement? For success in a future job, the ability to relate well to people is more important than studying hard in school. Use specific reasons and examples to support your answer.

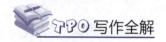

◆ 2. 思路大纲

主观点：与他人处理好关系的能力更加重要
分论点一：比好的学习成绩要更加难得
分论点二：可以减少矛盾，利于合作

◆ 3. 高分范文和思维导图

1) With the ever increasing pressure upon young people, people wonder which is considered more essential when it comes to securing a promising job, academic performance or interpersonal skills. 2) As for me, there is nothing more compelling in manifesting a person's ability than an individual's extraordinary ability to relate to people.

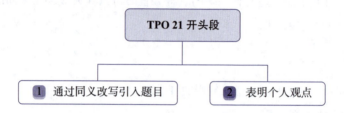

1) For one thing, it is harder to learn skills concerning how to build solid relationships with people than to acquire technical knowledge in class. 2) Interpersonal skills are not something common that you can easily master from textbooks; instead, the reality is, cultivating the capacity of relating well to strangers requires nothing but real-world practice in daily business life. 3) As a result, corporate profits may be jeopardized if they hired the wrong people who didn't have interpersonal skills and most companies can't afford such a huge loss. 4) Consistent with the above rationale is the prevalent phenomenon in the job fair that more and more positions give priority to the applicants who are swift at building connections with strangers, which implicates that the younger generation should put efforts into honing this skill. 5) On the contrary, it's never too late to acquire academic knowledge, since written words will never fade, and all it counts is an individual's determination and diligence.

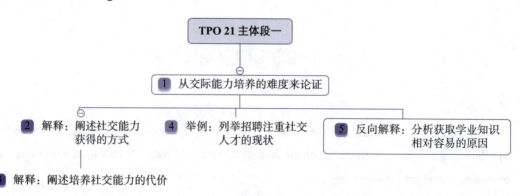

1) Another conspicuous function of having strong interpersonal skills is to mitigate conflict and facilitate cooperation, which is crucial to professional success. 2) Inevitably, disagreements and conflicts with coworkers or clients will occur in a workplace. 3) Only through productive communication can employees in the company work in harmony without being skeptical or displeased and earn trust from customers, which ensures that the whole enterprise functions at a full speed. 4) To be specific, ad designers need to negotiate with partners in order to achieve a satisfying consensus, and similarly salesmen need to persuade customers to buy the most profitable items and further boost sales. 5) We can easily observe that in one's career, countless occasions will arise calling for outstanding interpersonal skills.

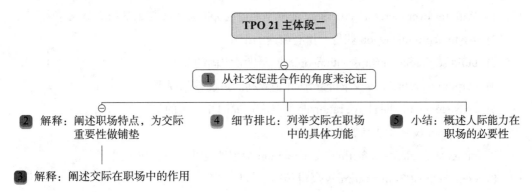

In conclusion, a person's communication skills can be applied beyond just working situations, and this kind of people can pursue a profession beyond ordinary constraints as long as they are persistent and willing to arm themselves with requisite expertise.

◆ 4. 范文译文

1）随着年轻人的压力越来越大，人们往往会想知道在获得前途光明的工作时，什么被认为是最重要的：学业成绩还是人际交流能力。2）对我而言，在表现一个人的能力方面没有什么比与他人交际的能力更有吸引力。

1）首先，学会如何与人建立牢固关系的技能比从课堂上获得技术知识更难。2）交际技能不是很容易从教科书中掌握的东西，事实上，培养与陌生人良好关系的能力除了在日常商业生活中的现实世界实践之外别无他法。3）因此，企业如果雇用了不懂人际关系的错误的人，其利润可能受到损害，大多数公司不能承受如此巨大的损失。4）与上述表述相一致的是招聘会中普遍存在的一种现象，越来越多的职位优先考虑能够迅速与陌生人建立联系的申请人，这意味着年轻一代应该努力培养这方面的能力。5）相反，学习学术知识永远不晚，因为书面文字永远不会褪色，只要这个人有决心且勤奋。

1）具有强大的人际交往能力的另一个显著功能是缓解冲突并促进合作，这对于职业成

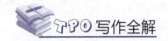

功至关重要。2）工作场所不可避免地会与同事或客户发生分歧和冲突。3）只有通过有效的沟通，公司员工才能和谐一致地工作，不会产生怀疑或不满，同时得到客户的信任，从而确保整个企业全速运转。4）具体而言，广告设计师需要与合作伙伴进行谈判以达成令人满意的共识，同样，推销员需要说服顾客购买最有利可图的商品，并进一步促进销售。5）我们可以很容易地看到，在自己的职业生涯中，无数场合需要杰出的人际交往能力。

总之，一个人的沟通技巧不仅仅用在工作环境中，只要他坚持不懈，愿意以必要的专业知识武装自己，这种人就可以追求超越一般限制的职业。

◆ 5. 重点场景表达

1) With the ever increasing pressure upon young people 随着年轻人的压力越来越大

2) secure a promising job 获得一份有前途的工作

3) build solid relationships with people 与人建立牢固的关系

4) corporate profits may be jeopardized 企业利润可能受到损害

5) consistent with the above rationale is 与上述原因相一致的是

6) give priority to 优先考虑

7) mitigate conflict and facilitate cooperation 缓解冲突并促进合作

8) earn the trust from customers 赢得顾客的信任

9) the whole enterprise functions at a full speed 整个企业全速运转

10) boost sale 促进销售

TPO 22 独立写作

◆ 1. 题目

Do you agree or disagree with the following statement? Teachers should not make their social or political views known to students in the classroom. Use specific reasons and examples to support your answer.

◆ 2. 思路大纲

主观点：老师在课堂上不应该向学生表达自己的社会或政治观点
分论点一：为了更好地培养学生的批判性思维
分论点二：为了更好地履行教师的本职工作

◆ 3. 高分范文和思维导图

1) The stress the whole society puts on education is stronger than ever, resulting in various

teaching approaches adopted by teachers. 2) Some teachers tend to include their personal views toward certain matters in the teaching process while some other teachers who are just the opposite, that is, they only pass information relevant to the materials they teach. 3) As for me, I think the second type of teacher definitely meets my satisfaction.

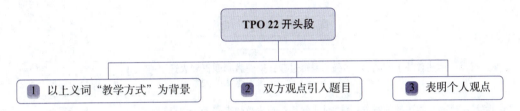

1) The first consideration must come from the concern that too many personal views from teachers jeopardize students' critical thinking, the concrete basis of independent thinking. 2) Teachers' personal insights might serve as impediments so that students cannot think critically. 3) There is a term in psychology called "familiarity principle", which demonstrates that when people had previous experience with something, they tend to prefer the same thing even though it is beyond their awareness that they had been exposed to it. 4) Following this logic, teachers are eager to impart their predilections to their students, which will have tremendous impact on their thinking. 5) It is a potential threat to students from the moment when students perceive them, making them less likely to think independently.

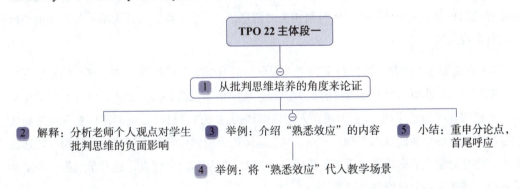

1) Also, the top priority of teachers is to impart knowledge to students rather than influencing students by their social and political perspectives. 2) Indeed, teachers are ultimately responsible to prepare students for the future job market, and equip them with knowledge and skills necessary to assume greater responsibilities. 3) Thus, teachers should encourage, motivate, and inspire students to be curious about the world and thus more willing to learn. 4) In fact, good educators do not try to sway their students' views but try to address all sides of an argument or issue. 5) Impartial lessons without any political view benefits students' study. 6) However, when spreading political and social

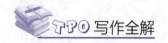

views in class, teachers, especially those who have extreme social and political views, will hinder students' active thinking and learning.

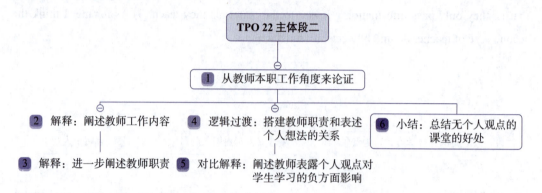

In conclusion, spreading political and social views in class jeopardize students' independent and critical thinking while an impartial lesson can stimulate students' curiosity and inspire them to learn.

◆ 4. 范文译文

1）全社会对教育的压力比以往任何时候都要强烈，导致教师采取各种教学方式。2）在教学过程中，有些教师倾向于将自己的个人观点纳入其中，而另外一些教师则恰恰相反，这意味着他们只能传递与他们教授的材料相关的信息。3）至于我，我认为第二种类型的教师绝对符合我的满意度。

1）首先要考虑的是，教师过多的个人观点会危及学生的批判性思维，这是独立思考的具体基础。2）教师的个人见解可能成为障碍，使学生不能批判性地思考。3）心理学中有一个术语叫作"熟悉原则"，它表明当人们以前经历过一件事情时，他们往往更喜欢之前接触过的东西，尽管他们意识不到这一点。4）遵循这个逻辑，教师渴望将自己的偏好传递给学生，将会对学生的思维造成巨大的影响。5）从学生认知的角度看，这对学生是一种潜在的威胁，使他们不太可能独立思考。

1）此外，教师的首要任务是传授知识，而不是影响学生的社会和政治观点。2）的确，教师最终有责任是为学生应对未来的就业市场做好准备，并使他们具备知识和技能，以承担更大的责任。3）因此，教师应该鼓励、激励学生对世界的好奇心，从而更愿意学习。4）事实上，好的教育者不会试图影响学生的观点，而是试图提出争论或问题的各个方面。5）没有任何政治偏见的课程有利于学生的学习。6）然而，在课堂上传播政治和社会观点时，教师，尤其是那些持有极端的社会和政治观点的教师，会阻碍学生积极思考和学习。

总之，在课堂上传播政治和社会观点危害学生的独立和批判性思维，而教师没有偏见的授课可以激发学生的好奇心，激励他们学习。

◆ 5. 重点场景表达

1) various teaching approaches 各种教学方法

2) personal views 个人观点

3) teaching process 教学过程

4) jeopardize students' critical thinking 危及学生的批判性思维

5) the concrete basis of independent thinking 独立思考的具体基础

6) serve as impediments 作为障碍

7) familiarity principle 熟悉原则

8) have tremendous impact on students' thinking 对学生的思维造成巨大的影响

9) social and political perspectives 社会和政治观点

10) equip them with knowledge and skills 使他们具备知识和技能

11) encourage, motivate, and inspire students to be curious 鼓励、激励学生对世界的好奇心

12) spread political and social views 传播政治和社会观点

13) hinder students' active thinking and learning 阻碍学生积极思考和学习

TPO 23 独立写作

◆ 1. 题目

Do you agree or disagree with the following statement? In today's world, it is more important to work quickly and risk making mistakes than to work slowly and make sure that everything is correct.

◆ 2. 思路大纲

主观点：工作缓慢不好

分论点一：容易错失机遇

分论点二：容易导致工作热情下降

◆ 3. 高分范文和思维导图

1) People tend to have different approaches when they do projects. 2) Some people mull over all aspects of a project, and do it very slowly, and thus they have few mistakes while others tend to work quickly and risk making mistakes. 3) Personally, working slowly is a bad quality based on the following reasons.

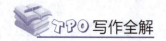

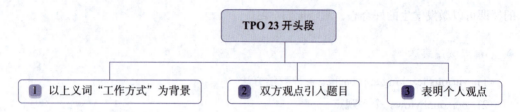

1) First of all, if a person spends too much time finishing his or her work, chances are that he or she might lose valuable opportunities that do not come around too often. 2) More often than not, those who are more motivated to finish their work earlier can enjoy better chances and opportunities since timing is an important factor for someone to capitalize on them. 3) For example, my supervisor Alex motivates his members to finish business projects very quickly. 4) Last year, the team led by Alex used only a month to come up with a new design makeover of a product. 5) It turned out our new product was put to market earlier than our competitors', which eventually helped our company made lots of profits.

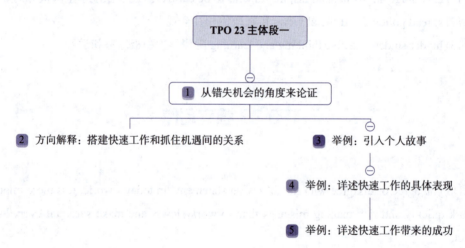

1) Additionally, taking a long time to finish a project can cause low employee morale. 2) Actually, people who spend a long time finishing up their work tend to overanalyze the situation and procrastinate through the whole work day, ending up achieving nothing at all. 3) The resulting sense of frustration leads to negative feelings and self-hatred, which eventually kills employee morale and results in lower productivity. 4) According to a recent survey conducted by a magazine titled *Weekly Business*, the speed of task completion is in proportion to the intensity of employee morale, which shows that if a group of employees spend too much time attacking a project without any achievement, employees will begin to make complaints and feel disappointed about their company.

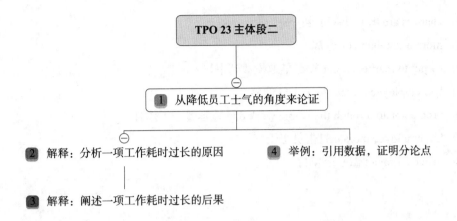

In all, despite the fact that working quickly might cause mistakes, it helps to spot valuable opportunities that do not come around too often. One the other hand, being meticulous about one's work causes lower working efficiency.

◆ 4. 范文译文

1）人们在做项目时倾向于采用不同的方法。2）有些人仔细研究项目的各个方面，并且做得非常慢，因此他们几乎没有错误，而另一些人倾向于快速工作并冒着犯错的风险。3）就个人而言，基于以下原因，慢慢工作不是一个好品质。

1）首先，如果一个人花费太多时间完成他或她的工作，他或她可能会错过不经常出现的宝贵机会。2）通常情况下，那些能够提前完成工作的员工可以享受更好的机会和机遇，因为时间安排是个人利用机会的重要因素。3）例如，我的主管亚历克斯会激励他的员工快速完成商业项目。4）去年，由 Alex 领导的团队仅用了一个月的时间就对产品进行了新的设计改造。5）结果我们的新产品早于竞争对手的产品投放到市场，最终帮助我们公司获得了很多利润。

1）此外，花费很长时间来完成一个项目可能会导致员工士气低落。2）实际上，花很长时间完成工作的人往往会过分分析情况，拖延整个工作日，结果什么都没有完成。3）由此产生的挫折感导致消极情绪和自我仇恨，最终导致员工士气低落，甚至导致生产力下降。4）一份名为《每周商业》的杂志最近进行的一项调查显示，任务完成速度与员工士气强度成正比，这表明如果一群员工花费太多时间做一个项目而没有取得任何成就，员工开始抱怨并对公司感到失望。

总而言之，尽管迅速工作可能会导致错误，但它有助于发现不经常出现的宝贵机会。另一方面，对工作一丝不苟，导致工作效率低下。

◆ 5. 重点场景表达

1）risk making mistakes 冒着犯错的风险

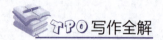

2) chances are that 很有可能……

3) more often than not 通常

4) be put to market earlier 被更早地投放到市场

5) low employee morale 员工士气低落

6) procrastinate through the whole work day 拖延整个工作日

7) kill employee morale 打击员工士气

8) attack a project 做一个项目

TPO 24 独立写作

◆ 1. 题目

Do you agree or disagree with the following statement? One of the best ways that parents can help their teenage children prepare for adult life is to encourage them to take a part-time job.

◆ 2. 思路大纲

主观点：鼓励孩子做兼职

分论点一：培养金钱意识

分论点二：加强时间管理能力

分论点三：丰富工作和生活经验

◆ 3. 高分范文和思维导图

1) Parents tend to place different priorities on their children's education. 2) Some regard good academic performance as the most important matter while others believe that a part-time job can get teenagers better prepared for adulthood. 3) From my perspective, taking a part-time job can be very beneficial to kids since children can learn the value of money, develop time management skills and gain a lot of valuable experience for their future life and career.

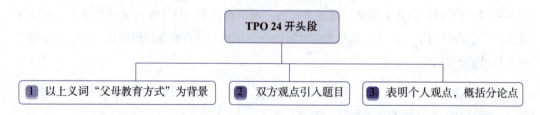

1) To begin with, taking a part-time job can make the children realize the value of money and spend their hard-earned dollars more wisely. 2) Kids who have never taken part-time jobs don't

recognize the value of money since they can just ask for some pocket money from their parents whenever they want to buy something. 3) However, if kids have a part-time job, they will be more likely to spend their hard-earned money in a more rational way since they have worked so hard to get it. 4) They can use the money to pay their tuition, buy useful textbooks, pay for their daily necessities, and even have some fun within the limit of their budget. 5) With the money earned, they have more choices when buying things they aspire for. 6) Eventually, having a part-time job makes the kids more financially responsible and appreciate the value of money, both of which are really important qualities for becoming a responsible adult.

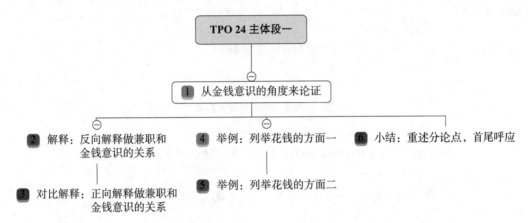

1) In addition, kids who take part-time jobs can develop time management skills. 2) As is common sense, nowadays students are pretty overwhelmed with their assignments like writing papers, preparing for exams, or even delivering presentations, leaving limited amount of leisure time for them. 3) In this case, kids who take part-time jobs tend to have less free time compared with non-working students. 4) Therefore, working kids will value their time since not only do they need to fulfill their working responsibility, but also they have to weigh their priorities so that they can finish their assignments before deadline. 5) Being able to do multiple tasks at the same time can be a great advantage when they are in adulthood.

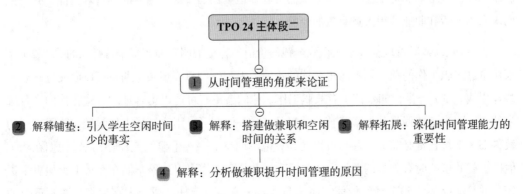

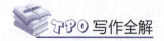

1) Lastly, kids who have done simple part-time jobs can gain more experience and this will give them a better shot to land a sweet job in their future. 2) While working part time, students will have the chance to be exposed to the real working environment and thus will be equipped with more professional skills and knowledge related to work. 3) In this way, students will have an edge over other competitors in hunting for a job and adapting to future work and thus win the favor of their prospective bosses. 4) To be specific, almost every position requires interns to work in a group so that they understand that they might fail to satisfy customers if they don't work in a cooperative spirit. 5) Consequently, those who have worked before are more adaptable when working together with others.

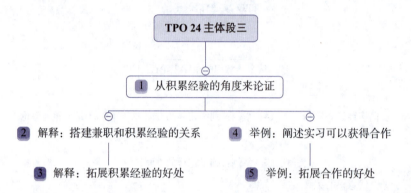

All in all, from the above analysis, we can safely draw the conclusion that taking a part-time job can make the kids better prepared for the future since they can learn the value of money and spend within the budget, develop time management skills, and gain valuable experience, all of which will be great assets for their future life and career.

◆ 4. 范文译文

1）父母对孩子的教育有不同的优先考虑的因素。2）有些人认为良好的学习成绩是最重要的事情，而另一些人认为兼职可以让青少年更好地为成年做准备。3）从我的角度来看，兼职可以让孩子们非常受益，因为孩子们可以知道金钱的价值，培养时间管理技能，并为他们未来的生活和职业获得大量宝贵的经验。

1）首先，兼职可以让孩子认识到金钱的价值，并更加明智地花费辛苦赚来的钱。2）从未从事过兼职工作的孩子们不懂得金钱的价值，因为他们只要想买东西就可以向父母索要一些零用钱。3）但是，如果孩子有兼职工作，他们会更有可能以更合理的方式花他们辛苦赚来的钱，因为这些钱是他们辛辛苦苦获得的。4）他们可以用这笔钱支付学费，购买有用的教科书，支付日常必需品，甚至可以在预算范围内享受一些乐趣。5）赚钱后，他们在购买他们渴望的东西时有更多的选择。6）最后，做兼职工作可以让孩子们在经济上承担更多责任，并且能够体会到金钱的价值，而这两者对于成为负责任的成年人来说都是非常重要的品质。

1）此外，兼职工作的孩子可以培养时间管理技能。2）按照常识，现在的学生对他们的学习任务比如写论文、准备考试，甚至做展示等感到压力山大，这也给他们留下有限的休闲时间。3）在这种情况下，与不做兼职的学生相比，从事兼职工作的孩子往往空闲时间更少。4）因此，工作的孩子会重视自己的时间，因为他们不仅需要履行自己的工作责任，还必须权衡自己的优先事项，以便他们能够在截止日期之前完成任务。5）能够同时完成多项任务在成年时具有很大的优势。

1）最后，做过简单兼职工作的孩子可以获得更多的经验，这将使他们有更好的机会在未来找到一份好工作。2）在兼职工作的同时，学生将有机会接触真实的工作环境，从而拥有更多与工作有关的专业技能和知识。3）通过这种方式，学生可以在寻找工作和适应未来工作方面优于其他竞争对手，从而赢得未来老板的青睐。4）具体而言，几乎每个职位都要求实习生在团队中协作，以便让他们明白，如果他们不以合作精神工作，就可能无法满足客户。5）因此，工作过的人在与他人合作时更具适应性。

总而言之，通过以上分析，我们可以得出结论：兼职工作可以帮助孩子们为未来做好准备，因为孩子们可以懂得金钱的价值，量入为出，发展时间管理技能并获得宝贵的经验，所有这些将成为他们未来生活和事业的重要资产。

◆ 5. 重点场景表达

1) different priorities 不同的重点

2) good academic performance 良好的学习成绩

3) gain a lot of valuable experience 获得很多宝贵的经验

4) develop time management skills　培养时间管理技能

5) pocket money　零用钱

6) part-time job 兼职工作

7) in a more rational way 以更合理的方式

8) pay their tuition, buy useful textbooks, pay for their daily necessities 交学费，买有用的教科书，支付日常必需品

9) financially responsible 财务负责

10) appreciate the value of money 懂得金钱的价值

11) cooperative spirit 合作精神

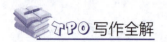
TPO 25 独立写作

◆ 1. 题目

Do you agree or disagree with the following statement? Young people nowadays do not spend enough time helping their communities.

◆ 2. 思路大纲

主观点：现在年轻人更愿意帮助社区

分论点一：对社区活动的重视程度提升

分论点二：参与社区活动的机会增多

◆ 3. 高分范文和思维导图

1) Volunteer and charitable activities of all forms are applauded and cherished by people. 2) When it comes to the question of whether young people are willing to help their communities, people tend to give different answers. 3) I, personally, am very affirmative that young people are more generous to help their communities than the past based on the following reasons.

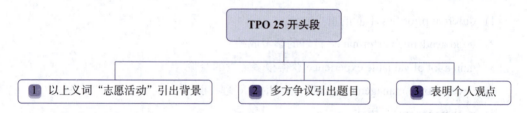

1) First of all, with the ever-increasing educational level, young people are more aware of the importance of volunteer activities. 2) Universities tend to evaluate the candidates' involvement in community service and those who have done certain hours of community service will enjoy a better shot to get admission letters than those who have not. 3) Professionals are also encouraged by their corporations to engage in community service. 4) Thus, fully aware of the benefits brought by community service, young people know that giving a helping hand to the community is a very rewarding experience and consciously donate their time and energy to make the community a better place to live in. 5) Many students who want to study abroad may engage in graffiti cleanup or animals habitat restoration, which will be valued by the admissions office of their dream school.

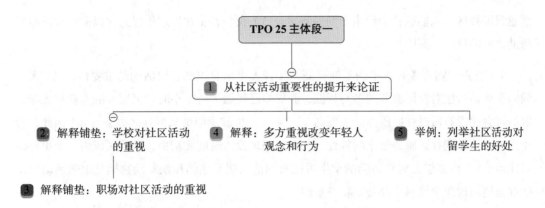

1) Additionally, schools and universities offer a myriad of volunteer and charitable activities for students. 2) For instance, a high school in my neighborhood offers students various volunteer programs and every student can check bulletin boards for activities which they are interested in. 3) To be specific, students can help to collect food, manage inventory and distribute food to those in need. 4) They can also volunteer in homeless shelters to prepare food or even work behind the scene in the business office. 5) With these programs offered by schools, young students are motivated to take the initiative and contribute their time and energy to the community. 6) Such a philanthropic atmosphere can be very contagious, getting everyone involved in community service.

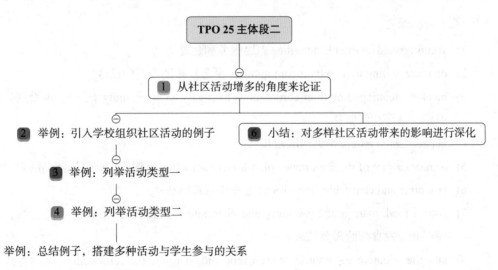

In conclusion, with the increasing awareness of the significance of community service and various volunteer programs offered by universities, young people are more willing to give a helping hand to their community.

◆ 4. 范文译文

1）各种形式的志愿服务和慈善活动都会受到人们的热烈追捧。2）谈到年轻人是否更

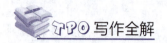

愿意帮助社区，人们往往会给出不同的答案。3）我个人非常肯定年轻人比以前更加慷慨地帮助他们的社区，原因如下。

1）首先，随着教育水平的不断提高，年轻人更加意识到志愿活动的重要性。2）大学倾向于评估考生对社区服务的参与程度，而那些已经做了一定小时社区服务的人获得大学录取的机会比没有做过社区服务的人要高 。3）公司也鼓励职员从事社区服务。4）因此，青年人充分认识到社区服务带来的好处，并有意识地投入时间和精力，使社区成为一个更好的居住地。5）许多想去海外留学的学生可能参加清除胡乱涂鸦和恢复动物栖息地的活动，这些都是他们理想学校召生办公室将看重的。

1）此外，学校和大学还为学生提供无数志愿者和慈善活动。2）例如，我附近的一所高中为学生提供各种志愿者项目，每个学生都可以到布告栏里查看自己感兴趣的活动。3）具体地说，学生可以帮助收集食物、管理存货并给有需要的人分发食物。4）他们也可以自愿在收容所里准备食物，甚至从事商务办公室的幕后工作。5）有学校提供这些项目，青年学生非常积极主动地为社会贡献自己的时间和精力。6）这样的慈善氛围很有感染力，促使每个人都参与社区服务。

总而言之，随着社区服务意识的提高和大学提供的各种志愿服务项目的日益增多，年轻人更愿意向社区伸出援助之手。

◆ 5. 重点场景表达

1) volunteer and charitable activities 志愿服务和慈善活动

2) be more willing to help their communities 更愿意帮助他们的社区

3) be also encouraged by their corporations to engage in community service 也受到公司的鼓励，从事社区服务

4) get admission letters 得到录取通知书

5) be more aware of the importance of volunteer activities 更加意识到志愿活动的重要性

6) volunteer and charitable activities 志愿者和慈善活动

7) collect food, manage the inventory and distribute food to those in need 收集食物、管理库存和分发食物给需要的人

8) take the initiative and contribute their time and energy to the community 主动为社会贡献自己的时间和精力

9) philanthropic atmosphere 慈善的氛围

TPO 26 独立写作

◆ 1. 题目

Do you agree or disagree with the following statement? It is better for children to choose jobs that are similar to their parents' jobs than to choose jobs that are very different from their parents' jobs.

◆ 2. 思路大纲

主观点：选择和父母一样的工作

分论点一：可以收获职业必需的特质

分论点二：可以在职场中获得必要的帮助

◆ 3. 高分范文和思维导图

1) A myriad of factors can contribute to one's career decision making like educational background, characters, and skill sets. 2) However, when it comes to the question of whether it is better for children to follow the footsteps of their parents professionally, people tend to give different answers. 3) I, personally, reckon that it is better to choose the same profession as our parents based on the following reasons.

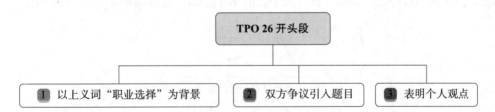

1) First of all, people are inherently influenced by their parents, who help them shape values, qualities, and ideologies that are important to parents' career. 2) Thus, people tend to have qualities that are required by their parents' professions. 3) Indeed, not only do parents influence us in terms of our values, habits and behaviors, but also they pass on a significant number of genes to us, making us have favorable qualities to follow our parents' footstep professionally. 4) For instance, my cousin was born and raised by parents who worked in the military for their whole life. 5) As is known to all, military professionals follow rigid rules, have absolute loyalty to their superiors, and get things done quickly. 6) Consequently, because of the fact that my cousin has better self-discipline and tougher character than his peers, he can be more successful in the military than in

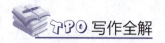

other professions.

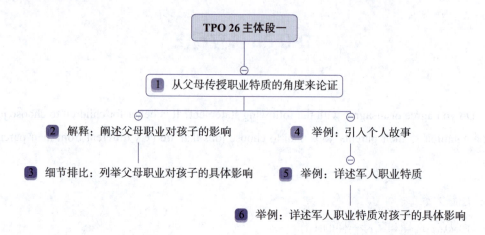

1) Additionally, following parents' footsteps professionally means that we can get more help in our career advancement. 2) Our parents might have worked in their professions for a few decades, during which time they have accumulated rich working experience and already established very useful social networks. 3) These resources can be very helpful for us if we choose the same occupation as our parents did. 4) For instance, my college friend Alex's dad is a very successful banker in the local community. 5) Naturally, he helped Alex land a job in a local bank and whenever Alex has problems dealing with customers and clients, his dad can provide timely assistance and guidance to him. 6) With staunch support from his dad, Alex was awarded the most valuable employee of the year by his bank. 7) Consequently, our parents can assist us professionally.

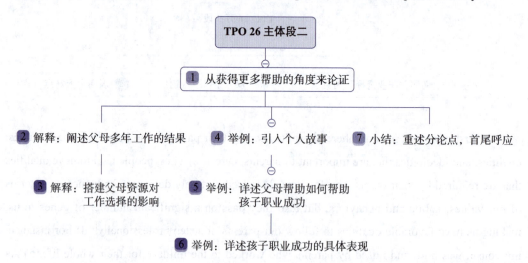

In all, it is in the best interest of individuals to follow their parents' footsteps professionally since they have qualities and skill sets required by the same job as their parents and they can benefit professionally from their parents.

◆ 4. 范文译文

1）无数的因素可以影响职业决策，如教育背景、性格特质和技能。 2）但是，当谈到孩子职业选择上追随父母的脚步是否更好的问题时，人们往往会给出不同的答案。 3）我个人认为，基于以下原因，选择与我们父母相同的职业更好。

1）首先，人们天生受到父母的影响，父母帮助他们塑造对父母职业很重要的价值观、素质和意识形态。 2）因此，人们倾向于拥有父母职业所需的品质。 3）的确，父母不仅在我们的价值观、习惯和行为方面影响我们，而且他们还传给我们大量的基因，使我们有良好的品质来从事父母的专业。 4）例如，我的表弟生于军人家庭。 5）众所周知，军人遵循严格的规则，对上级绝对忠诚，并迅速完成任务。 6）因此，由于我的表弟比同龄人有更好的自律和更坚强的品格，在军队里他可以比在其他职业里更为成功。

1）另外，职业上子随父（母）业意味着人们可以在职业发展中获得更多的帮助。 2）我们的父母可能在他们的专业工作了几十年，在此期间他们积累了丰富的工作经验，并且已经建立了非常有用的社交网络。 3）如果我们选择与他们相同的职业，这些资源对我们非常有帮助。 4）例如，我的大学朋友亚历克斯的父亲是当地社区非常成功的银行家。 5）当然，他帮助亚历克斯在当地银行找到工作，并且每当亚历克斯遇到与顾客和客户打交道的问题时，他的父亲都可以及时向他提供帮助和指导。 6）在他父亲的坚定支持下，亚历克斯被他的银行授予了年度最有价值的员工。 7）因此，我们的父母可以在职业上协助我们。

总之，追随父母的职业符合个人的最佳利益，因为这些人具有与其父母同样工作所需的素质和技能，并且他们可以受益于父母的职业。

◆ 5. 重点场景表达

1) a myriad of factors 无数的因素

2) shape values, qualities, and ideologies 塑造价值观、素质和意识形态

3) pass on a significant number of genes 传给我们大量的基因

4) follow our parents' footstep professionally 从事父母的专业

5) follow rigid rule, have absolute loyalty to their superiors 遵循严格的规则，对上级绝对忠诚

6) establish very useful social networks 建立非常有用的社交网络

7) provide timely assistance and guidance to 及时向……提供帮助和指导

8) be in the best interest of individuals 符合个人的最佳利益

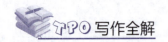

TPO 27 独立写作

◆ 1. 题目

Do you agree or disagree with the following statement? If people have the opportunity to obtain a secure job, they should take it right away rather than wait for a job that may be more satisfying.

◆ 2. 思路大纲

主观点：立刻抓住一份稳定的工作

分论点一：有利于尽早接触社会

分论点二：有利于拓展社交圈

◆ 3. 高分范文和思维导图

1) People have different expectations out of a job like personal satisfaction, higher pay, respect, and social recognition. 2) When it comes to the question of whether people should take the job offer they have just received or wait for a more satisfying position, people tend to give different opinions. 3) I, personally, reckon that taking the job right away is a better choice.

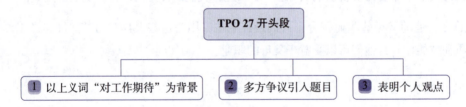

1) First of all, taking a job early means early exposure to the real world, which is very important for future professional development. 2) Eventually, it helps one to find his or her real expectation and ultimate career goal in the long run. 3) For example, if one gets a job offer from a small company, it is worth taking even though it is not something that makes one feel especially proud of. 4) One will learn to follow strict regulations and procedures when conducting business and how to cooperate with other coworkers to achieve ultimate efficiency. 5) Also, working early means more working experience in different industries, which will make the employees more flexible and adaptable in distinctive working environments. 6) Future employers will value those who have had exposure to a variety of challenges and can bring new ideas and changes to their companies.

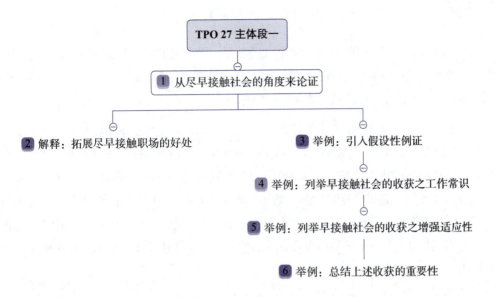

1) Additionally, starting off early in the corporate world also means that an individual has more opportunities to explore new social networks, thus enjoying a much more promising career in the near future. 2) Obviously, whatever jobs one engages in much earlier, more useful connections with fellow employees or managers can be created. 3) Eventually, these connections will open up one's career path in unexpected ways. 4) For example, many well-known international companies prefer to hire managers and supervisors not from the newly-graduated students but from within the business. 5) This is because they look not only for people with the necessary skills and personality traits, but also for people that are well known, especially by current managers in these fields. 6) Therefore, the more connections one makes in one's place of employment, the more leaders will take notice when it is time for promotions.

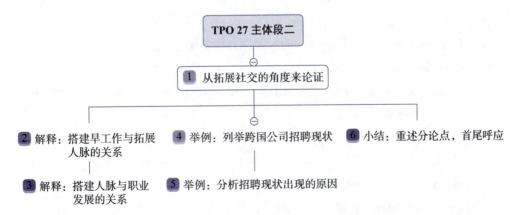

To conclude, taking a job right away means early exposure to the real world and more opportunities to broaden social and professional networks, both of which will lay a solid foundation for future professional development.

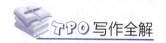

◆ 4. 范文译文

1）人们对工作有不同的期望，如个人满意度、更高的工资、尊重和社会认可。2）当谈到人们是否应该接受他们刚刚收到的工作邀请或等待更满意的职位时，人们往往持不同的意见。3）我个人认为立即开始工作是更好的选择。

1）首先，尽早工作意味着尽早接触现实世界，这对未来的专业发展非常重要。2）最终，从长远来看，这有助于找到他或她的真正期望和终极职业目标。3）例如，如果有人从一家小公司获得工作机会，即使这不是让人感到特别自豪的事情，也值得立刻拿下。4）一个人在开展业务时学到如何遵循严格的规定和程序，以及如何与其他同事合作以达到最高效率。5）早期工作意味着在不同行业有更多的工作经验，这将使员工在不同的工作环境中更具灵活性和适应性。6）未来的雇主将重视那些能够应对各种挑战并能给公司带来新想法和变化的人。

1）此外，更早进入职业世界，也意味着个人有更多机会探索新的社交网络，因此在不久的将来享有更有前途的职业生涯。2）很显然，无论你更早参与哪种工作，都可以创建与同事或经理更有用的联系。3）最终，这些关系将以意想不到的方式开辟你的职业道路。4）例如，许多著名的国际公司更愿意从企业内部而不是新毕业的学生中筛选经理和主管人员。5）这是因为他们不仅关注具有必要技能和人格特质的人，还关注在当前领域小有名气的人。6）因此，你在就业岗位上建立的关系越多，领导者在提拔人才时就会更多注意到你。

总而言之，立马工作就意味着尽早接触现实世界，并有更多的机会拓宽社交和专业网络，这将为未来的专业发展奠定坚实的基础。

◆ 5. 重点场景表达

1）early exposure to the real world 尽早接触现实世界

2）ultimate career goal 终极职业目标

3）follow strict regulations and procedures 遵循严格的规定和程序

4）conduct business 开展业务

5）more flexible and adaptable in distinctive working environments 在不同的工作环境中更具灵活性和适应性

6）enjoy a much more promising career in the near future 在不久的将来享有更有前途的职业生涯

7）open up one's career path in unexpected ways 以意想不到的方式开辟你的职业道路

8）lay solid foundation for 为……奠定坚实的基础

TPO 28 独立写作

◆ 1. 题目

Do you agree or disagree with the following statement? Parents today are more involved in their children's education than parents were in the past.

◆ 2. 思路大纲

主观点：现在父母更多地参与到孩子的教育中

分论点一：父母受教育水平更高

分论点二：父母对教育的重视程度更高

◆ 3. 高分范文和思维导图

1) Education, especially that during the early period of kids' development, can be crucial to their future life and career. 2) When it comes to the question of whether parents are more engaged in kids' education than parents were in the past, I, personally, am in favor of the statement due to parents' more advanced education level and their ever-increasing educational awareness.

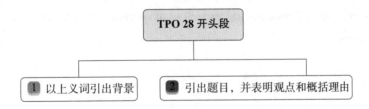

1) First of all, more advanced education level of parents makes it easier and more likely for them to get involved in kids' education. 2) Currently, most of the kids' parents get a decent degree from an accredited higher institution. 3) They know the value of education and how better education can help kids to be successful in both life and career. 4) Thus, they can motivate their children to study well and provide necessary resources to improve kids' academic performance. 5) For instance, my uncle held a Ph.D degree in math from Yale University. 6) When my cousin had a hard time understanding some difficult concepts and ideas in calculus, my uncle would chip in to help him learn. 7) Well educated in the discipline of math, my uncle can explain complex formulas and concepts in plain language, making it very intuitive for my cousin to learn. 8) Actually, parents like my uncle are good role models for children, motivating kids to achieve better academic performance.

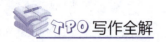

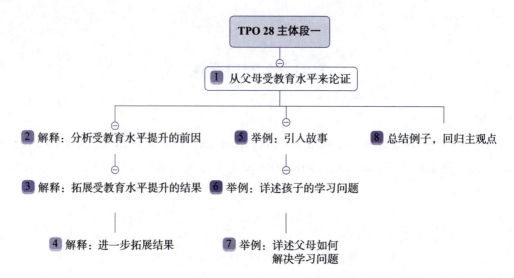

1) Additionally, with the increase in education awareness, parenting now is playing a much more active role in kids' education. 2) In terms of what is expected for a child to achieve parents have a tendency to compare their kids and other kids in the class, and accordingly they are getting more concerned about the kids' academic performance and how best they can do to help their children to be successful in school. 3) Consequently, parents participate in their children's education in a variety of ways both at home and in school. 4) At home they read with their children, provide a quiet place for studies, supervise assignments, and promote school attendance. 5) At school, parents attend teacher conferences, "open houses" as well as other events. 6) They are also invited to serve on advisory committees.

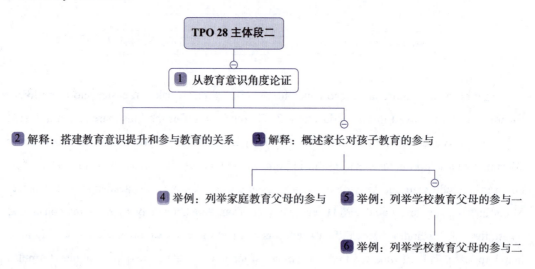

In all, with parents' more advanced education level and their ever-increasing educational awareness, parents are more involved in kids' education.

◆4. 范文译文

1）教育，尤其在孩子发展的早期阶段，对于孩子未来的生活和事业至关重要。2）当谈到父母是否比过去更多地参与孩子的教育时，我个人赞成这个说法，由于家长有较高的教育水平和不断提高的教育意识。

1）首先，父母教育程度越高，越容易参与孩子的教育。2）目前，大多数孩子的父母有一个从被认可的高等院校获得的相当不错的学位。3）他们知道教育的价值以及教育如何能够帮助孩子在生活和事业上取得成功。4）因此，他们可以激励他们的孩子好好学习，并提供必要的资源，以提高孩子的学习成绩。5）例如，我的叔叔拥有耶鲁大学数学博士学位。6）当我的表弟很难理解微积分中的一些困难的概念时，我的叔叔就会帮助他学习。7）由于在数学学科中接受过良好的教育，叔叔可以用简单的语言解释复杂的公式和概念，使我表弟非常直观地学习。8）其实，像我叔叔那样的父母是孩子的好榜样，他们激励孩子取得更好的学习成绩。

1）此外，随着教育意识的提高，育儿现在在儿童教育中扮演着更加积极的角色。2）在对孩子的期望方面，家长倾向于把他们的孩子与班上的其他孩子做比较，因此他们越来越关心孩子的学习成绩，以及他们如何能够最好地帮助孩子在学校成功。3）因此，家长在家里和学校都以各种方式参与子女的教育。4）在家里，他们和孩子一起阅读，提供一个安静的学习场所，监督作业，并提高学生出勤率。5）在学校，家长参加教师会议、"开放日"以及其他活动。6）他们也被邀请担任咨询委员会成员。

总之，随着家长教育水平的提高和教育意识的不断提高，家长更多地参与孩子的教育。

◆5. 重点场景表达

1) more advanced education level of parents 父母教育程度更高

2) get a decent degree from an accredited higher institution 有一个从被认可的高等院校获得的相当不错的学位

3) provide necessary resources to improve kids' academic performance 提供必要的资源以提高孩子的成绩

4) chip in to help sb. 参与进来帮助某人

5) explain complex formulas and concepts in plain language 用简单的语言解释复杂的公式和概念

6) be good role models for 是……的好榜样

7) participate in their children's education in a variety of ways 以各种方式参与子女的教育

8) supervise assignments 监督作业

9) promote school attendance 提高出勤率

10) attend teacher conferences 参加教师会议

11) serve on advisory committees 在咨询委员会中任职

TPO 29 独立写作

◆ 1. 题目

Do you agree or disagree with the following statement? To improve the quality of education, universities should spend more money on salaries for university professors.

◆ 2. 思路大纲

主观点：给教师涨工资可以提高教育质量

分论点一：利于提升教师的教学热情

分论点二：利于吸引优秀人才

◆ 3. 高分范文和思维导图

1) It is universally known that a solid education level can be conducive to a country's social and economic development. 2) Many educators and experts claim that increasing professors' salaries can improve the quality of education. 3) Personally, I am in the favor of the statement based on the following reasons.

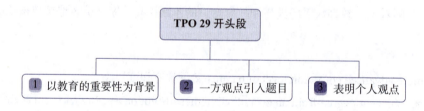

1) Firstly, increasing professors' salaries can greatly improve their performance. 2) Monetary incentive can be an important source of motivation and happiness, which is proved by a recent study on the correlation between monetary compensation and employee satisfaction published by *Harvard Business Review*. 3) Indeed, monetary reward can make professors very happy and eventually more devoted to teaching and cultivating the next generations. 4) To be specific, they will teach the young students more patiently, increasing chances for students to acquire knowledge and develop abilities, and will delve more deeply into the improvement of their teaching techniques. 5) Without a decent salary, professors cannot afford the daily necessities like paying rents and covering living expenses, to say nothing about dedicating themselves to educating students.

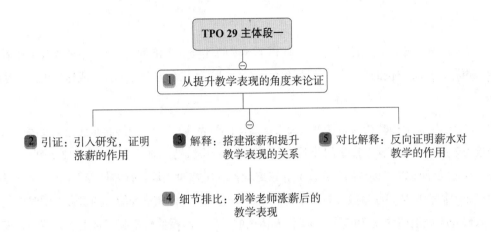

1) Additionally, the job itself, with more pay, can attract more famous professors. 2) Undoubtedly, professors, especially well-known ones, are the driving force behind a prestigious university. 3) With more satisfying salaries, the famous professors hired by the school will be more committed to publishing papers and scientific discoveries, which in turn attracts lots of scientific fund. 4) Therefore, the university will have abundant financial resources to renovate their facilities. 5) To be specific, the library will be installed with an electronic search engine, which can help students search for reference more easily. 6) Also, universities can build research centers and science labs, so students can apply theories into practice. 7) Eventually, with famous professors and advanced teaching facilities in place, students can get a better educational experience.

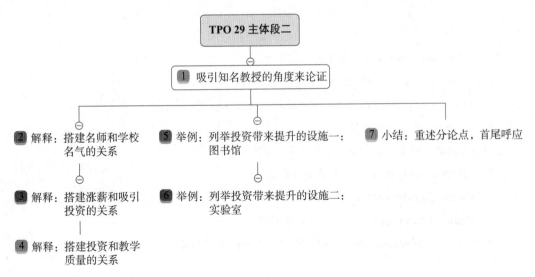

In all, increasing professors' salaries helps to attract talented young people to be professors and indirectly improve university facilities, which eventually enhances the quality of education.

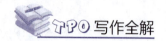

◆ 4. 范文译文

1）众所周知，扎实的教育水平有利于国家的社会和经济发展。2）许多教育工作者和专家声称，增加教授的薪水可以提高教育质量。3）就我个人而言，我赞成这种说法，原因如下。

1）首先，增加教授的薪水可以大大提高他们的表现。2）《哈佛商业评论》发表的一篇最近关于报酬与员工满意度之间关系的研究表明，货币激励是动机和幸福的重要来源。3）的确，金钱奖励可以让教授们非常高兴，最终他们会更加投入地教育并培养下一代。4）具体而言，他们会更加耐心地教导青年学生，增加学生获取知识和培养能力的机会，同时他们会深入研究改进他们的教学技巧。5）没有体面的工资，教授们付不起日常生活必需品，如支付租金和支付生活费用，更不用说奉献自己、教育学生了。

1）此外，工作本身有了更多的薪水可以吸引更多的著名教授。2）毫无疑问，教授，尤其是知名教授，是著名大学背后的推动力。3）学校聘请的知名教授工资较高，他们将更加致力于发表论文和科学发现，从而吸引大量科学基金。4）因此，大学会有丰富的经济资源装备设施。5）具体而言，图书馆将安装电子搜索引擎，学生可以更轻松地搜索参考书。6）大学也可以建立研究中心和科学实验室，让学生将理论运用到实践中。7）最终，有了著名的教授和先进的教学设施，学生可以获得更好的教育体验。

总而言之，增加教授的薪水有助于吸引有才能的年轻人担任教授，并间接改善大学设施，最终提高教育质量。

◆ 5. 重点场景表达

1) a solid education level 扎实的教育水平

2) improve the quality of education 提高教育质量

3) an important source of motivation and happiness 动机和幸福的重要来源

4) monetary reward 金钱奖励

5) cultivate the next generations 培养下一代

6) afford the daily necessities 负担日常必需品

7) a prestigious university 一所著名的大学

8) abundant financial resources 丰富的经济资源

9) research centers and science labs 研究中心和科学实验室

TPO 30 独立写作

◆ 1. 题目

Do you agree or disagree with the following statement? It is more enjoyable to have a job where you work only three days a week for longer hours than to have a job where you work five days a week for shorter hours.

◆ 2. 思路大纲

主观点：每周工作三天，每天工作时间长更好

分论点一：更好地放松和增进家人关系，提升生活质量

分论点二：避免拖延，提升工作效率

◆ 3. 高分范文和思维导图

1) People tend to have different expectations out of a job like personal satisfaction, higher pay, respect, and social recognition. 2) When it comes to the question of whether people should work only three days a week for longer hours or have a job where people work five days a week for shorter hours, people tend to give different opinions. 3) I, personally, reckon that having to work only three days a week for longer hours is a better option based on the following reasons.

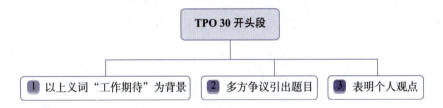

1) First of all, working for only three days means that people have enough leisure time to relax and spend quality time with family members. 2) Working for three days means that employees have a four-day break every week, which is a whole lot of time. 3) One can use this leisure time to develop a new skill or hobby like learning to play the piano or playing golf with a friend. 4) Besides, with a four-day break, one can spend some quality time with their families and maintain a harmonious bond with them. 5) Not only is it good to one's mental health, but also it will make one more productive in a professional setting.

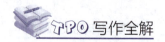

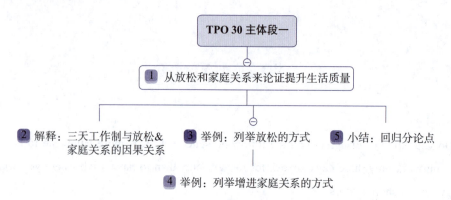

1) Additionally, working longer hours means that employees can be motivated to finish their projects quickly and avoid putting things off. 2) Working longer hours a day also means that employees can have enough time to finish their business projects without too many interruptions. 3) On the contrary, if they only work for shorter hours a day, chances are that they have to constantly stop their projects and then restart the projects the next day, which tend to prolong the project period. 4) In fact, research conducted by *Harvard Business Review* shows that too many interruptions of business projects because of shorter working hours lead to negative feelings and self-hatred. 5) Moreover, prolonged project period jeopardizes confidence and morale, which eventually results in lower productivity.

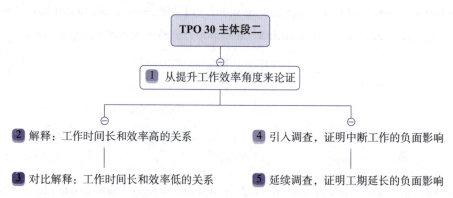

To conclude, working three days a week with longer hours affords employees a chance to have more breaks, during which time they can develop a new skill or hobby and spend quality time with their family. However, working five days a week with shorter hours leads to too many interruptions of business projects, which results in lower productivity.

◆ 4. 范文译文

1）人们倾向于从工作中获得不同的期望，如个人满意度、更高的工资、尊重和社会认可。
2）当谈到人们是应该每周只工作三天但是每天工作较长时间，还是做一份让人们每周工作五天但是每天工作较短时间的工作时，人们有不同的意见。3）我个人认为，每周只工作三天但是每天工作较长时间是一个更好的选择，原因如下。

1）首先，只工作三天意味着人们有足够的空闲时间来放松，并与家人共度美好时光。2）工作三天意味着员工每周休息四天，这是一个很长的时间。3）人们可以利用这段闲暇时间来培养新的技能或兴趣，如学习弹钢琴或与朋友打高尔夫球。4）此外，休息四天意味着可以与家人共度美好时光，与他们保持和谐的关系。5）这不仅对个人的心理健康有好处，而且在职业环境中也能提高个人的生产力。

1）此外，长时间工作意味着员工可以尽快完成项目，避免延期。2）每天较长时间工作意味着员工可以有足够的时间完成他们的业务项目，同时不会有太多的中断。3）相反，如果他们每天只工作几个小时，那么他们有可能不得不经常停止他们的项目，然后在第二天重新启动项目，这往往会延长项目周期。4）事实上，《哈佛商业评论》进行的研究显示，工作时间短，对业务项目的干扰太多，会导致消极情绪和自我憎恨。5）而且，拉长的项目周期危及信心和士气，最终导致生产力下降。

总而言之，每周工作三天，每天工作较长的时间，可以让个人有更多的休息时间，在这段时间内，他们可以培养新的技能或爱好，并与家人共度美好时光。但是，每周工作五天，每天工作较短的时间会导致业务项目太多的中断，从而导致生产力下降。

◆ 5. 重点场景表达

1) spend some quality time with their families and maintain a harmonious bond with them 与家人共度美好时光，与家人保持和谐的关系

2) one's mental health 个人的心理健康

3) make one more productive in a professional setting 在职业环境中也能提高个人的生产力

4) restart the projects the next day 在第二天重新启动项目

5) prolonged the project period 项目周期延长

6) too many interruptions of business projects 商业项目的中断太多

7) lead to negative feelings and self-hatred 导致消极情绪和自我憎恨

8) prolonged project period jeopardizes confidence and morale 拉长的项目周期危及信心和士气

9) result in lower productivity 导致生产力下降

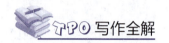

TPO 31 独立写作

◆ 1. 题目

Do you agree or disagree with the following statement? Because the world is changing so quickly, people now are less happy or less satisfied with their lives than people were in the past.

◆ 2. 思路大纲

主观点：人们更加满意现在的生活

分论点一：收入增加带来幸福

分论点二：社会福利制度完善带来幸福

◆ 3. 高分范文和思维导图

1) Taking a panoramic picture of human evolution, one can see people's lives have improved significantly despite twists and turns. 2) Even though pessimists are unhappy since environment degradation, resource depletion and population explosion make the world a worse place to live in, I reckon that people are generally happier and more satisfied than they were in the past.

1) First of all, with ever-increasing salary, people are happy to have higher living standard. 2) With a strong economy, employees especially those in developed countries are get better pay and salary. 3) More disposable income makes it possible for people to invest in themselves, their children and their community. 4) For instance, they can buy a bigger house, a luxurious car, and finance their kids' college education to reduce their financial pressure of paying off a student loan. 5) People might even plan a family trip to a foreign country and spend quality time with family members. 6) All the above was totally unobtainable for people in the past due to low income. 7) Indeed, with more money in their pocket, people have less pressure and higher satisfaction about life.

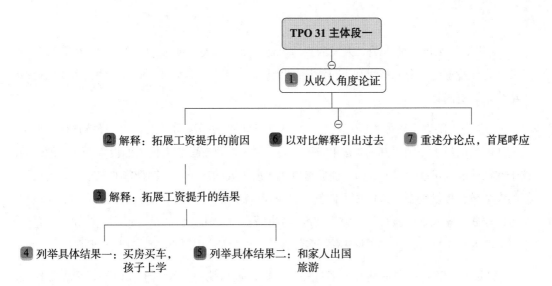

1) Additionally, with the sophistication of social welfare system, everyone, including the unlucky ones that are marginalized by society, is happier than people were in the past. 2) Most countries around the globe have their own social welfare systems, significantly improving people's living standard. 3) As long as an individual is a legal citizen of a certain country, he or she is entitled to enjoy a series of social welfare like food stamps, unemployment benefit, and even medicare. 4) To be specific, food stamps are aimed to help those low-income people to buy food; unemployment assistance is offered to workers who have lost their jobs; medicare intends to cover people's health and medical costs. 5) These social programs help millions of families get out of poverty and live a decent life, which eventually makes people happier than ever before.

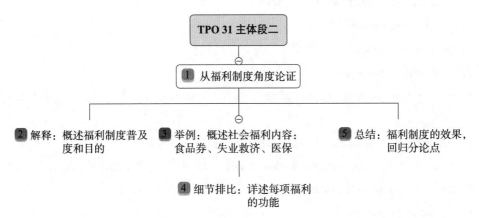

In all, people nowadays are happier and more satisfied than those who lived decades ago since currently there are a myriad of social programs in place and people generally have better pay.

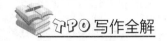

◆ 4. 范文译文

1）纵观人类进化的全貌，人民的生活虽然曲折，却有了明显的改善。2）尽管悲观主义者因为环境退化、资源枯竭和人口激增使世界变得更糟而不高兴，但是，我认为人们比过去更快乐、更满足。

1）首先，随着工资的不断提高，人们为生活水平的提高而高兴。2）经济强劲，特别是发达国家的员工得到更好的报酬和薪水。3）更多的可支配收入使人们投资自己、他们的孩子和社区成为可能。4）例如，他们可以买一所更大的房子、一辆豪华的汽车，并为孩子们的大学教育提供资金，这样孩子们就可以减轻他们偿还学生贷款的经济压力。5）人们甚至可以计划全家到外国旅行，与家人共度美好时光。6）由于收入低，所有这些在过去是完全不可能的。7）事实上，口袋里有更多的钱，人们生活的压力减少，满足感更强。

1）此外，随着社会福利制度的进一步发展，包括社会边缘人士在内的每个人都比过去更加幸福。2）全球大多数国家都有自己的社会福利制度，大大提高了人民的生活水平。3）只要是某个国家的合法公民，人人有权享受一系列的社会福利，如食品券、失业补助金，甚至医疗保险。4）具体地说，食品券旨在帮助低收入人群购买食品；失业人员领取失业救济；医疗保险旨在支付人们的健康和医疗费用。5）这些社会方案帮助数百万家庭摆脱贫困，过上体面的生活，最终使人们比以往更加快乐。

总的来说，现在的人比几十年前的人更幸福、更满足，因为现在有大量的社会福利项目，人们的薪水也比较高。

◆ 5. 重点场景表达

1) environment degradation 环境退化

2) resource depletion 资源枯竭

3) population explosion 人口激增

4) more disposable income 更多可支配收入

5) reduce their financial pressure of paying off a student loan 减轻偿还学生贷款的财政压力

6) the sophistication of social welfare system 社会福利制度的完善

7) be entitled to enjoy a series of social welfare 有权享受一系列社会福利

8) cover people's health and medical costs 支付人们的健康医疗开销

9) get out of poverty 脱贫

10) a myriad of social programs 大量的社会福利项目

TPO 32 独立写作

◆ 1. 题目

Do you agree or disagree with the following statement? Young people today have no influence on the important decisions that determine the future of society as a whole.

◆ 2. 思路大纲

主观点：现在年轻人对重大决策有影响

分论点一：年轻人受教育水平提升了

分论点二：科技进步丰富了参与方式

◆ 3. 高分范文和思维导图

1) Politics is an indispensable part of modern people's life. 2) When it comes to the question of whether young people have impact on decision-making that concerns the public, some people argue that young people are marginalized in the critical decision-making process. 3) However, I reckon that young people nowadays can influence major social decisions based on the following reasons.

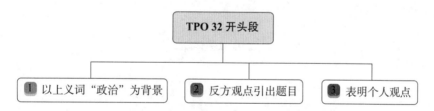

1) First of all, with the increasing educational level of young people, they tend to be more aware that participation in political and governmental activities has big impact on their well-being. 2) Indeed, most of the youngsters today get diplomas from accredited higher institutions. 3) Taking political science class, where students learn political systems, political actions, and issues related with politics, is a requirement to graduate. 4) Consequently, students are more and more aware of the importance of civil and political involvement. 5) They hold rallies, stage demonstrations, and raise fund for their favorite political candidates to express their concerns and dissatisfaction. 6) In response to these voices, government agencies are pressured and have to consider these dissident opinions in important decision-making processes.

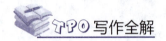

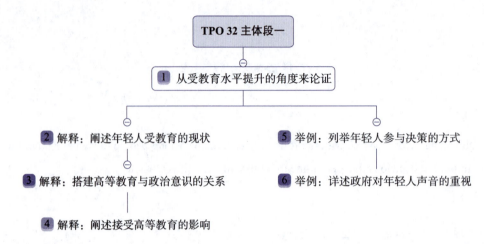

1) Additionally, young people are more creative by using effective tools and means to get involved in political activities. 2) With the advent of state-of-the-art technologies and the invention of cutting-edge technological gadgets like tablets, laptops, and even smart phones, young people can use social networks easily like Facebook, Twitter, or even Instagram to voice their opinions at an unprecedented speed. 3) Young people post their thoughts about civic and political issues, react to others' postings, and press friends to act on issues and vote. 4) With the help of the Internet, they can spread their political views and raise fund for their candidates. 5) Thus, the Internet can really help them to shape their ideology and make a difference.

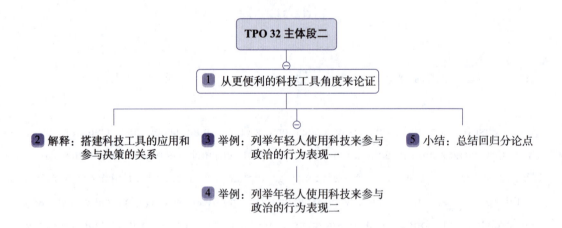

In a nutshell, with the ever-increasing awareness of the significance of political engagement and the convenience brought by the Internet, young people tend be more influential in critical decision-making processes.

◆ 4. 范文译文

1）政治是现代人生活中不可或缺的一部分。2）谈到年轻人是否影响与公众有关的决策的问题时，有人认为年轻人在关键决策过程中被边缘化。3）但我认为，现在的年轻人可以影响重大社会决策，原因如下。

1）首先，随着年轻人文化水平的提高，他们更加意识到参与政治和政府活动对他们的幸福有很大的影响。2）的确，今天大多数年轻人都获得了被认可的高等院校的文凭。3）政治科学课可以让学生了解政治制度、政治行为和与政治相关的问题，这都是毕业要求。4）因此，学生越来越意识到公民和政治参与的重要性。5）他们举行集会、游行，为他们喜欢的政治候选人筹集资金来表达他们的关切和不满。6）针对这些声音，政府机构受到压力，重要的决策过程中必须考虑这些持不同政见者的意见。

1）此外，年轻人更具创造性地通过使用有效的工具和手段参与政治活动。2）随着最先进技术的出现以及平板电脑、笔记本电脑甚至智能手机等尖端科技产品的发明，年轻人可以轻松使用Facebook、Twitter甚至Instagram等社交网络以前所未有的速度表达他们的意见。3）年轻人发表关于公民和政治问题的看法，对其他人的帖子做出反应，并督促朋友就一些社会问题投票行事。4）在互联网的帮助下，他们可以传播他们的政治观点并为他们的候选人筹集资金。5）因此，互联网可以真正帮助他们塑造自己的意识形态并发挥作用。

简而言之，随着政治参与重要性的意识不断提高和互联网带来的便利，年轻人在关键决策过程中往往更具影响力。

◆ 5. 重点场景表达

1) is an indispensable part of 是不可或缺的一部分

2) decision-making that concerns the public 关乎公众的决策

3) decision-making process 决策过程

4) educational level 受教育程度

5) get diplomas from accredited higher institutions 从被认可的高等院校取得文凭

6) hold rally, stage demonstrations, and raise fund 举行集会，发起游行，筹集资金

7) express their concerns and convey their dissatisfaction 表达他们的关切并表达他们的不满

8) state-of-the-art technologies 最先进的技术

9) post their thoughts about civic and political issues 发表他们关于公民和政治问题的看法

10) raise fund for their candidates 为他们的候选人筹集资金

11) shape their ideology 塑造他们的意识形态

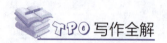

TPO 33 独立写作

◆ 1. 题目

Do you agree or disagree with the following statement? When teachers assign projects on which students must work together, the students learn much more effectively than when they are asked to work alone on projects.

◆ 2. 思路大纲

主观点：与他人协作学习效果更好

分论点一：任务完成速度很快

分论点二：培养领导组织能力，受益终身

◆ 3. 高分范文和思维导图

1) Educators and researchers have never stopped the examination of the importance and relevance of collaborative learning that are encouraged by middle schools. 2) I personally believe that studying with a group is far more beneficial to students than studying alone, for the following reasons.

1) First of all, working with a group enables students to finish their project more quickly. 2) The saying "many hands make light work" remains as relevant today as it did a century ago. 3) Obviously, when a group attacks a project, the whole project can be divided into different parts, which means that each group member only needs to do their own part and the speed of task completion will increase. 4) For example, suppose a teacher organizes his students into small study groups to do a research about the water quality of the local town. 5) Chances are that one or two students may go to the water supplier to learn about the manufacturing procedure, and the other may search for some data about water pollution from the Internet, analyze information from multiple sources, and finish the paper smoothly. 6) However, if just one student attempted to muddle through

the whole research, there is a higher likelihood that he might spend much more time getting it done.

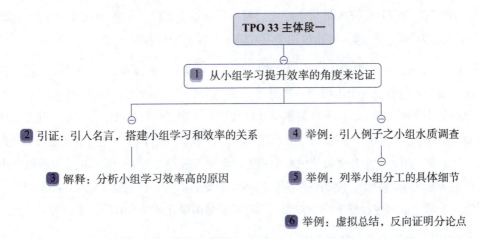

1) Additionally, working with a group helps to hone communicative skills, which goes a long way to students' future. 2) When learning with a group, every single student gains a chance to voice his views to the group members and simultaneously gets exposed to distinctive perspectives from others. 3) In order to reach an agreement, they need learn to accept different points of view and find common ground. 4) Such an educational experience will not only be helpful for their future study, but also beneficial to them when they have to deal with coworkers, clients, and teammates in a professional setting in the future. 5) Numerous studies have shown that students who have prior experiences of working with others enjoy a better chance to be successful in their future career.

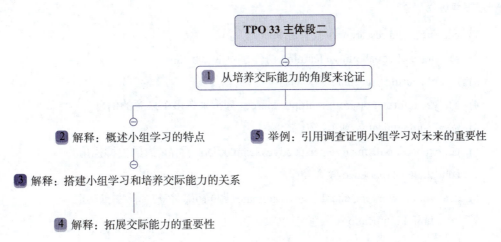

In conclusion, working with a group has far more meaningful implications than working alone since collaborative learning helps students to learn much more effectively and develop important skills that are vital for their future study and career.

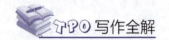

◆ 4. 范文译文

1）教育工作者和研究人员从未停止过对中学鼓励合作学习的重要性和相关性的研究。2）我个人认为与学生一起学习比单独学习对学生更有利，原因如下。

1）首先，在一个小组中工作使学生能够更快地完成他们的项目。2）"许多人让工作轻松"这句话今天仍然与一个世纪前一样重要。3）显然，当一个团队攻关一个项目时，整个项目可以分为不同的部分，这意味着每个团队成员只需要完成自己那部分任务，任务完成的速度就会增快。4）例如，假设一位教师组织学生在小型研究小组中对当地城镇的水质进行研究。5）有一两个学生有机会到供水公司去了解生产过程，另一个人可能会从互联网上搜索一些有关水污染的数据，他们将分析来自多个来源的信息并顺利完成论文。6）但是，如果只有一个学生试图完成整个研究，那么极有可能他需要花费更多时间完成研究。

1）另外，团队合作有助于提高交际能力，这对学生的未来有很大的帮助。2）在小组学习时，每个学生都有机会向组员发表自己的观点，并同时接触到别人的独特视角。3）为了达成协议，他们需要学会接受不同的观点并找到共同点。4）这样的教育经历不仅有助于他们未来的学习，而且在将来他们必须在专业环境中与同事、客户和队友打交道时也会对他们有益。5）大量研究表明，有与他人合作经历的学生在未来的职业生涯中获得成功的机会更大。

总而言之，在一个小组中工作比单独工作更有意义，因为协作式的学习可以帮助学生更有效地学习，并培养对他们未来的学习和职业至关重要的技能。

◆ 5. 重点场景表达

1）educators and researchers 教育者和研究人员

2）relevance of collaborative learning 协作学习的重要性

3）manufacturing procedure 生产程序

4）analyze information from multiple sources 分析来自多个来源的信息

5）hone communicative skills 磨炼交际能力

6）get exposed to distinctive perspectives from others 了解别人的独特视角

7）educational experience 教育经验

8）deal with coworkers, clients, and teammates 跟同事、客户和队友打交道

9）meaningful implications 有意义的影响

TPO 34 独立写作

◆ 1. 题目

Do you agree or disagree with the following statement? Educating children is a more difficult task today than it was in the past because they spend so much time on cellphone, online games, and social networking websites. Use specific reasons and examples to support your answer.

◆ 2. 思路大纲

主观点：网络游戏和社交网站让教育孩子变得更加容易

分论点一：网络游戏可以激发学生的兴趣，从而更容易教育

分论点二：社交网站丰富孩子获取知识的途径，从而更容易受教育

◆ 3. 高分范文和思维导图

1) Taking a panoramic picture of human evolution, one can see education has been playing a very important role, especially in modern days, in that a solid education experience is essential in determining a person's future. 2) When it comes to the question of whether educating kids is more difficult than before as currently kids are distracted by smart phones, online games and social networking websites, I, personally, reckon that educating kids is easier even with the emergence of smart phones, online games and social networking websites based on the following reasons.

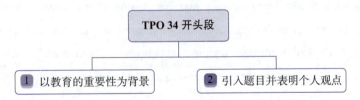

It is true that these so-called distractions like playing online games, socializing with peers online are addictive to kids. However, with proper guidance and supervision, parents can manage the time that kids spend on these activities, and playing online games and socializing with peers online might bring potential benefits.

1) First of all, video games are very conducive to stirring students' interest and help students to acquire certain knowledge more actively. 2) As is known to all, due to the boredom of the current curricula offered in school, most students are passive learners, which means that their passion for exploring knowledge by themselves is at a low level. 3) However, once online games are applied to students' learning, it will be a totally different picture. 4) Take video games including *Civilization,*

Age of Empires and the *Story of Three Kingdoms* as an example. 5) These games often allow children to design and exchange maps or other customized contents, sparking their interest in world history, geography, and ancient cultures. 6) To be more specific, while having fun children can pick up a wide range of historical events and locations of famous cities that serve as preparation for future learning.

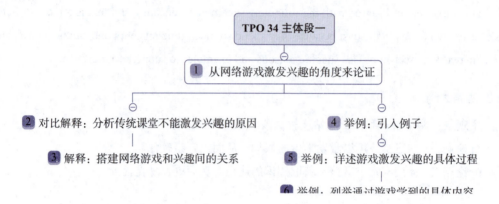

1) Additionally, social networking websites can also help kids to acquire knowledge more easily. 2) Educational resources shared on online social networking front page diversify the channels of gaining information. 3) For instance, as a high school student, I follow the TED Facebook page. 4) As a platform for scientists, businesspeople, philanthropists, and even talented young people to share their inventions, ideas and perspectives with a large audience, TED helps me to gain knowledge in science, know more about other countries' cultures, and eventually broaden my horizons. 5) Plus, by following massive on-line open courses on Facebook pages, I can gain specific knowledge in different disciplines like computer science, coding, or even foreign languages. 6) However, had it not been for the development of Internet and modern technological gadgets, I would not have been able to gain access to so much useful information and knowledge.

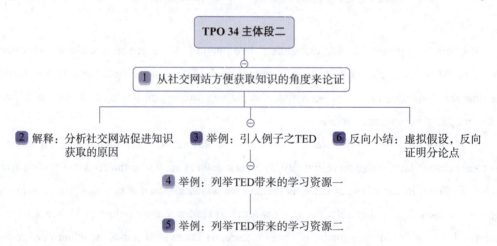

In all, under the proper guidance of parents, kids can benefit from modern technology since it helps kids to bond with peers, dedicate themselves to a noble cause, gain more knowledge and eventually broaden their horizons.

◆ 4. 范文译文

1）纵观人类进化的全景，教育一直在发挥着非常重要的作用，特别是在现代，坚实的教育经历对确定一个人的未来至关重要。2）谈到教育孩子是否比以前更困难，因为目前孩子们被智能手机、网络游戏和社交网站分心了，我个人认为，智能手机网络游戏和社交网站的出现让教育孩子变得更容易，原因如下。

确实，这些所谓的分心，比如玩网络游戏，在线与同龄人交流会让孩子们上瘾。然而，通过适当的指导和监督，家长可以管理孩子在这些活动上花费的时间，玩在线游戏并在线与同龄人交流可能会带来潜在的好处。

1）首先，电子游戏非常有利于激发学生的兴趣，帮助学生更积极地获得某些知识。2）众所周知，由于目前学校提供的课程很无聊，大多数学生都是被动学习者，这意味着他们自己探索知识的热情处于低水平。3）然而，一旦网络游戏适用于学生的学习，这将是一个完全不同的情况。4）以《文明》、《帝国时代》和《三国演绎》等视频游戏为例。5）这些游戏通常让儿童设计和交换地图或其他定制内容，引发他们对世界历史、地理和古代文化的兴趣。6）更具体一点，孩子们在玩的同时，可以了解各种历史事件和著名城市的地点，这将为将来的学习做好准备。

1）此外，社交网站还可以帮助孩子更容易地获得知识。2）在线社交网络首页共享的教育资源让获取信息的渠道更加的多元化。3）例如，作为高中生，我关注 TED Facebook 页面。4）作为让科学家、商人、慈善家，甚至有才华的年轻人向大量观众分享他们的发明、想法和观点的平台，TED 帮助我获得科学知识，更多地了解其他国家的文化，并最终拓宽我的视野。5）另外，通过关注大量的在线开放课程 Facebook 页面，我可以获得计算机科学、编码，甚至语言学习等不同学科的具体知识。6）但是，如果不是因为互联网和现代科技小装置的发展，我不可能获得这么多有用的信息和知识。

总而言之，在父母的适当指导下，现代科技可以让孩子们受益，因为它可以帮助孩子与同龄人结缘，致力于崇高事业，获得更多知识并最终拓宽视野。

◆ 5. 重点场景表达

1) a solid education experience 扎实的教育经历

2) emergence of smart phones 智能手机的出现

3) socialize with peers 与同龄人交往

4) spark their interest 引发他们的兴趣

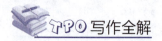

5) serve as preparation for future learning 作为未来学习的准备

6) educational resources 教育资源

7) share their inventions, ideas and perspectives with a large audience 将他们的发明、想法和观点分享给广大观众

8) modern technological gadgets 现代科技小装置

TPO 40 独立写作

◆ 1. 题目

Do you agree or disagree with the following statement? Some parents offer their school-age children money for each high grade (mark) they get in school. Do you think this is a good idea?

◆ 2. 思路大纲

主观点：应该使用金钱奖励取得好成绩的孩子

分论点一：激发学习动力

分论点二：培养金钱意识

◆ 3. 高分范文和思维导图

1) How to motivate kids to achieve high academic performance has been subject to constant debate among parents, teachers and researchers. 2) Some argue that giving kids money is a good way to achieve this goal while others dispute such a claim. 3) I, personally, reckon that rewarding kids with money for high grade can benefit kids in many ways.

1) First of all, monetary reward can serve as a kind of motivation for kids to achieve better academic performance. 2) Giving kids money for their good grade is a positive feedback of their hard work. 3) This can help kids develop a sense of self value, and boost their self-esteem, which in turn motivate them to do better in schoolwork. 4) For instance, my uncle knows money can motivate not only adults but also kids. 5) So, he would give my cousin Alex some allowance if he got high grade or made great progress in his study. 6) For Alex, the money can be used in whatever

way he wants like buying things he like, going out with friends, and buying his favorite CD. 7) Thus, Alex feels a sense of control, and he is very active and devoted to his academic work.

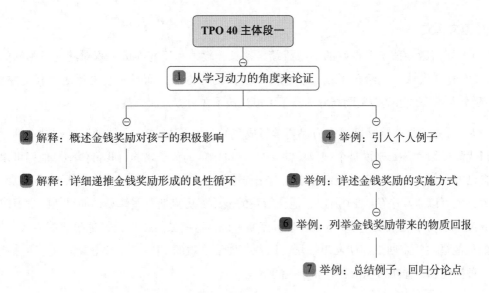

1) Additionally, rewarding kids with money for their school performance makes them better understand the value of money and their personal choices, and helps them know the importance of making ends meet. 2) Actually, this is far better than just lecturing the kids about the importance of money, since kids who are not mature enough might find it hard to understand. 3) Fortunately, giving kids monetary reward makes them have the real world experience of managing money, and they will figure out how to balance the expected purchase and their budget. 4) This will be a great asset for kids' future and they will not "bite more than she can chew" when it comes to spending money. 5) Instead they will figure out how to save money for the things they really need rather than maxing out their credit card.

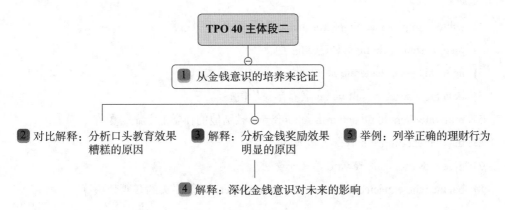

In a nutshell, rewarding kids with money for high grade helps kids to develop a sense of self

value and motivate them to score higher achievements. Also, monetary reward helps kids to be financially responsible in the future.

◆ 4. 范文译文

1）如何激励孩子取得好的学习成绩，家长、教师和研究人员一直对此进行不断的争论。2）有些人认为，给孩子钱是实现这一目标的好方法，而另一些人反对这样的主张。3）我个人认为，用金钱奖励高分的孩子可以让孩子在很多方面受益。

1）首先，金钱奖励可以作为提高学习成绩的一种动力。2）金钱的奖励对勤奋学习而取得优质成绩的孩子来说是个积极反馈。3）这可以帮助孩子培养自我价值感，他们可以提高自己的自信心，从而激励他们在学业上做得更好。4）例如，我叔叔知道钱不仅可以激励大人，也可以激励小孩。5）所以，他会给我的表弟亚历克斯一些津贴，如果他的学习成绩优异或者取得了很大的进步。6）对亚历克斯来说，这些钱可以以任何他想要的方式使用，比如买他喜欢的东西，和朋友出去玩，以及买他最喜欢的 CD。7）因此，亚历克斯感觉到了一种控制感，他非常积极和专注于他的学业。

1）此外，用金钱奖励孩子们取得的好的学习成绩，使他们更好地了解金钱的价值和个人的选择，并帮助他们知道收支相抵的重要性。2）实际上，这比仅仅向孩子们讲授金钱的重要性要好得多，因为不够成熟的孩子可能会觉得难以理解。3）幸运的是，给孩子们金钱奖励使他们拥有真实世界的管理金钱的经验，他们将弄清楚如何平衡要买的东西和预算。4）这对于孩子们的未来来说将是一笔巨大的财富，他们花钱时就不会 "不自量力"。5）反而他们会为了买真正需要的东西而省钱，而不是疯狂地刷卡。

简而言之，用金钱奖励高分的孩子可以帮助孩子培养自我价值感，激励他们取得更高的成就。而且，金钱奖励有助于孩子在未来承担经济方面的责任。

◆ 5. 重点场景表达

1) achieve high academic performance 取得好的学习成绩

2) dispute such a claim 反对这样的主张

3) achieve better academic performance 提高学习成绩

4) develop a sense of self value 培养自我价值感

5) motivate them to do better in schoolwork 激励他们在学业上做得更好

6) make great progress 取得了很大的进步

7) give kids monetary reward 给孩子金钱奖励

8) balance the expected purchase and their budget 平衡要买的东西和预算

TPO 41 独立写作

◆ 1. 题目

Do you agree or disagree with the following statement? Teachers were more appreciated and valued by society in the past than they are nowadays.

◆ 2. 思路大纲

主观点：现在老师更受重视

分论点一：科技进步让更多人接受教育

分论点二：父母更加忙碌，没时间教育孩子

◆ 3. 高分范文和思维导图

1) Taking a panoramic picture of human evolution, one can see school education has been playing a very important role, especially in modern days. 2) When it comes to the question of whether teachers were more valued in the past than today, opinions vary from person to person. 3) However, I reckon that teachers are more appreciated than they were in the past based on the following reasons.

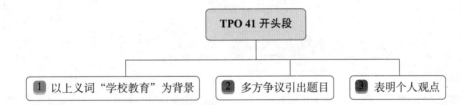

1) First of all, the advent of technological gadgets makes it possible for people from common family backgrounds to gain access to education, enabling teachers to play a more dominant role in their educational experience. 2) To be more specific, with the appearance of smart phones, tablets and computer laptops, it is easier for people to get access to all kinds of better educational resources provided by teachers. 3) Consequently, teachers are not only valued by students from cities but also are more respected by kids from poverty-stricken areas, who can take online classes offered by famous teachers. 4) Thus, compared with the past, teachers especially those highly established teachers are more valued nowadays.

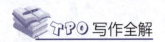

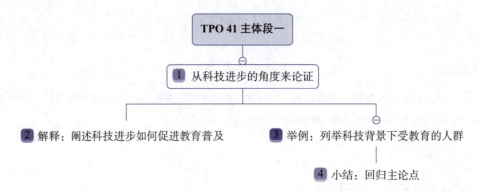

1) Additionally, parents live a hectic life and have no time get involved in kids' education, which in turn makes teachers play a more important role in this process. 2) To be more specific, as employees, parents are overwhelmed with an enormous amount of workload like attending business meetings, writing reports to their supervisors, going on business trips, or even addressing customers' problems. 3) Also, they are under huge financial pressure, struggling to pay mortgage and paying their kids' tuition, and medical bills. 4) Thus, a busy schedule and enormous pressure of parents make teachers play a more active role in education.

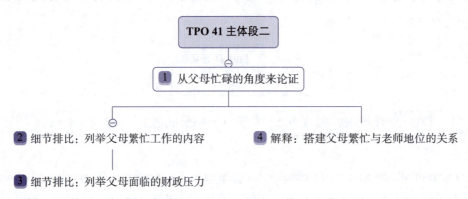

In conclusion, modern technology and parents' busy schedule make teachers play a more dominant role in education. Consequently, teachers are more appreciated and valued in the community than they were in the past.

◆ 4. 范文译文

1）纵观人类进化的全景，学校教育一直扮演着非常重要的角色，特别是在现代。2）谈到过去教师是否比今天更受重视的问题时，人们有不同的看法。3）但是，我认为教师比以往更加受到重视，原因如下。

1）首先，技术产品的到来使普通家庭背景的人们有机会接受教育，使教师在教育经历中扮演更重要的角色。2）更具体地说，随着智能手机、平板电脑和笔记本电脑的出现，人们更容易获得教师提供的各种更好的教育资源。3）因此，教师不仅受到城市学生的重视，而且受到来自贫困地区的孩子的更多尊重，他们也可以接受著名教师提供的在线课程。4）因此，与过去相比，现在教师尤其是那些名师更受重视。

1）此外，父母过着紧张的生活，他们没有时间参与孩子的教育，这反过来使得教师在这个过程中扮演更重要的角色。2）更具体地说，作为员工，父母被巨大的工作量弄得焦头烂额，例如参加商务会议、向上司提交报告、出差，甚至解决客户的问题。3）而且，他们还承受着巨大的经济压力，努力支付抵押贷款，支付孩子的学费和医疗费用。4）因此，父母忙碌的工作时间和巨大的压力使教师在教育中扮演更积极的角色。

总而言之，现代科技和家长的繁忙日程让教师在教育中发挥更大的优势。因此，教师在社区中比在过去更受重视。

◆ 5. 重点场景表达

1) the advent of technological gadgets 技术产品的到来

2) gain access to education 获得教育的机会

3) to be more specific 更具体地说

4) with the appearance of smart phones, tablets and computer laptops 随着智能手机、平板电脑和笔记本电脑的出现

5) poverty-stricken areas 贫困地区

6) be overwhelmed with an enormous amount of workload 被巨大的工作量弄得焦头烂额

7) attending business meetings, writing reports to their supervisors, going on business trips, and even addressing customers' problems 参加商务会议、向主管撰写报告、出差，甚至解决客户的问题

8) under huge financial pressure 承受巨大的经济压力

9) play a more active role in education 在教育中扮演更积极的角色

TPO 42 独立写作

◆ 1. 题目

Do you agree or disagree with the following statement? Workers are more satisfied when they have many different types of tasks to do during the workday than when they do similar tasks all day long.

◆ 2. 思路大纲

主观点：做相同的工作更满足

分论点一：做相同工作更加专注，更高效
分论点二：做相同工作更容易成为专家

◆ 3. 高分范文和思维导图

1) Job satisfaction is attributed to several factors like high salary, flexible working hours, and even friendly coworkers. 2) When it comes to the question of whether people get great satisfaction from doing different kinds of tasks or similar tasks every day, people tend to give different answers. 3) I, personally, would say that workers are more satisfied when doing similar tasks all day long.

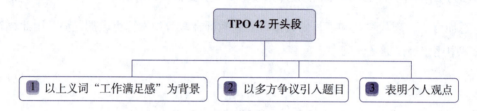

1) First of all, doing similar tasks can help employees stay more concentrated and more productive, while working on several tasks at the same time hurts performance and lowers efficiency. 2) In the course of working on several tasks during a single day, the multi-taskers' cognitive capacity functions at such an inefficient level that they can neither organize their thoughts nor filter information. 3) To make things worse, when switching from one task to another, their brains need to constantly change from one thinking pattern to another, which seriously lowers working efficiency. 4) Countless researches on cognitive psychology have shown that multi-taskers cannot pay attention to, recall and process information as well as those who focus on one task at a time can. 5) Indeed, it is quite self-evident that people's brain can function better and they perform better when they have fewer things to worry about.

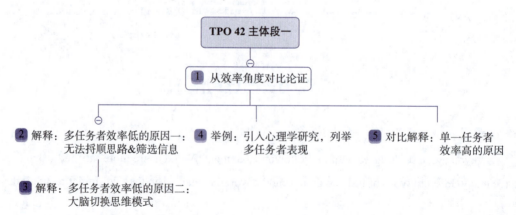

1) Additionally, working on similar tasks all day long promotes proficiency while doing

several different tasks all together might lead to negative feelings and self-hatred. 2) For people who do different tasks during a single day, they are under a lot of pressure. 3) If they could not finish all the tasks well, they will lack confidence and morale. 4) In contrast, those who focus on similar tasks all day long have higher proficiency and are less likely to make mistakes. 5) In fact, according to the "rule of 10,000 hours of practice" invented by Malcom Gladwell, the author of *Outlier*, people who have done repetitive tasks in an extended period of at least 10 years will achieve expert level of performance. 6) Even though so many hours of deliberate practice might be repetitive, it is worthwhile since proficiency in certain tasks can help one get better paying jobs and thus live a happy life.

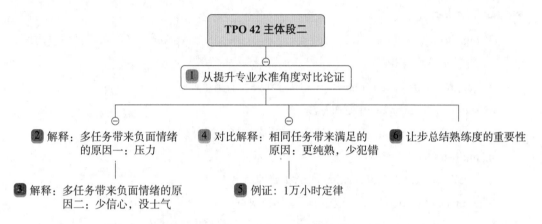

In conclusion, doing similar and repetitive jobs helps improve productivity and promote expert level of performance. So many hours of deliberate practice in one single task is worthwhile since it helps an individual to land a better job, which in turn makes them happy in life.

◆ 4. 范文译文

1）工作满意度归功于几个因素，如高薪、灵活的工作时间，甚至友好的同事。2）当谈到人们每天做不同的任务还是类似任务才能得到很大满足这个问题时，人们往往会给出不同的答案。3）我个人认为，工人整天做类似的任务会比较满意。

1）首先，做类似的任务可以有助于员工更专注和更有成效，同时从事多项任务会损害性能和降低效率。2）在一天的工作中，多任务者的认知能力效率低下，不能组织他们的想法和处理信息。3）更糟糕的是，从一个任务转换到另一个任务时，他们的大脑需要不断从一种思维模式转换到另一种思维模式，这严重降低工作效率。4）认知心理学的无数研究表明，多任务者不能像只有一个任务的人那样专注、回忆和处理信息。5）的确，不言而喻的是，当没有什么可担心的事情时，人们状态更好，同时大脑也可以更好地发挥作用。

1）另外，全天做类似的任务可以提高熟练度，同时做几项不同的任务可能会导致

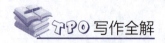

负面的情绪和自我憎恨。2）对于一天中做不同任务的人来说，他们承受着很大的压力。3）如果他们不能很好地完成所有的任务，就会导致缺乏自信和士气。4）相比之下，那些整天专注于类似任务的人更熟练，更不会犯错误。5）事实上，根据《异类》作者 Malcom Gladwell 提出的"10 000 小时练习规则"，那些至少在 10 年中重复同一个任务的人将达到专家级的表现。6）即使这么多小时的刻意练习可能是重复的，但值得一提的是，精通某些任务可以帮助人们找到更好的工作，从而过上幸福的生活。

总之，做类似的重复性任务有助于提高生产力，提升工作效率。这么多小时的刻意从事单一的任务是值得的，因为它帮助一个人找到更好的工作，从而使他们生活愉快。

◆ 5. 重点场景表达

1) high salary, flexible working hours, and even friendly coworkers 高薪、灵活的工作时间，甚至友好的同事

2) get great satisfaction from 从……中得到很大的满足

3) stay more concentrated 更加专注

4) hurt performance and lower efficiency 损害性能，降低效率

5) multi-tasker 多任务者

6) recall and process information 回忆和处理信息

7) brain can function better 大脑可以运作得更好

8) cognitive capacity functions at an inefficient level 认知能力处在一个低效的水平

9) change from one thinking pattern to another 从一种思维模式转变到另一种思维模式

10) promote proficiency 提高熟练程度

11) lead to negative feelings and self-hatred 导致消极情绪和自我憎恨

12) lack confidence and morale 缺乏自信和士气

13) repetitive task 重复的任务

14) in an extended period 长期

15) deliberate practice 刻意从事

TPO 43 独立写作

◆ 1. 题目

Imagine that you are in class or a meeting. The teacher or the meeting presenter says something incorrect. In your opinion, which of the following is the best thing to do?

—Interrupt and correct the mistake right away.

—Wait until the class or meeting is over and the people are gone, and then talk to the teacher or meeting presenter.

　　—Say nothing.

◆ 2. 思路大纲

　　主观点：课后或会后与老师或发言者沟通
　　分论点一：直接打断会影响其他听众的体验
　　分论点二：默不作声会影响获取信息的正确性

◆ 3. 高分范文和思维导图

　　1) When it comes to the question of whether we should correct the teacher in class or the presenter in a meeting right way when they make a mistake, people tend to have different options. 2) Some correct them right away or talk to them after class or the meeting while others just do nothing. 3) I, personally, reckon talking to the teacher or presenter afterwards is the best choice.

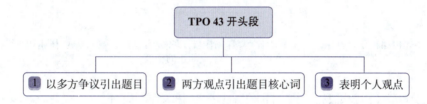

　　1) First of all, correcting the teacher or presenter the moment they make a mistake will disturb them，having impact on the audience's experience. 2) Interrupting teachers in class or a presenter in front of a large audience will make them embarrassed, so they may suffer from a lack of confidence and cannot think straight. 3) Because of the interruption and disturbance, the speaker cannot organize their thought clearly, retain information, and deliver their message clearly and coherently. 4) Eventually, the audience will have a bad experience in class or at the meeting. 5) However，if the audience keep quiet in classroom or professional settings, the class or meeting will not be chaotic.

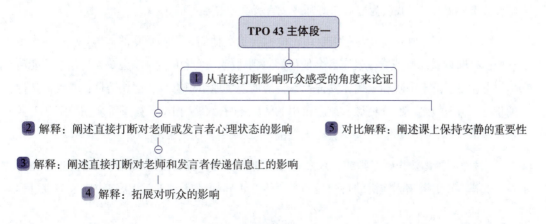

1) Additionally, pretending nothing happened when you recognize the mistakes made by the teacher or presenter is not a good option. 2) The purpose of lectures and presentations is to get the right message delivered to the audience. 3) If one spots a mistake during the lecture or presentation and is not willing to do anything, chances are that the teacher or presenter will continue to convey wrong ideas and perceptions to future audience. 4) However, if someone corrects the teacher or presenter afterward, they will appreciate the help. 5）By discussing and exchanging ideas with them, teachers can correct their mistakes made in class, meanwhile presenters will convey their idea more accurately and precisely. 6) Thus, correcting the teacher or the meeting presenter afterward provides a win-win outcome for all the parties involved.

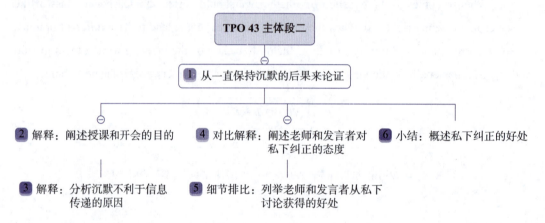

In all, correcting the teacher or the meeting presenter right away can be disruptive to the teacher, the meeting presenter and their audience. Correcting them afterward is a better choice since it helps to clear up wrong message or information and benefits all the parties involved.

◆ 4. 范文译文

1）当涉及我们是否应该在课堂上纠正老师或者在会议中纠正发言者的问题时，人们往往有不同的选择。2）有些人马上纠正他们或者在课堂或会议结束之后与他们交谈，另一些人则什么都不做。3）我认为之后与老师或发言者交谈是最好的选择。

1）首先，在老师或发言者犯错时纠正他们会扰乱他们，影响听众的体验。2）在大量听众面前打断课堂老师或会议发言者会使他们感到尴尬，因此他们可能会缺乏自信，不能清晰地思考。3）由于中断和干扰，发言者不会清晰连贯地组织思想、记住信息，并且传达他们的信息。4）最终，听众在课堂或会议中的体验不好。5）相反，如果听众在教室和专业环境中保持安静，课堂或会议将不会陷入混乱。

1）另外，当你认识到老师或会议发言者犯的错误时，假装任何事情都没有发生不是一个好的选择。2）讲座和演讲的目的是向听众传达正确的信息。3）如果在讲座或演讲过程中发现错误并且不情愿做任何事情，那么老师或演讲者可能会继续向未来的观众传达错误的观点和看法。4）但是，如果有人在之后更正了老师或演讲者，他们会感谢你的帮助。5）通过与他们讨论和交流意见，教师可以纠正他们在课堂上犯的错误，同时发言者会更准确地传达他们的想法。6）因此，过后纠正老师或会议发言者会有一个双赢的结果。

总而言之，立即纠正老师或发言者可能会对他们和他们的听众产生干扰。过后对他们的错误进行修正是一个更好的选择，因为这样有助于清除错误的信息，对所有相关方都有利。

◆ 5. 重点场景表达

1) interrupt teachers in class 课堂中打断老师

2) suffer from a lack of confidence 缺乏信心

3) interruption and disturbance 中断和干扰

4) deliver their message clearly and coherently 清楚而连贯地传达他们的信息

5) convey wrong ideas and perceptions 传达错误的观点和看法

TPO 44 独立写作

◆ 1. 题目

Some people believe that when busy parents do not have enough time to spend with their children, the best use of that time is to have fun playing games or sports. Others believe that it is best to use that time doing things together that are related to schoolwork. Which of the two approaches do you prefer?

◆ 2. 思路大纲

主观点：孩子应该花时间去和朋友玩游戏或做体育锻炼

分论点一：有利于孩子放松

分论点二：有利于孩子获得社交技能

◆ 3. 高分范文和思维导图

1) Living a hectic life, seldom do parents spend quality time with their kids. 2) Consequently, some people argue that it is best for parents to help kids do their schoolwork rather than leisurely activities like games and sports together. 3) However, I tend to disagree with this idea based on the following reasons.

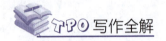

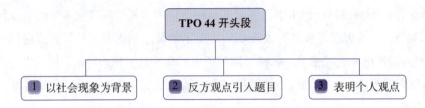

1) First of all, playing games or doing sports with parents provides a chance for kids to get away from their busy life and study, and switch off. 2) As is known to all, kids' academic life can be overwhelming. 3) Students are constantly under lots of academic pressure like presentations, group projects, final exams, so on and so forth, but barely do they have chances to release their pressure. 4) Fortunately, when playing with parents or involving in sports activities, they can switch off and unwind. 5) As the saying goes, "all work and no play makes Jack a dull boy." 6) Indeed, recent research on the correlation between leisure time and students' academic performance conducted by National Association of Psychiatrists shows that a student with certain amount of time spent on entertainment activities is observed to have higher grade than those who don't. 7) Consequently, doing leisurely activities helps to improve students' academic performance.

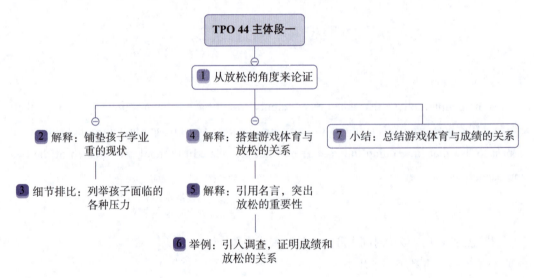

1) Additionally, playing together with parents teach kids some important lessons of life. 2) Most of the time, playing with parents are more interactive and requires kids to work with each other to achieve the common goal. 3) Kids can develop willingness to cooperate with others, because they will realize that an individual's capability to achieve something is limited and close collaboration with teammates is mandatory. 4) For instance, playing basketball games is a good case in point. 5) Different offensive and defensive strategies have to be executed together in order to win the game. 6) To be more specific, in the pick and roll strategy, the big man needs to read the

gesture of the guard handling the ball and sets a screen for him in time, and the guard also has to pass the ball back to the center player, only through which can the whole team has a nice offence. 7) Such an experience is going to serve as very valuable and intangible assets for one's future and one will benefit from such a memorable experience that they had with their parents.

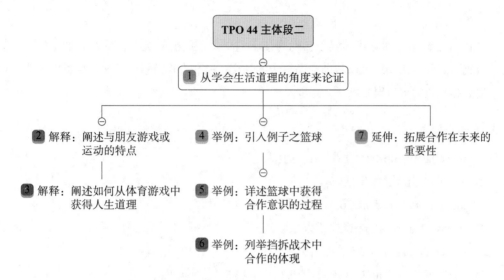

In all, entertaining activities like sports and games provide kids with the opportunity to unwind, which in turn helps to improve their academic performance. Such activities can also help to improve kids' social skills and cooperation awareness, both of which will be valuable assets for their future life and career.

◆ 4. 范文译文

1）父母生活繁忙，他们很少与孩子共度美好时光。2）因此，有些人认为最好让孩子专注于学业，而不是像游戏和运动这样的悠闲活动。3）但是，我不同意这个想法，原因如下。

1）首先，跟父母一起玩游戏或做运动为孩子们摆脱忙碌的生活和学习，并为放松提供了机会。2）众所周知，孩子们的学校生活可能会令人应接不暇。3）学生经常承受诸如演讲、小组项目、期末考试等诸多学习压力，但他们几乎没有机会释放压力。4）幸运的是，当与父母一起玩或参与体育活动时，他们可以放松。5）俗话说："整天工作没有放松会让人变傻。"6）事实上，国家精神科医师协会对休闲时间与学生学习表现之间的相关性进行的最新研究表明，有一定时间用于娱乐活动的学生比没有参加娱乐活动的学生成绩更好。7）因此，悠闲活动有助于提高学生的学习成绩。

1）另外，和父母一起玩耍教会孩子们一些重要的人生教训。2）大多数时候，与父母玩耍更具互动性，需要彼此合作才能实现共同目标。3）孩子们可以发展与其他人合作的意愿，因为他们会意识到一个人获得某些东西的能力是有限的，并且与队友的密切合作是很有

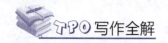

必要的。4）例如，打篮球比赛就是一个很好的例子。5）为了赢得比赛，不同的攻守战略必须一起执行。6）更具体一点来说，在挡拆策略中，大个子需要读懂控球后卫的手势，并及时为他打掩护，而后卫也必须将球传给中锋，只有这样整个球队才有一个不错的进攻。7）这样的经历将成为人们未来的宝贵和无形资产，人们将从这样一个跟父母一起的难忘的经历中受益。

总而言之，体育和游戏等娱乐活动为孩子们提供了放松的机会，从而有助于提高他们的学习成绩。此类活动还可以帮助提高孩子的社交技能和合作意识，这两方面都将成为他们未来生活和职业的宝贵财富。

◆ 5. 重点场景表达

1) live a hectic lifestyle 过着繁忙的生活

2) academic life 学校生活

3) under lots of academic pressure 承受很多学习压力

4) release their pressure 释放压力

5) switch off and unwind 放松

6) National Association of Psychiatrists 国家精神科医师协会

7) academic performance 学习成绩

8) achieve the common goal 达到共同的目标

9) offensive and defensive strategies 攻击和防御策略

10) pick and roll strategy 挡拆策略

11) improve kids' social skills and cooperation awareness 提高孩子的社交技能和合作意识

12) valuable assets 宝贵财富

TPO 45 独立写作

◆ 1. 题目

Do you agree or disagree with the following statement? In the past, young people depended too much on their parents to make decisions for them; today young people are better able to make decisions about their own lives.

◆ 2. 思路大纲

主观点：现在年轻人更有能力独自做决策

分论点一：受教育水平的提升，自身能力变强

分论点二：科技的帮助，更容易收集信息

◆ 3. 高分范文和思维导图

1) With the changes of time, the independence of the young has become one of the most controversial topics among the general public. 2) Parents and teachers claim that today young people are more dependent on others when making decisions about their own lives, while the young generation casts serious doubt on the above claim. 3) I think indeed young people now have a stronger ability to make decisions about their own life than before.

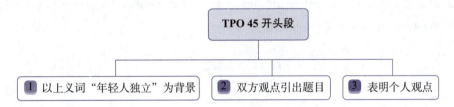

1) Above all, better educational background of the young today has improved their capability of decision-making. 2) As we all know, in the past, due to lack of adequate educational resources, many young adults didn't receive formal education and were even just illiterate. 3) In this case, parents with richer experience in life and work were prone to make decisions for their children in order to prevent their kids from making terrible mistakes. 4) For example, in ancient China, the marriage and future jobs of young people were arranged by their parents. 5) Nevertheless, with the significant development of education, modern schools cultivate intelligent students who are psychologically mature and knowledgeable enough to analyze the problems they encounter. 6) As a result, these well-educated youths are more likely to make decisions themselves, whether on marriage or on career.

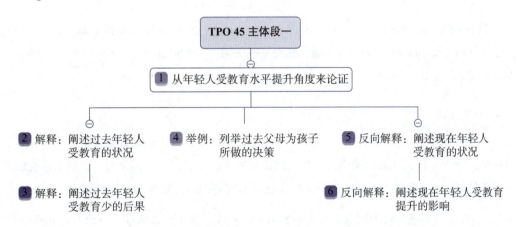

1) Furthermore, the availability of various information resources contributes to the success of student's decision-making without parents. 2) The past two decades has witnessed a great leap in the technology that promotes access to information. 3) As a result, young people today can

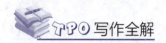

easily collect information necessary for decision-making without consulting their parents. 4) My own experience of searching for my ideal college is a good case in point. 5) In the process of application, I can log onto the official website of my ideal school to get to know the faculty members and school facilities. 6) Also, I can initiate a discussion about the pros and cons of choosing a certain university on the online forum. 7) All the above information can be gained thanks to the advances of communication technology. 8) However, this was something unimaginable several decades ago, when the only reliable information source was nothing but your parents so that you had to rely on them to make decisions.

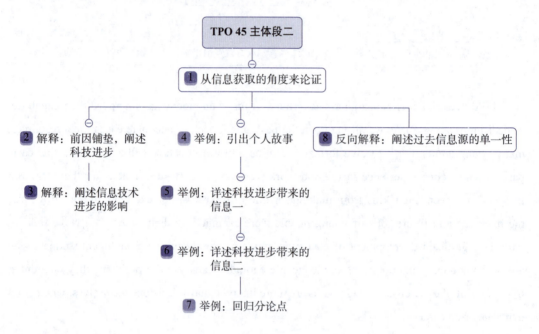

Judging from what has been discussed above, we can draw the conclusion that today young people are more able to make decisions about their own lives on account of the improvement of their educational background and different approaches to acquire information.

◆ 4. 范文译文

1）随着时间的变迁，年轻人的独立性成为公众中争议最大的话题之一。 2）家长和老师声称，今天年轻人在做出关于自己生活的决定时更加依赖他人，而年轻一代对上述说法表示严重怀疑。3）我认为现在的年轻人确实比以前有更强的决定自己生活的能力。

1）首先，当今年轻人拥有更好的教育背景，提高了他们的决策能力。 2）大家都知道，过去由于缺乏足够的教育资源，许多年轻人没有受过正规教育，甚至是文盲。3）在这种情况下，有着更丰富的生活和工作经验的父母很容易为他们的孩子做决定，以防止他们的孩子犯下可怕的错误。 4）例如，在中国古代，年轻人的婚姻和未来工作是由父母包办的。

5）然而，随着教育的显著发展，现代学校培养出智力良好的学生，他们的心理成熟程度和知识足以分析他们遇到的问题。6）因此，这些受过良好教育的年轻一代更有可能做出适合自己的决定，无论是在婚姻还是择业上。

1）此外，各种信息资源的可用性有助于学生在没有父母的情况下成功地决策。2）过去二十年来，信息获取技术取得了巨大飞跃。3）因此，今天的年轻人可以在不咨询父母的情况下轻松收集决策所需的信息。4）我自己寻找理想大学的经历就是一个很好的例子。5）在申请学校的过程中，我可以登录我理想学校的官方网站，了解教学人员和学校设施。6）另外，我可以在网络论坛上讨论选择某所大学的利弊。7）由于通信技术的进步，所有上述信息都可以获得。8）然而，这是几十年前无法想象的，当时唯一可靠的信息来源只不过是你的父母，所以你必须依靠他们来做决定。

从以上讨论的结果来看，我们可以得出这样的结论：由于他们的教育背景和信息获取途径的多样化，今天的年轻人能够更好地为自己的生活做决定。

◆ 5. 重点场景表达

1) controversial topics 争议的话题
2) adequate educational resources 充足的教育资源
3) make terrible mistakes 犯下可怕的错误
4) well-educated youths 受过良好教育的青年人
5) ideal college 理想的大学
6) communication technology 通信技术
7) on account of 由于

TPO 46 独立写作

◆ 1. 题目

Do you agree or disagree with the following statement? The opinions of celebrities, such as famous entertainers and athletes, are more important to young people than they are to old people. Use specific reasons and examples to support your answer.

◆ 2. 思路大纲

主观点：名人观点对年轻人更重要
分论点一：年轻人不成熟
分论点二：年轻人与名人接触更多

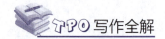

TPO写作全解

◆ 3. 高分范文和思维导图

1) People tend to respond differently to the comments and opinions of celebrities in the entertaining and sports fields because people have different educational and family backgrounds, ages and perspectives. 2) When it comes to the question of whether young people are more susceptible to celebrities' opinions than old people, I would say that youngsters are more influenced by celebrities because of their immaturity and extensive exposure to celebrities.

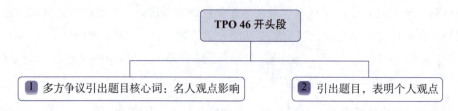

1) First of all, young people especially adolescents who are in their formative years are less mentally mature, thus more easily influenced by the comments and opinions of celebrities. 2) Children tend to imitate whatever their idols say and do since they think their idols are so cool. 3) Rock stars might use lots of curse words on stage, and professional sportsmen might trash talk on court. 4) Movie stars might use flirtatious language in a movie. 5) All of these comments and language have tremendous impact on kids' attitudes and behaviors. 6) Thus, it is no wonder that young students tend to use derogatory language, sing suggestive song lyrics, and even flirt with each other in a classroom. 7) In sharp contrast, with entrenched values and beliefs deep inside themselves, adults are less likely to be influenced by pop culture idols and celebrities of other sorts.

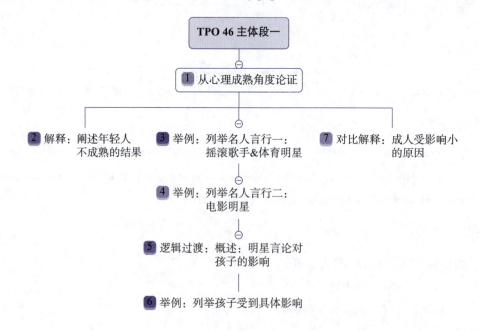

1) Additionally, the younger generation has much more intensive exposures to celebrities' opinions and lifestyles, making themselves more susceptible to celebrities' ideas and comments. 2) Actually, lots of kids nowadays waste too much time on technological gadgets like laptops, cell phones and other kinds of electronic devices. 3) Obviously, the omnipresence of the reports about celebrities are made possible by the advancement of modern technologies like laptops, smart phones, and tablets such as iPad. 4) To further illustrate, news about celebrities' life can be updated very quickly. 5) In fact, what the celebrities said before might show up on the Internet a few hours later. 6) Since the younger generation account for a huge proportion of electronic device users, the main media of spreading viewpoints of famous people, they are much more easily influenced than adults who might not even own a smart phone.

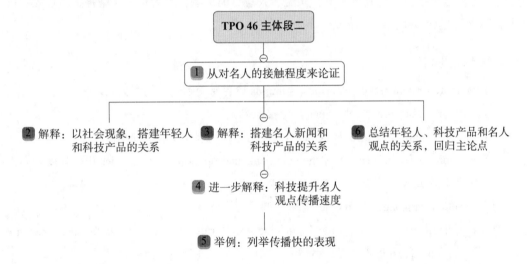

In all, youngsters are more easily influenced by celebrities' opinions than adults because young people are not mentally mature and they are extensively exposed to celebrities' language and behaviors.

◆ 4. 范文译文

1）人们对娱乐和运动领域的名人的评论和意见反应不同，因为人们有着不同的教育背景、年龄和观点。 2）谈到年轻人是否比老年人更容易受到名人意见的影响，我想说年轻人更多地受到名人的影响，因为他们不成熟并且广泛接触到名人。

1）首先，年轻人尤其是处于成长期的青少年精神上不太成熟，因此他们更容易受到名人的评论和意见的影响。 2）年轻的孩子们喜欢模仿他们偶像说的话，因为他们认为他们的偶像非常酷。 3）摇滚明星可能会在舞台上使用很多脏词，专业运动员可能会在场上讲垃圾话。 4）电影明星可能会在电影中使用调情的语言。 5）所有这些评论和语言都会对孩子的态度和行为产生巨大的影响。 6）因此，难怪年轻学生倾向于使用贬义语言、唱出暗示性的

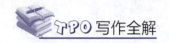

歌词，甚至在教室里互相调情。7）与之形成鲜明对比的是，对于成人来说，根深蒂固的价值观植根于他们的内心深处，所以成人不太可能受流行文化偶像和其他名人的影响。

1）此外，年轻一代对名人的观点和生活方式的接触更为密集，使他们更容易受到名人的想法和评论的影响。2）实际上，现在很多孩子在笔记本电脑、手机等技术设备和其他种电子设备上浪费太多时间。3）显然，现代技术（如笔记本电脑、智能手机和 iPad 等平板电脑）的发展，使得有关名人的报道无所不在。4）进一步说，关于名人生活的新闻可以很快更新。5）事实上，几个小时后，名人所说的话可能会在互联网上出现。6）由于年轻一代在电子设备用户中所占的比例很大，而知名人士的观点在网上很快传播，年轻人比那些甚至没有智能手机的成年人更容易受影响。

总而言之，年轻人比成年人更容易受名人意见的影响，因为年轻人精神上不成熟，同时他们广泛接触名人的语言和行为。

◆ 5. 重点场景表达

1) be more susceptible to celebrities' opinions 更容易受到名人的意见的影响

2) extensive exposure to celebrities 广泛接触名人

3) imitate whatever their idols say and do 模仿他们的偶像所说和所做

4) be more easily influenced by the comments and opinions of celebrities 更容易受到名人的评论和意见的影响

5) flirtatious language in a movie 电影中调情的语言

6) use derogatory language, sing suggestive song lyrics, and even flirt with each other in a classroom 使用贬义语言、唱暗示性歌词，甚至在课堂上互相调情

7) technological gadgets like laptops, cell phones and other kinds of electronic devices 诸如笔记本电脑、手机等技术设备和其他种电子设备

8) account for a huge proportion of electronic devices users 占电子设备用户的比例很大

TPO 47 独立写作

◆ 1. 题目

Do you agree or disagree with the following statement? It is important to know about events happening around the world, even if it is unlikely that they will affect your daily life. Use specific reasons and examples to support your answer.

◆ 2. 思路大纲

主观点：了解时事很重要

分论点一：可以增进关系

分论点二：符合人性，改善世界

◆ 3. 高分范文和思维导图

1) Taking a panoramic picture of human evolution, we can see information has been playing a very important role, especially in modern times. 2) We are overwhelmed with all kinds of information, such as sensational stories in our everyday mundane lives, or news that attracts international attention. 3) When it comes to whether people should care about the things happening around the globe that does not even affect their lives, I would say people, indeed, should follow them closely for the following reasons.

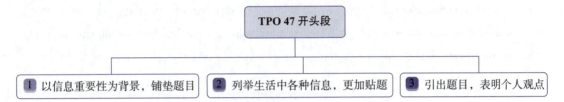

1) In the first place, following the news around the globe，even though it might seem to be far away from our lives，can keep us posted about the most up-to-date domestic and international affairs, and thus we have something to talk about when spending time with our friends. 2) This is because these reports serve as great conversation ice breakers. 3) For example, I am very keen to keep myself informed of world events, including the US presidential elections, the nuclear crisis of Iran and North Korea, or even the Wimbledon Tennis Championship. 4) Every time I try to connect with a friend or my family members, I make use of such information that I obtained on newspapers and TV, and not surprisingly, I feel like it can bring my friendship or relationship with families to a new level by exchanging ideas with them on these global events. 5) Therefore, sharing our perspectives on world events actually brings us closer than ever before.

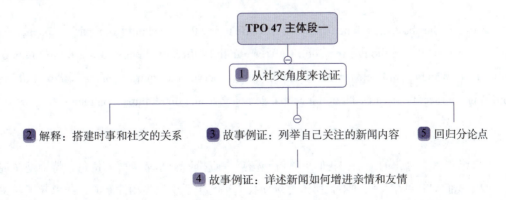

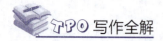

1) More importantly, humans are gregarious, meaning that we depend on each other to survive and thrive. 2) When one has proper shelter and daily necessities to live, he or she should be compassionate about those who are less fortunate. 3) As citizens in a civilized world, we have to follow the news that has nothing to do with us, since there might be some catastrophic events happening in other places, and hence we can give victims a helping hand when they are desperately in need of help. 4) Recently, a journalist shot a picture about a desperate father who tried to buy some pencils for his daughter so that she could learn to write, but unfortunately, he was so destitute that he could not even afford it. 5) But, the dad finally made it because this very picture drew attention from the people around the globe on the Internet and then money was raised for his daughter. 6) Such touching stories can be so contagious that it helps to spread positive energy not only to the community but to the whole world at large. 7) What happened in the picture has nothing to do with others, but if we stop and take a look at it, we will be aware that there are millions of people who are compassionate about the unlucky ones, thus making the world a better place to live in.

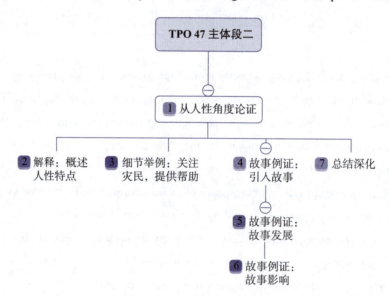

Through the above-mentioned analysis, it is safe to say that we should know things happening around the world even though they don't affect our lives directly since sharing these kinds of information brings people closer. More importantly, it serves the interests and livelihood of the entire human race if one cares about things that do not have any direct impact on them.

◆ 4. 范文译文

1）纵观人类进化的全景，我们可以看到信息一直扮演着非常重要的角色，特别是在现代。2）我们对各种信息感到不知所措，例如我们平凡生活中的轰动性新闻，或引起国际关注的新闻。3）当谈到人们是否应该关心全球范围内甚至不影响我们生活的事情时，我想说人们应该关注，理由如下。

1）首先，在全球各地的新闻发布之后，尽管它似乎离我们的生活很遥远，但是可以让我们了解最新的国内和国际事务，因此我们与朋友在一起的时间可以有谈资。2）这是因为这些报道是非常棒的谈话破冰利器。3）例如，我非常热衷于了解世界各地的事件，包括美国总统选举、伊朗和朝鲜核危机，甚至温布尔登网球锦标赛。4）每次尝试与朋友或家人联系时，我都会利用我在报纸和电视上获得的信息，并且毫不奇怪，我觉得通过就这些全球性事件彼此交换意见，我可以将我与家人的友谊或关系提升到一个新的水平。5）因此，分享我们对世界事件的观点实际上使我们比以往任何时候都更加亲近。

1）更重要的是，人类是群居的，这意味着我们依靠彼此生存和发展。2）当一个人有适当的住所和日常生活必需品时，他或她应该对那些不幸的人有同情心。3）作为文明世界的公民，我们必须关注与我们毫无关系的新闻，因为在其他地方可能会发生一些灾难性事件，他们迫切需要我们帮忙。4）最近，一名记者拍摄了一张绝望的父亲的照片，他试图为女儿购买铅笔，这样她才能够学写字，但不幸的是，他太穷了，甚至连铅笔都买不起。5）但是，爸爸终于成功了，因为这张照片引起了全球网民的注意，为他的女儿筹集了资金。6）这些感人的故事非常具有传染性，不仅有助于向社区，而且向整个世界传播积极的能量。7）图片中发生的事与其他人没有任何关系，但如果我们停下来看看它，我们就会意识到有数百万人对不幸的人产生了同情心，从而使世界变得更加美好。

通过上述分析，可以说尽管不会直接影响我们的生活，但我们应该了解世界各地的情况，因为分享这些信息会使人们更加亲密。更重要的是，如果人们关心那些对他们没有任何直接影响的事物，这样符合全人类的利益。

◆ 5. 重点场景表达

1) sensational stories in our everyday mundane lives 平凡生活中的轰动性新闻

2) keep us posted about the most up-to-date domestic and international affairs 让我们随时了解最新的国际国内事务

3) great conversation ice breakers 谈话破冰利器

4) exchange ideas with 与……交流观点

5) daily necessities 日常必需品

6) be compassionate about 同情……

7) be desperately in need of help 极度需要帮助

8) shoot a picture about 拍了一张关于……的照片

9) spread positive energy 传递正能量

10) bring people closer 让人们更加亲近

TPO 48 独立写作

◆ 1. 题目

Do you agree or disagree with the following statement? Because modern life is very complex, it is essential for young people to have the ability to plan and organize. Use specific reasons and examples to support your answer.

◆ 2. 思路大纲

主观点：组织计划能力很重要

分论点一：有助于孩子取得好的学业成绩

分论点二：有助于孩子未来的求学和就业

◆ 3. 高分范文和思维导图

1) The question of what kind of skills that kids should develop to be more successful has never failed to attract attention from parents, educators and researchers. 2) Since people of all age groups are limited by their time and energy, it is important to develop skills that help them to use their time more effectively. 3) Thus, I, personally, believe that planning and organization skills are very decisive skills that kids cannot live without.

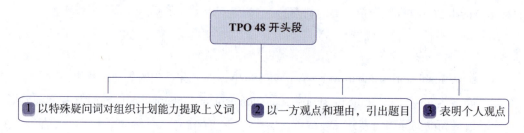

1) First of all, excellent planning and organization skills can help kids to achieve better academic performance in school. 2) As is common sense, young children ranging from 5 to 10 years old are under lots of academic pressure in primary school. 3) For instance, they have to write book reports, do experiments in the lab, go on field trips organized by the school, and in some cases kids have to attend piano classes, dancing classes and taekwondo classes after regular class sessions in school. 4) Due to lack of certain skills to manage their time effectively, it is not surprising to see that lots of children tend to put things off and procrastinate quite often when it comes to their assignments. 5) If kids develop good time management skills and organization skills, they will listen more attentively during class and finish their assignments in time, thus making their study

more productive.

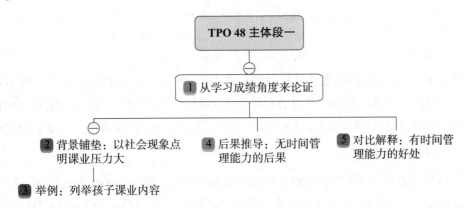

1) Additionally, good planning and organizational skills can be beneficial to kids' future when they pursue further study in high school and university and even when they eventually become professionals. 2) When kids enter high school and university, they will enjoy better chances to get involved in social activities like doing community service, organizing a school play or raising fund for a local charity. 3) Students who have organizational skills tend to be more successful in organizing these activities than those who don't. 4) For example, when organizing a school play, a student director is responsible for lots of issues like selecting the play, choosing the cast and designing the set. 5) When having to face multiple responsibilities, students who don't have organizational skills are less likely to present a nice school play to the audience and even screw it up. 6) Moreover, research conducted by National Society of Developmental Psychologists shows that students who developed organizational skills in their formative years are more likely to get better pay and benefits after graduation, thus having a more promising career than those without these essential skills.

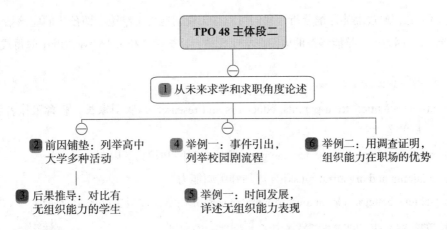

In summary, through the above careful analysis, we can safely draw the conclusion that kids

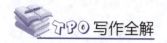

should develop planning and organizational skills since these skills will help them to be successful in academic performance, social activities and future career.

◆ 4. 范文译文

1）孩子应该发展哪些技能才能取得更大成功这个问题一直吸引家长、教育工作者和研究人员的关注。2）由于所有年龄组的人都受到时间和精力的限制，因此发展能够帮助他们更有效地利用时间的技能很重要。3）因此，我个人认为，规划和组织技能是非常决定性的技能，孩子们不能没有。

1）首先，出色的计划和组织能力可以帮助孩子在学校取得更好的学业成绩。2）5至10岁的小孩在小学时承受着很大的学业压力，这是常识。3）例如，他们必须写读书报告，在实验室做实验，参加学校组织的实地考察，有些孩子在学校的正规课程后还必须上钢琴课、舞蹈课和跆拳道课。4）由于缺乏一定的技能来有效地管理他们的时间，很多孩子倾向于做事推迟，在完成作业时经常拖延，这并不奇怪。5）如果孩子培养出良好的时间管理技能和组织能力，他们会在课堂上更专心地听讲，并课下及时完成任务，从而提高他们的学习效率。

1）另外，良好的计划和组织能力有益于孩子在高中和大学继续深造，甚至有益于孩子成为职业人士。2）当孩子进入高中和大学时，他们将享受更好的机会参与诸如做社区服务、组织校园剧或为当地慈善机构募集资金等社交活动。3）具有组织能力的学生比那些没有组织能力的学生更能成功地组织这些活动。4）例如，在组织校园剧时，学生导演负责诸如选择精彩剧目、选择剧组和设计场景等许多问题。5）当面对多重责任时，没有组织能力的学生不太可能为观众呈现一场精彩的校园剧，甚至会把它搞砸。6）此外，由国家发展心理学家协会进行的研究表明，那些在成长期间培养了组织技能的学生在毕业后更有可能获得更好的薪酬和福利，因此他们比没有这些基本技能的人更有前途。

总而言之，通过上述仔细分析，我们可以毫无疑问地得出结论，即孩子们应该培养规划和组织能力，因为这些技能将帮助他们在学业成绩、社交活动和未来职业生涯中取得成功。

◆ 5. 重点场景表达

1) attract attention from parents, educators and researchers 吸引家长、教育工作者和研究人员的关注

2) be limited by their time and energy 受到他们时间和精力的限制

3) planning and organization skills 规划和组织能力

4) achieve better academic performance in school 在学校取得更好的学业成绩

5) manage their time effectively 有效管理他们的时间

6) put things off and procrastinate 做事推迟和拖延

7) write book reports, do experiments in the lab, go on field trips organized by the school 写

读书报告，在实验室做实验，参加学校组织的实地考察

8) attend piano classes, dancing classes and taekwondo classes after regular class sessions 在正规课程后参加钢琴课、舞蹈课和跆拳道课

9) become professionals 成为专业人士

10) organize a school play and raise fund for a local charity 组织校园剧和为当地慈善机构筹集资金

11) face multiple responsibilities 面对多重责任

12) present a nice school play to the audience 为观众呈现一场精彩的校园剧

13) get better pay and benefits 得到更好的福利待遇

14) have a more promising career 有一个更有前途的职业

TPO 49 独立写作

◆ 1. 题目

Do you agree or disagree with the following statement? The ability to maintain friendship with a small number of people over a long period of time is more important for happiness than the ability to make many new friends easily. Use specific reasons and examples to support your answer.

◆ 2. 思路大纲

主观点：和少数人保持友谊更好

分论点一：保证友谊的质量，带来快乐

分论点二：节省时间，有更多私人空间

◆ 3. 高分范文和思维导图

1) Friends are a big part of our lives. 2) Sometimes it is our friends who give us timely support and encouragement so that we can hang in there in face of hardships and barriers in our life. 3) Some people argue more friends mean more happiness while others believe in the philosophy "less is more" when making friends. 4) I, personally, think that having fewer friends is a better choice.

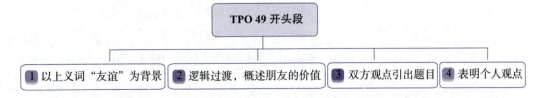

TPO 49 开头段			
① 以上义词 "友谊" 为背景	② 逻辑过渡，概述朋友的价值	③ 双方观点引出题目	④ 表明个人观点

1) First of all, having fewer friends guarantees quality friendship, which in turn makes people

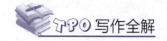

happier. 2) It is common sense that if a person has a huge number of friends, he or she is cooler and more popular than those who don't have so many friends. 3) However, just because someone has your phone number doesn't mean he or she is a friend of yours. 4) Just because someone was your friend at some point doesn't mean he or she is your friend now or in the future. 5) In fact, having fewer friends means that we can have more quality time together and we can be committed to our friendship. 6) Given the fact that we have just a few friends, we can spend more time together hanging out, grabbing some food together, watching a game, and even going to a concert together.

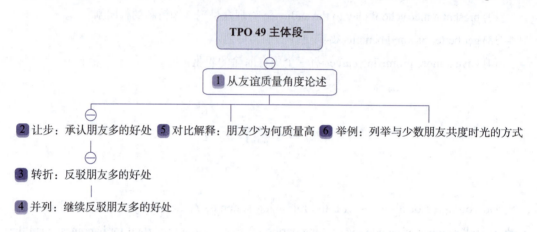

1) Additionally, maintaining close relationship with fewer friends means that we can have time to enjoy our personal space, which in turn brings more happiness to our life. 2) Maintaining a quality friendship takes time as we have already discussed in the last paragraph. 3) Indeed, we have to comfort our friends when things go wrong, listen to our friends vent their feelings about their work, and even empathize with our friends when they are in bad mood. 4) Having too many superficial friends takes up too much of our time. 5) It involves a big-time commitment, leaving us not much time to enjoy our personal space. 6) Life is not about pleasing others. 7) It is more important to learn to enjoy personal space like reading a book, watching a movie and even taking a walk. 8) These kinds of activities can help people to relax and reflect.

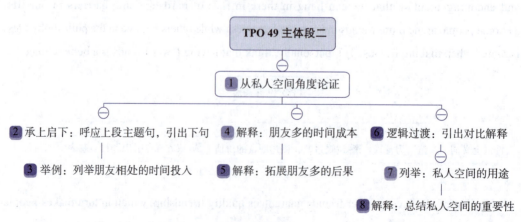

In all, keeping fewer friends is better since it ensures more quality friendship and leaves more time for us to enjoy our personal space, which in turn makes us happier people.

◆ 4. 范文译文

1）朋友是我们生活中很重要的一部分。 2）有时候是我们的朋友给予我们适时的支持和鼓励，让我们在生活中遇到困难和障碍的时候坚持下去，3）有些人认为，更多的朋友意味着更多的快乐，而另外一些人信奉"少就是多"的交友哲学。4）我个人认为交较少的朋友是更好的选择。

1）首先，少交朋友保证高质量的友谊，反过来使人更快乐。2）一般人认为，如果一个人有很多的朋友，他就比那些没有那么多朋友的人更酷、更受欢迎。3）然而，仅仅因为有人有你的电话并不意味着他或她是你的朋友。4）某个时候某人是你的朋友，并不意味着他或她现在或将来还是你的朋友。5）事实上，少交朋友意味着我们可以共度美好时光，我们可以更投入我们的友谊中。6）由于我们只有几个朋友，所以我们可以花时间在一起闲逛，一起吃东西，看比赛，甚至一起去听音乐会。

1）另外，与少数朋友保持密切的关系，意味着我们有时间享受我们的个人空间，反过来给我们的生活带来更多的快乐。2）保持高质量的友谊需要时间，正如我们在上一段已经讨论的那样。3）事实上，当事情出错时，我们必须安慰我们的朋友，听朋友发泄他们对工作的感受，甚至在朋友心情不好的时候我们要同情他们。4）太多肤浅的朋友占用我们太多的时间。5）交更多朋友涉及一个巨大的时间承诺，使得我们没有太多的时间来享受我们的个人空间。6）生活不是取悦别人。7）学会享受个人空间更重要，比如看书，看电影，甚至散步。8）这些活动可以帮助人们放松和反思。

总之，少交朋友比较好，因为它确保了更优质的友谊，留给我们更多的时间享受个人空间，使我们更快乐。

◆ 5. 重点场景表达

1) give us timely support and encouragement 给予我们适时的支持和鼓励

2) hang in there in face of hardships and barriers in our life 让我们在生活中面对困难和障碍的时候要坚持下去

3) the philosophy "less is more" "少就是多" 的哲学

4) guarantee quality friendship 保证高质量的友谊

5) spend quality time together 共度美好时光

6) be committed to our friendship 投入我们的友谊中

7) to hang out, grab some food together, watch a game, and even go to a concert together 出去闲逛，一起吃东西，看比赛，甚至一起去听音乐会

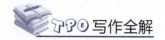

8) enjoy our personal space 享受我们的个人空间

9) comfort our friends when things go wrong 朋友出现问题时，安慰我们的朋友

10) listen to our friends vent about their work 听我们的朋友发泄他们对工作的感受

11) empathize with our friends when they are in bad mood 当他们心情不好的时候我们要同情他们

12) too many superficial friends 太多肤浅的朋友

13) involve a big-time commitment 涉及大量时间的承诺

14) please others 取悦别人

15) read a book, watch a movie and even take a walk 看书，看电影，甚至散步

16) help people to relax and reflect 帮助人们放松和反思

TPO 50 独立写作

◆ 1. 题目

Do you agree or disagree with the following statement? People will spend less time cooking and preparing food in twenty years than they do today. Use specific reasons and examples to support your answer.

◆ 2. 思路大纲

主观点：人们未来会花更少的时间在做饭上

分论点一：生活更加富裕

分论点二：生活方式转变

◆ 3. 高分范文和思维导图

1) The preparation of food is a topic that has not been discussed with constant fervor. 2) When it comes to the time people will spend on cooking in next twenty years, the answer might be different since a myriad of factors could be at play such as family income, professions, and even eating habits. 3) Taking such changes into consideration, I would say generally people will devote less time to cooking and preparing for food in twenty years based on the following reasons.

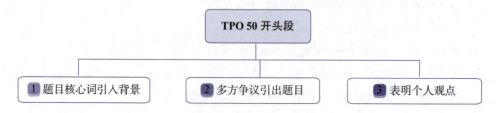

1) In the first place, with the masses' increasing affluence, it is more likely for people to spend less time preparing and cooking food. 2) Family income and financial conditions are closely related with the time spent on cooking. 3) According to a research by National Bureau of Statistics, people in developed countries that belong to the Organization for Economic Cooperation Development spend significantly less time on household chores including cooking, cleaning, mowing the lawn, or walking the dog. 4) One possible explanation for this phenomenon is that when people are getting wealthier, they tend to eat out in a nice restaurant. 5) Another trend that might give people an incentive to devote less time to cooking is that restaurants featuring cuisines in different countries are burgeoning in a way that people can eat whatever food they want, whether it is Pad Thai, Italian pizza, Belgian macaroons or Chinese dumplings. 6) These featured restaurants target different customers regardless of meat lovers or vegetarians. 7) With the increase of people's income as well as the types of restaurants, more people will dine out instead of cooking at home.

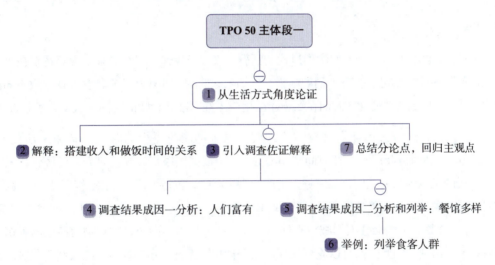

1) In the second place, people now are living an overwhelmingly hectic life, and the situation will worsen in twenty years, leaving people no time to prepare and cook food. 2) Our obsession with productivity is a reflection of our deep-rooted belief, an idea that our potential happiness is intricately tied to the amount of wealth we have. 3) When people think that the majority will be wealthier and richer than themselves, chances are that a great number of people would live their lives as in a race and competition to beat the odds. 4) It is not surprising for us to work harder and longer, and squeeze more time out of our day than other people so that we can finally accumulate sufficient wealth to escape the drudgery of work. 5) Therefore, people's insatiable desire to achieve infinite fortune and wealth is hard to satisfy, leaving us no time to cook.

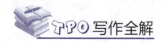

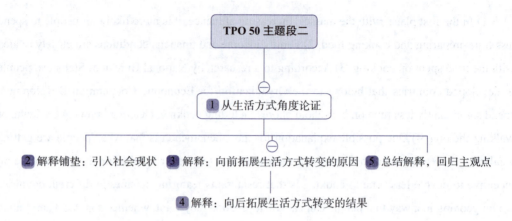

TPO 50 主题段二

① 从生活方式角度论证

② 解释铺垫：引入社会现状　③ 解释：向前拓展生活方式转变的原因　⑤ 总结解释，回归主观点

④ 解释：向后拓展生活方式转变的结果

In conclusion, with the masses' increasing affluence and overwhelmingly hectic lifestyles, it is more likely for people to spend less time preparing and cooking food in twenty years.

◆ 4. 范文译文

1）准备食物不是一个人们激烈讨论的话题。2）当谈到人们在未来二十年花费在烹饪上的时间如何改变，可能会有不同的因素，例如家庭收入、职业甚至是饮食习惯导致不同的答案。3）考虑到这些变化，人们在二十年内用于烹饪和准备食物的时间会减少，理由如下。

1）首先，随着人民群众日益富裕，人们更有可能花更少的时间准备和烹饪食物。2）家庭收入和财务状况与烹饪时间密切相关。3）根据国家统计局的研究，经济合作发展组织所属的发达国家的人们花在家务上的时间大大减少，包括做饭、打扫、修剪草坪、遛狗。4）对这种现象的一种可能的解释是，当人们越来越富有时，他们往往在一家不错的餐馆就餐。5）另外一个趋势可能会让人们减少烹饪的时间，那就是以不同国家的食物为特色的餐馆如雨后春笋般出现，因此人们可以吃到任何国家的食物，无论是泰式米粉、意大利比萨饼、比利时蛋白杏仁饼干还是中国水饺。6）这些特色餐厅面向不同的顾客，不论是肉类爱好者还是素食主义者。7）既然这些特色餐厅针对不同人群，更多的人会外出用餐，而不是在家做饭。

1）其次，现在人们的生活非常忙碌，未来二十年情况会恶化，人们没有时间准备和烹饪食物。2）我们对生产力的痴迷是对我们根深蒂固的信念的反映，这个信念是我们的潜在幸福与我们拥有的财富有着错综复杂的关系。3）当人们认为大多数人比他们自己更富裕时，很有可能会有很多人把自己的生活过得像比赛一样以便成功。4）不足为奇的是，我们工作越来越努力，时间越来越长，比其他人挤出更多时间，这样我们最终可以积累足够的财富以便逃避工作的苦差事。5）人们对无穷无尽财富的欲望难以满足，因此，没有时间做饭。

总而言之，随着人民群众日益富裕，生活方式非常忙乱，人们在未来二十年内会花更少的时间准备和烹饪食物的可能性就更大了。

◆ 5. 重点场景表达

1) family income, professions, and even eating habits 家庭收入、职业甚至饮食习惯

2) the masses' increasing affluence 群众日益增加的财富

3) Family income and financial conditions 家庭收入和财务状况

4) Organization for Economic Cooperation Development 经济合作发展组织

5) household chores, including cooking, cleaning, mowing the lawn, and walking the dog 做家务，包括做饭、打扫卫生、修剪草坪、遛狗

6) Pad Thai, Italian pizza, Belgian macaroons or Chinese dumplings 泰国米粉、意大利比萨饼、比利时蛋白杏仁饼干或中国饺子

7) meat lovers or vegetarians 肉类爱好者或素食者

8) live an overwhelmingly hectic life 过着紧张繁忙的生活

9) a reflection of our deep-rooted belief 反映了我们根深蒂固的信念

10) squeeze more time out of our day 挤出更多的时间

11) escape the drudgery of work 逃避工作的苦差事

12) achieve infinite fortune and wealth 获得无限的财富

附录 1　TPO 1-50 综合写作话题一览表

TPO 1　四天工作制好吗？

TPO 2　小组协作完成任务好吗？

TPO 3　油画的作者是伦勃朗吗？

TPO 4　恐龙是恒温动物吗？

TPO 5　巨型石屋的作用是什么？

TPO 6　网上百科全书比纸质百科全书好吗？

TPO 7　美国木材公司愿意获取环保认证吗？

TPO 8　塞恩加尔骑士写的回忆录是真的吗？

TPO 9　燃料电池发动机能代替内燃机吗？

TPO 10　到底是污染还是捕食者导致海獭数量下降？

TPO 11　公众文学阅读量下降会带来负面影响吗？

TPO 12　油画上的主人公是简·奥斯汀吗？

TPO 13　化石卖给私人收藏家是福还是祸？

TPO 14　挽救式伐木对经济和森林好吗？

TPO 15　控制甘蔗蟾蜍蔓延的方式有效吗？

TPO 16　英国考古学面临的困境能打破吗？

TPO 17　美国鸟类的数量会持续下降吗？

TPO 18　防止香榧灭绝的方式有效吗？

TPO 19　商业中的"托儿"是否应该被禁止？

TPO 20　放任森林大火燃烧的政策应该被实施吗？

TPO 21　种植转基因树是福还是祸？

TPO 22　乙醇可以代替汽油吗？

TPO 23　黄松减少的原因是什么？

TPO 24　霸王龙化石中有活组织吗？

TPO 25　陶罐子是古代电池吗？

TPO 26　斑马蚌的蔓延不可阻挡吗？

TPO 27　小冰川时代怎样形成的？

TPO 28　罗伯特·皮尔里去过北极吗？

TPO 29　爱德蒙托龙迁徙吗？

TPO 30　燃烧的镜子存在吗？

附录2　TPO 1-50 独立写作话题一览表

TPO 1　社会活动和体育一样重要

TPO 2　说真话对维持人际关系不重要

TPO 3　维系老朋友比交新朋友更重要

TPO 4　未来车辆会越来越少

TPO 5　现在人们将更多时间投入应该做的事情上

TPO 6　现在的生活比过去更加轻松

TPO 7　理解概念比学习事实更重要

TPO 8　应该禁播针对年幼孩子的广告

TPO 9　科技让孩子更加有创造力

TPO 10 玩游戏不浪费时间

TPO 11 网络提供了有价值的信息

TPO 12 掌握多门学科知识更好

TPO 13 大家庭不如过去重要

TPO 14 出国游比国内游好

TPO 15 从小管钱有助于培养对自己财务负责的人

TPO 16 个人出游比团队游要好

TPO 17 广告美化了产品

TPO 18 学生受朋友的影响要比受教师影响大

TPO 19 应该从多种信息源获取信息

TPO 20 成功人士会更爱尝试新事物和冒险

TPO 21 交际能力比努力学习更有助于成功

TPO 22 老师在课堂上不应该向学生表达自己的社会或政治观点

TPO 23 冒着犯错的风险快速工作好于不犯错但工作缓慢

TPO 24 鼓励孩子做兼职有助于准备未来

TPO 25 现在年轻人更愿意帮助社区

TPO 26 子承父业好处多

TPO 27 立刻抓住一份稳定工作好于等待满意的工作

TPO 28 现在父母更多地参与到孩子的教育

TPO 29 给教师涨工资可以提高教育质量

TPO 30 三天工作制好于五天工作制

图书在版编目（CIP）数据

TPO 写作全解 / 孟炎，赵波编著 . —北京：中国人民大学出版社，2019.3
ISBN 978-7-300-26706-7

Ⅰ . ①T… Ⅱ . ①孟… ②赵… Ⅲ . ①英语–写作–水平考试–自学参考资料 Ⅳ . ①H315

中国版本图书馆 CIP 数据核字（2019）第 028169 号

TPO 写作全解

孟 炎 赵 波 编著

TPO Xiezuo Quanjie

出版发行	中国人民大学出版社	
社　　址	北京中关村大街31号	**邮政编码** 100080
电　　话	010-62511242（总编室）	010-62511770（质管部）
	010-82501766（邮购部）	010-62514148（门市部）
	010-62515195（发行公司）	010-62515275（盗版举报）
网　　址	http://www.crup.com.cn	
	http://www.1kao.com.cn（中国 1 考网）	
经　　销	新华书店	
印　　刷	北京玺诚印务有限公司	
规　　格	185 mm×260 mm　16 开本	**版　　次** 2019 年 3 月第 1 版
印　　张	15	**印　　次** 2019 年 3 月第 1 次印刷
字　　数	299 000	**定　　价** 48.00 元